Understanding
DIGITAL
Marketing

Marketing strategies for engaging the digital generation

DAMIAN RYAN & CALVIN JONES

KOGAN
PAGE

London and Philadelphia

First published in Great Britain and the United States in 2009 by Kogan Page Limited

120 Pentonville Road
London N1 9JN
United Kingdom
www.koganpage.com

525 South 4th Street, #241
Philadelphia PA 19147
USA

ISBN 978 0 7494 5389 3

British Library Cataloguing-in-Publication Data

A CIP record for this book is available from the British Library.

Library of Congress Cataloging-in-Publication Data

Ryan, Damian.
    Understanding digital marketing : marketing strategies for engaging the digital generation / Damian Ryan and Calvin Jones.
        p. cm.
    Includes index.
    ISBN 978-0-7494-5389-3
    1. Internet marketing. 2. Social media. 3. Strategic planning. 4. Marketing-- Management. I. Jones, Calvin. II. Title.
    HF415.1265.R93 2008
    658.8'72--dc22

                                        2008034688

Typeset by JS Typesetting Ltd, Porthcawl, Mid Glamorgan
Printed and bound in India by Replika Press Pvt Ltd

Contents

Preface: Welcome to a brave new world

The world of digital media is changing at a phenomenal pace. Its constantly evolving technologies, and the way people are using them, are transforming not just how we access our information, but how we interact and communicate with one another on a global scale. It's also changing the way we choose and buy our products and services.

People are embracing digital technology to communicate in ways that would have been inconceivable just a few short years ago. Digital technologies are no longer the preserve of tech-savvy early adopters, and today ordinary people are integrating them seamlessly into their everyday lives. From SMS updates on their favourite sports teams, to a free video call with relatives on the other side of the globe, to collaborative online gaming and much, much more: ordinary people – your customers – are starting to use digital media without giving it a second thought.

The global online population was around 1.3 billion at the end of 2007. Projections suggest that figure will hit 1.8 billion by 2010. In the developed world internet access is becoming practically ubiquitous, and the widespread availability of always-on broadband connections means that people are now going online daily to do everything from checking their bank statement, to shopping for their groceries, to playing games.

What makes this digital revolution so exciting is that it's happening right now. We're living through it, and we have a unique opportunity to jump in and be part of this historical transition.

In the pages that follow we'll take you on a journey into the world of digital marketing. We'll show you how it all started, how it got to where it is today, and where thought leaders in the industry believe it's heading in the future. Most importantly of all we'll show you – in a practical, no-nonsense way – how you can harness the burgeoning power of digital media to drive your business to the crest of this digital marketing wave, and how to keep it there.

This book will:

- help you and your business to choose online advertising and marketing channels that will get your ideas, products and services to a massive and ever-expanding market;
- give you that elusive competitive edge that will keep you ahead of the pack;
- future-proof your business by helping you to understand the origins of digital marketing and the trends that are shaping its future;
- give you a concept of the scale of the online marketplace, the unfolding opportunities and the digital service providers who will help your business to capitalize on them;
- provide practical, real-world examples of digital marketing successes – including leading brands that have become household names in a relatively short space of time;
- offer insight through interviews, analysis and contributions from digital marketing experts;
- ultimately, give you the tools you need to harness the power of the internet to take your business wherever you want it to go.

We set out to unravel the mysteries of digital marketing by taking you on a journey. As we travel into this digital world we'll reveal how leading marketers in sectors as diverse as travel, retail, gambling and adult entertainment have stumbled on incredibly effective techniques to turn people on to doing business online, reaping literally millions as a result. We'll show you how to apply their experience to transform your own digital enterprise.

Whether you are looking to start up your own home-based internet business, work for a large multinational or are anywhere in between, if you want to connect with your customers today and into the future, you're going to need digital channels as part of your marketing mix. The internet has become the medium of choice for a generation of consumers: the first generation to have grown up taking instant access to digital information for granted. This generation integrates digital media into every facet of its daily lives, in ways we could never have conceived of in even the recent past. Today this generation of digital natives is entering the workplace and is spending like never before. This is the mass market of tomorrow, and for businesspeople and marketers the challenge is to become fluent in this new digital language so that we can talk effectively to our target audience.

Television froze a generation of consumers to the couch for years; now digital media are engaging consumers and customers in ways that the early architects of the technology could never have dreamed of.

When the Apple Mac came along it opened up the art of publishing, and as a result print media boomed. Today, the same thing is happening online, through the phenomenon of user-generated content (UGC) and social networking: ordinary people are becoming the directors, producers, editors and distributors of their own media-rich content – the content they, their friends and the world want to see. But that's only the start.

Prime-time television audiences are falling, print media are coming under increasing pressure to address dropping circulation figures and – while the old school sits on the sidelines, bloated and slowly atrophying – digital media have transformed themselves into a finely tuned engine delivering more power, opportunity and control than any other form of media could dream of. In other words – it's time to follow the smart money!

Over the last 15 years I've had the absolute pleasure and pain of working at the coalface of the burgeoning and insistent new media. I've met lots of smart people and spoken to literally hundreds of organizations with massively diverse and challenging agendas. The one common factor was a hunger for data and knowledge: anything that would give their particular brand that elusive competitive edge.

When putting this book together we wanted to make it as informative and practical as possible. Each chapter begins with a summary of its content, so you can easily browse through the chapters and select the one that addresses the topic you're interested in. We've purposely left out the jargon – and where technical terms have been absolutely necessary we supply a clear definition in the text, backed up by a complete glossary at the back of the book that explains all of the terms we use in plain English. The result, we hope, is a book that is clear, informative and entertaining, even for the complete digital novice.

In your hands you hold what independent marketers around the world have been crying out for: a book that shows you how to use the internet successfully to sell your products or services. We begin with the origins of the medium and take you through the various disciplines of digital marketing campaigns. We travel around the world collecting facts, figures, comment and opinion from acknowledged experts, brands and organizations in different fields, getting them to spill the beans on how the net delivered the goods for them.

We'll look in detail at areas like search marketing and affiliate marketing, we'll delve into e-mail marketing and creative online executions and look at various digital marketing strategies, some moral, some less so.

In Amsterdam last year, I was granted a late-night audience with some of the best 'Black Hat' marketers in the world. These people, who will remain nameless, earn their living scuppering the efforts of competing brands in the digital marketplace. Black Hat marketing is real – and it can do real damage to your business. We explain what it is and, more importantly, give you some practical steps you can take to help protect your business against it.

It took television 22 years to reach 50 million households – it took the internet just five to achieve the same level of penetration. Things are progressing at an unbelievable rate, and we're approaching a pivotal point in marketing history – a time when digital marketing will overtake traditional mass media as the medium of choice for reaching the consumer of tomorrow.

In the summer of 1993 I interviewed Jerry Reitman, head of direct marketing for Leo Burnett in Chicago, for my magazine *goDirect*. During our conversation Jerry pointed at the computer on his desk and said: 'And that... that's where it's going.' I wondered what he was talking about.

Fifteen years on and practically the entire population is online. Consumers have grown tired of mass media marketing and are turning instead to the internet. They want more engagement, more interaction. They're starting to spend most of their leisure time in a digital world, and creative digital marketing is the way your business will reach them.

Welcome to my world...

Damian Ryan

Acknowledgements

Damian Ryan

There are so many people to thank – it would be so much more convenient, less environmentally aggressive, accountable and faster if I was to text all of you or send you a gratitude link or whack something on Facebook... this book medium, however, *is* the message!

The book began in 2001 and then again in 2002, 2004 (I skipped 2003 because of the arrival of my daughters), (in 2005 I went to journalist school to improve my writing skills) and then I started it again in 2006. This led me to meet the great Calvin Jones without whom I can honestly say this book would not have happened and I would now be starting it again in 2009, 2054 and so on.

Calvin has extraordinary powers of patience combined with a sense of diligence and work ethic that completely clashes with my personality – we are the ideal writing partnership!

Having Calvin as a writing partner meant the book never 'began again'. Throughout the 15 months of writing, research, celebratory nights out in Cork (a lesson in how not to mix drinks!), e-mails, texts, instant messages etc we managed to craft something which we sincerely hope will be of benefit to readers. At a minimum our target was everyone should be able to get *one idea* to help their business get the best from digital marketing.

Calvin has mentioned the many contributors who helped us in our quest. I would like to thank Annie Knight and her colleagues from Kogan Page for giving us enough rope and for being an ongoing source of encouragement too!

To my family and friends and particularly to everyone who ever worked with me in either the publishing era or the digital era, THANKS!

Some of course have to be singled out – they know their role: Simon Ferguson, Michael Byers, Declan Kennedy, Charles Blandford, Sinead Ryan, Clare McAndrew, Roisin Joyce, Patrick Stewart – your support and encouragement will never be forgotten.

To my wife Suzanne who was very supportive throughout this entire episode and who got on board by collecting case studies and writing on the creative chapter – thanks.

I would like to dedicate this book to my daughters Katie and Alannah – the apples of my eyes! Sorry I hogged the computer guys – now you can play with Cbeebies again!

And finally this book is for my Mum – mother of seven, opera singer, cordon bleu chef, constant source of inspiration, likes my jokes and someone who showed me that persistence pays off!

Calvin Jones

Writing this book has been something of an adventure for me.

Damian first contacted me about the project in April 2007. Since then we've been on a veritable roller-coaster ride of discovery, insight and learning. It's been a year full of highs, lows, and, for the last six months at least, very hard, and at times relentless work.

Writing a book with as broad a scope as the one you're holding is challenging in all sorts of ways. Culling material was inevitable, and we spent long hours labouring over what to include, realising all the time that what we chose to leave out would be just as crucial as what we left in. It's taken long, frustrating days, and some even longer nights at the keyboard to produce the end result, and I think it's fair to say the project has absorbed more time and energy than either of us anticipated at the outset. The results, we hope, are worth it.

This book wouldn't exist without the help of a lot of people. First, of course, there's Damian; this project was his brainchild – born of his boundless enthusiasm and immense experience in this space. His inspiration, guidance and support moulded its evolution from the outset. Damian has a talent for looking beyond the technology to the human story beneath, and that ability has been instrumental in making this work what it is.

I also have to thank the digital marketing experts who helped fast-track my education – particularly John and Noel Coburn of PraxisNow (www.praxisnow.com) who got me off to a flying start with their Internet Marketing seminars. Martin Murray of Interactive Return (www.interactivereturn.com) provided valuable input and guidance early in the process, and kindly extended an invitation to attend Search Marketing World 2008. While there I got to speak to such international Web 2.0 luminaries as Chris Sherman, Vanessa Fox, Brian Marin and Brian Clifton to name but a few, and to absorb the wisdom of many more from the podium. Thank you, one and all, for your insight.

Throughout the book we've punctuated our own text with interesting and informative articles from expert authors who kindly gave us permission to share their expertise with you: our thanks to Jill Whalen, Jeff Jarvis, Martin Murray, Brandt Dainow, Richard Foan, Richard Eyre and other contributors for allowing us to reproduce their valuable work. Thanks also to Kim Gilmour for her help with the e-mail marketing chapter, and Suzanne Ryan for her work on the online creative chapter and case studies, your efforts are much appreciated. I also have to thank Annie Knight, our editor at Kogan Page, for her patience as we battled to pull everything together.

To my daughters Ava, Nia and Lana – who were robbed of their Dad for long stretches during the course of writing this book – thank you girls, you can have Daddy back now!

Finally, and most important of all, to Sally Ann, my partner in everything, for proofreading the manuscript and correcting my inevitable shortcomings, and for her enduring love, support and guidance through good times and bad. Without you, none of this would matter!

Let the adventure continue...

1 Going digital – the evolution of marketing

We look at the present through a rear-view mirror. We march backwards into the future.

(Marshall McLuhan)

The press, the machine, the railway, the telegraph are premises whose thousand-year conclusion no one has yet dared to draw.

(Friedrich Nietzsche)

Whoever, or whatever, wins the battle for people's minds will rule, because mighty, rigid apparatuses will not be a match, in any reasonable timespan, for the minds mobilized around the power of flexible, alternative networks.

(Manuel Castells, author of The Network Society)

Our chapter pledge to you

When you reach the end of this chapter you'll have answers to the following questions:

- How did we reach the dawn of a digital age in marketing?
- What are the similarities between the internet and historical global communications revolutions?

- How many people are on the internet and how quickly is it growing?
- How is digital technology influencing consumer behaviour?

In the beginning. . .

Etched on a dusty kerbstone amidst the ruins of the ancient Roman city of Pompeii, you'll find an engraved penis, strategically carved to point the way to what, at the time, was one of the most popular brothels in the area. Guides will tell you it's the 'oldest advertisement in the world, for the oldest business in the world'. While the truth of that claim is debatable, the phallic ad is certainly very old.

The Pompeii penis was buried by the eruption of Mount Vesuvius, which destroyed the city on 24 August, AD 79, but the true origins of marketing go back much further than that. Although, according to business historians, marketing as a discrete business discipline wasn't born until the 1950s, marketing activities have played a fundamental role in the success of businesses from, well, the very first business. There are few certainties in the world of business, but one thing's for sure: if you don't let customers know about your business, you won't stay in business for very long.

But this is a book about marketing in the digital age – the present, and the future

That's true. We're here to talk about the exciting new world of digital marketing as it emerges from relative obscurity into the mainstream. We're going to look at how businesses just like yours can harness the power of this online revolution to connect with a new wave of consumers: consumers who take this pervasive technology and integrate it seamlessly into their everyday lives in ways we could never have conceived of as recently as a decade ago.

This book is about the future of marketing. So why are we starting it by looking backwards? In his 1960s classic *Understanding Media*, Canadian communications theorist and philosopher Marshall McLuhan notes: 'It is instructive to follow the embryonic stages of any new growth, for during this period of development it is much misunderstood, whether it be printing or the motor car or TV.' As is so often the case, having a basic grasp of the past can help our understanding of the present and ultimately illuminate our view of the future.

So buckle your seatbelt as we take a whistle-stop tour of how marketing has evolved over the years, and how advertising and technology have converged to define a new marketing landscape that is just beginning to mature and is still gravid with opportunity.

The changing face of advertising

Advertising can be intoxicating. The spin, the story, the message, the call to action, the image, the placement, the measurement, the refinement: it all adds up to a powerful cocktail that can ultimately change the world. At its core, advertising is all about influencing people – persuading them to take the actions we want, whether that's choosing a particular brand of toothpaste, picking up the phone, filling in a mailing coupon or visiting a website. Done well, advertising has a power that can achieve amazing things, and if you're in business you're already doing it and will continue to do so.

Advertising through the ages

Advertising, an essential component in the marketing of any business, has been around for a long time. The Pompeii penis is positively modern compared to some of the advertising relics archaeologists have unearthed in ancient Arabia, China, Egypt, Greece and Rome. The Egyptians used papyrus to create posters and flyers, while lost-and-found advertising (also on papyrus and often relating to 'missing' slaves) was common in both ancient Greece and ancient Rome. Posters, signs and flyers were widely employed in the ancient cities of Rome, Pompeii and Carthage to publicize events like circuses, games and gladiatorial contests.

People have been trying to influence other people since the dawn of human existence, utilizing whatever means and media they had at their disposal at the time. The human voice and word of mouth, of course, came first. Then someone picked up a piece of stone and started etching images on a cave wall: enduring images that told stories, communicated ideas and promoted certain ways of doing things. The first advertising? That's debatable, but these images, some of which are still around to this day, certainly demonstrate an early recognition of the power images and messages have to influence the perception and behaviour of others.

The development of printing during the 15th and 16th centuries heralded a significant milestone in advertising, making it more cost-effective for marketers to reach a much wider audience. In the 17th century, adverts began to appear in early newspapers in England and then spread across the globe. The first form of mass media advertising was born.

The 18th and 19th centuries saw a further expansion in newspaper advertising, and alongside it the birth of mail-order advertising – which would evolve into the massive direct-mail and direct-response industry we know and love today. It also saw the establishment of the first advertising agency, set up in Boston in 1843 by the pioneering Volney Palmer. Initially ad agencies acted as simple brokers for newspaper space, but before long they developed into full-service operations, offering a suite of creative and ad-placement services to their clients.

The 20th century saw the dawn of another new advertising age, with the advent of radio offering a completely new medium through which advertisers could reach out to prospective clients. Then came television, which shifted the advertising landscape yet again, and towards the end of the century a new force – the internet – began moving out of the realm of 'techies' and early adopters to become a valuable business and communication tool for the masses. The era of digital marketing was born.

Technological advances have punctuated the evolution of advertising throughout history, each fundamentally altering the way businesses could communicate with their customers. Interestingly, however, none of these ground-breaking developments superseded those that came before. Rather they served to augment them, offering marketers more diversity, allowing them to connect with a broader cross-section of consumers. In today's sophisticated age of paid search placement, keyword-targeted pay-per-click advertising and social networking, you'll still find the earliest forms of advertising alive and well.

Stroll through any market practically anywhere in the world – from the food markets of central London to the bazaars of North Africa, to the street markets of India – and you'll be greeted by a cacophony of noise as vendors use their voices to vie for the attention of passing customers. The human voice, the first marketing medium in history, is still going strong in the digital age.

The technology behind digital marketing

As we've already mentioned, developments in technology and the evolution of marketing are inextricably intertwined. Technology has underpinned major milestones in the history of marketing since its inception. The process tends to go something like this:

- New technology emerges and is initially the preserve of technologists and early adopters.
- The technology gains a firmer foothold in the market and starts to become more popular, putting it on the marketing radar.
- Innovative marketers jump in to explore ways they can harness the power of this emerging technology to connect with their target audience.
- The technology migrates to the mainstream and is adopted into standard marketing practice.

The printing press, radio, television and now the internet are all examples of major breakthroughs in technology that ultimately altered the relationships between marketers and consumers for ever, and did so on a global scale. But, of course, marketing isn't about technology; it's about people: technology is only interesting, from a marketing perspective, when it connects people with other people more effectively.

There are plenty of examples of technology through the ages having a significant impact on various markets – technology that may seem obscure, even irrelevant today. Remember Muzak, the company that brought elevator music to the masses back in the 1930s? The technology for piping audio over power lines was patented in 1922 by retired Major General George O Squier, and exclusive rights to the patent were bought by North American Company. In 1934, under the corporate umbrella of 'Muzak', they started piping music into Cleveland homes.

Muzak seemed to have hit on a winning formula, but the advent of free commercial radio sounded the death knell for the company's chosen route to market. With free music available on their shiny new wirelesses, households were no longer prepared to pay for the Muzak service. Undeterred the company focused its efforts on New York City businesses. As buildings in New York soared skywards, the lift or elevator became practically ubiquitous. Muzak had found its niche, and 'elevator music' was born.

So what, you might think. It's true that, compared to behemoths of contemporary media like radio, television and now the internet, elevator music is small potatoes. But back in its heyday this was cutting-edge stuff, and it reached a lot of people. Muzak had the power to sway opinions and influence markets, so much so that, for music artists of that era, having your track played on the Muzak network practically guaranteed a hit.

The point is that technology has the ability to open up completely new markets and to radically shake up existing ones. The mainstream adoption of digital technology – the internet, the software applications that run on it, and the devices that allow people to connect both to the network and to each other whenever, wherever and however they want to – promises to dwarf all that has come before it. It heralds the single most disruptive development in the history of marketing.

Whether that disruption represents an opportunity or a threat to you as a marketer depends largely on your perspective. We hope the fact that you're reading this book means that you see it as an opportunity.

The first global communications network: 'the highway of thought'

To understand the explosive growth of the internet we need to look back at how early communications technology evolved into the global network of interconnected computers that today we call the internet. The story of electronic communication begins with the wired telegraph – a network that grew explosively to cover the globe, connected people across vast distances in a way that seemed almost magical, and changed the world for ever.

In his book *The Victorian Internet*, Tom Standage looks at the wired telegraph and draws some astonishing parallels between the growth of the world's first electronic communications network and the growth of the modern-day internet. Standage describes the origins of the telegraph, and the quest to deliver information from point to point more rapidly in the days when speedy communication relied on a fast horse and a skilled rider:

> On an April day in 1746 at the grand convent of the Carthusians in Paris about 200 monks arranged themselves in a long, snaking line. Each monk held one end of a 25 foot iron wire in each hand connecting him to his neighbour on either side. Together the monks and their connecting wires formed a line over a mile long. Once the line was complete the Abbot, Jean-Antoine Nollet, a noted French scientist, took a primitive battery and, without warning, connected it to the line of monks – giving all of them a powerful electric shock.

These 'electric monks' demonstrated conclusively that electricity could transmit a message (albeit a painful one) from one location to another in an instant, and laid the foundation for a communications revolution.

In 1830 Joseph Henry (1797–1878), an eminent US scientist who went on to become the first director of the Smithsonian Institute, took the concept a step further. He demonstrated the potential of the electromagnet for long-distance communications when he passed an electric current through a mile-long cable to ring an electromagnetic bell connected to the other end. Samuel Morse (1791–1872), the inventor of Morse Code, took Henry's concept a step further and made a commercial success of it: the electronic telegraph was born.

In 1842 Morse demonstrated a working telegraph between two committee rooms in Washington, and Congress voted slimly in favour of investing $30,000 for an experimental telegraph line between Washington and Baltimore. It was a very close call: 89 votes for the prototype, 83 against and 70 abstentions by congressmen looking 'to avoid the responsibility of spending the public money for a machine they could not understand'.

Despite the reservations of the congressmen, the new network was a huge success. It grew explosively: by 1850 there were more than 12,000 miles of telegraph lines criss-crossing the United States; two years later there was more than twice that, and the network of connected wires was spreading rapidly around the globe.

This spellbinding new network delivered news in moments rather than the weeks and months people were used to. It connected people over vast distances in ways previously inconceivable, and to many remained completely incomprehensible. Governments tried and failed to control this raw new communications medium, its advocates hailed it as revolutionary, and its popularity grew at an unprecedented rate. Newspapers began publishing news hours rather than weeks after the event, romance blossomed over the wires, couples were married 'online', gamblers used the new network to 'cheat' on the horses, and it transformed the way business was conducted around the world. In the space of a generation the telegraph literally altered the fabric of society.

Does any of this sound familiar? A *New York Times* article published on Wednesday, 14 September 1852 describes the telegraph network as 'the highway of thought': not much of a stretch from the 'information superhighway' label we apply to our modern-day revolutionary network. If anything, the communications revolution instigated by the telegraph must have represented more of a cultural upheaval than the explosive growth of the internet today.

For the first time people grasped that they could communicate almost instantly with people across continents and even oceans. They felt a sense of closeness, a togetherness that simply hadn't been possible before. The telegraph system was hailed by some as a harbinger of peace and solidarity: a network of wires that would ultimately bind countries, creeds and cultures in a way hitherto unimaginable. Others, of course, used the network to wage war more efficiently. The sheer expansion of ideas and dreams that ensued must have been truly staggering, the opportunities and potential for change bewildering.

For rapid long-distance communications the telegraph remained the only game in town until 1877, when two rival inventors battled to be the first to patent another new technology set to turn the world of electronic communications on its head. Its name, the telephone; the inventors, Elisha Gray and Alexander Graham Bell. They submitted their patent applications within hours of one another – but Bell pipped Gray to the post, and a now-famous legal battle ensued.

The first words ever transmitted into a telephone were uttered by Bell, speaking to his research assistant, Thomas Watson, in the next room. He simply said: 'Mr Watson, come here. I want to see you.'

Early networks

The internet story really starts in 1957, with the USSR's launch of the Sputnik satellite. It signalled that the United States was falling behind the Soviet Union in the technology stakes, prompting the US government to invest heavily in science and technology. In 1958, the US Department of Defense set up the Advanced Research Projects Agency (ARPA), a specialist agency established with a specific remit: to make sure the United States stayed ahead of its Cold War nemesis in the accelerating technology race.

In 1962 a computer scientist called Joseph Carl Robnett Licklider, vice-president at technology company Bolt Beranek and Newman, wrote a series of memos discussing the concept of an 'intergalactic computer network'. Licklider's revolutionary ideas, amazingly, encompassed practically everything that the internet has today become. In October 1963, Licklider was appointed head of the Behavioral Sciences and Command and Control programs at ARPA. During his two-year tenure he convinced the agency of the importance of developing computer networks and, although he left ARPA before work on his theories began, the seed for ARPANET – the precursor to the internet – had been sown.

In 1965 researchers hooked up a computer at Massachusetts Institute of Technology's (MIT) Lincoln Lab with a US Air Force computer in California. For the first time two computers communicated with each other using 'packet'-based information transmitted over a network.

ARPA (since renamed DARPA – www.darpa.mil) started the ARPANET project in 1966, claiming that it would allow the powerful computers owned by the government, universities and research institutions around the United States to communicate with one another and to share valuable computing resources. IBM and other large computer companies at the time were sceptical, reportedly claiming that the network ARPA proposed couldn't be built.

ARPA ploughed on, and on 21 November 1969 the first two computers were connected to the fledgling ARPANET, one at the University of California, Los Angeles, the other at Stanford Research Institute. By 5 December the same year the network had doubled in size as they were joined by two other computers: one at the University of California, Santa Barbara, the other at the University of Utah's graphics department.

The new network grew quickly. By 1971, 15 US institutions were connected to ARPANET, and by 1974 the number had grown to 46 and had spread to include overseas nodes in Hawaii, Norway and London.

You've got mail

E-mail, which is still often described as the internet's 'killer application', began life in the early 1960s as a facility that allowed users of mainframe computers to send simple text-based messages to another user's mailbox on the same computer. But it wasn't until the advent of ARPANET that anyone considered sending electronic mail from one user to another across a network.

In 1971 Ray Tomlinson, an engineer working on ARPANET, wrote the first program capable of sending mail from a user on one host computer to another user's mailbox on another host computer. As an identifier to distinguish network mail from local mail Tomlinson decided to append the host name of the user's computer to the user login name. To separate the two names he chose the @ symbol.

'I am frequently asked why I chose the at sign, but the at sign just makes sense', writes Tomlinson on his website. 'The purpose of the at sign (in English) was to indicate a unit price (for example, 10 items @ $1.95). I used the at sign to indicate that the user was "at" some other host rather than being local.'

E-mail, one of the internet's most widely used applications, and one of the most critical for internet marketers, began life as a programmer's afterthought. Tomlinson created e-mail because he thought it 'seemed like a neat idea' at the time. 'There was no directive to "go forth and invent e-mail". The ARPANET was a solution looking for a problem. A colleague suggested that I not tell my boss what I had done because e-mail wasn't in our statement of work', he said.

From ARPANET to internet

The term 'internet' was first used in 1974 by US computer scientist Vinton Cerf (commonly referred to as the 'father of the internet', and now a senior executive and internet evangelist with Google). Cerf was working with Robert Khan at DARPA on a way to standardize the way different host computers communicated both across the growing ARPANET and between the ARPANET and other emerging computer networks. The Transmission Control Program (TCP) network protocol they defined evolved to become the Transmission Control Program/Internet Protocol (TCP/IP) protocol suite that's still used to pass packets of information backwards and forwards across the internet to this day.

In 1983 the ARPANET started using the TCP/IP protocol – a move that many consider to signal the true 'birth' of the internet as we know it. That year, too, the system of domain names (.com, .net, etc) was invented. By 1984 the number of 'nodes' on the still fledgling network passed 1,000 and began climbing rapidly. By 1989 there were more than 100,000 hosts connected to the internet, and the growth continued.

Making connections – birth of the web

It was in 1989 that Tim Berners-Lee, a British developer working at the European Organization for Nuclear Research (CERN) in Geneva, proposed a system of information cross-referencing, access and retrieval across the rapidly growing internet based on 'hypertext' links. The concept of a hypertext information architecture was nothing new, and was already being used in individual programs running on individual computers around the world. The idea of linking documents stored on different computers across the rapidly growing internet, though, was nothing short of revolutionary.

The building blocks for the world wide web were already in place – but it was Tim Berners-Lee's vision that brought them together. 'I just had to take the hypertext idea and connect it to the TCP and DNS ideas and – ta-da! – the World Wide Web', Berners-Lee comments on the World Wide Web Consortium (W3C) website.

The first web page on the internet was built at CERN, and went online on 6 August 1991. It contained information about the new world wide web, how to get a web browser and how to set up a web server. Over time it also became the first ever web directory, as Berners-Lee maintained a list of links to other websites on the page as they appeared.

The wild wide web – a new frontier

Up to this point, the internet had been the realm of technologists and scientists at research institutions. But the advent of the web changed the landscape, making online information accessible to a much broader audience. What happened next was explosive. Between 1991 and 1997 the web grew at an astonishing 850 per cent per annum, eclipsing all expectations. With more websites and more people joining the online party every day, it was only a matter of time before innovative tech-savvy marketers started to notice the web's potential as an avenue for the marketing message.

The mid-1990s saw a surge in new online ventures as pioneering entrepreneurs, grasping the burgeoning potential of this exciting new medium, scrambled to stake their claim on this virtual new frontier. In August 1995 there were 18,957 websites online; by August 1996 there were 342,081 ('Fifteen Years of the Web', Internet timeline, www.bbc.co.uk).

Silicon Valley was awash with venture capital as investors bet big bucks on the net's next big thing – some with viable business plans, others with charismatic founders riding on the coat tails of the prevailing net mania. New ventures sprang up almost daily, selling everything imaginable – or selling nothing at all. Fledgling companies spent vast amounts of money growing quickly with scant regard for turning a profit, betting their future on building strong online brands that could win the hearts and minds of net consumers. The profits would come later – at least, that was the theory. Some of these companies were destined to become household names in a few short years; others would vanish into obscurity just as quickly.

These were heady, almost euphoric times. The internet had acquired the mythical Midas touch: a business with .com in its name, it seemed, was destined for great things. Initial public offerings (IPOs) of dot.com companies made millionaires of founders, and made the headlines, fuelling further mania. It was an era that saw the birth of some of today's most well-known online brands: sites like Amazon, Yahoo!, eBay and, in September 1998, Google Inc.

Boom, boom... bang!

For a time it seemed as though the halcyon days of the late 1990s would continue for ever and that the dot.com bubble was impervious to bursting. Fuelled by speculative investment and high-profile high-tech IPOs, the Nasdaq Composite stock index continued to rocket upwards. Each new dot.com success fuelled the fervour for technology stocks, blowing the bubble up a little more. On 10 March 2000 the Nasdaq index hit an intraday high of 5,132.52 before settling to an all-time closing high of 5,046 points.

And then it went into free fall. What happened to the railways in the 1840s, radio in the 1920s and transistor electronics in the 1950s had finally hit the dot.com boom. Between March 2000 and October 2002 some US$5 trillion in all was wiped off the market value of technology stocks. Speculative investment suddenly stopped, venture capitalists were less cavalier with their cash, and high-risk start-ups with dubious business plans ran out of places to source funding. With profits still a distant dream, even for high-profile internet start-ups, the coffers soon began to run dry. It signalled the end of the road for many.

Despite the occasional 'blip', both the stock market index and the fortunes of internet businesses continued to wane until 2003, when, slowly but surely, the tide turned and things started to look up. Although there had been some high-profile closures, mergers and acquisitions in the wake of the crash, the reality is that, for the internet industry as a whole, the inevitable 'readjustment' had a positive impact. It essentially cleared the decks – sweeping away a plethora of unviable, poorly conceived and poorly managed businesses – and served as a poignant reality check to those that remained. Yes, there were casualties, but overall the industry emerged stronger, more focused and both optimistic and, crucially, realistic about its future.

Two other crucial elements helped fuel the recovery and to some extent the public fascination with the internet: one was the meteoric rise of Google from relative obscurity to dominate the world of internet search; the other was the accelerated roll-out of high-speed, always-on broadband access for residential users.

People could suddenly find what they were looking for online – could get access to what they wanted, when they wanted it – without having to go through the frustrating rigmarole of a dial-up connection. It transformed the online experience, turning it from a passing curiosity into a useful everyday tool for a much wider demographic of users. And the more people used the internet, the more indispensable it became.

Enough technology – let's talk about people

If you're non-technical the world of digital marketing may seem a bit daunting at first. All that technology must be really complicated... right? Not necessarily.

One of the key things to remember if you're new to digital marketing is this: digital marketing isn't actually about technology at all; it's all about people. In that sense it's similar to traditional marketing: it's about people (marketers) connecting with other people (consumers) to build relationships and ultimately drive sales.

Technology merely affords you, the marketer, new and exciting platforms that allow you to connect with people in increasingly diverse and relevant ways. Digital marketing is not about understanding the underlying technology, but rather about understanding people, how they're using that technology, and how you can leverage that to engage with them more effectively. Yes, you have to learn to use the tools at your disposal – but understanding people is the real key to unlocking the potential of digital marketing.

A huge and growing market

Although internet companies suffered bruised finances and a tarnished public image in the wake of the dot.com crash, the internet itself never stopped growing, in terms both of the number of websites online and, crucially from a marketing perspective, of the number of people with internet access. In March 2000, when the dot.com bubble burst, there were an estimated 304 million people in the world with internet access. By March 2003 that figure had doubled to 608 million, and in December 2005 the global online population passed 1 billion. As of December 2007 the figure sat at around 1.3 billion people. That's 20 per cent of the world's population – and climbing (Internet World Stats, www.internetworldstats. com).

As global and local online populations have spiralled upwards, so too have the levels of broadband penetration, which means that not only are there more people online but they're also online more often, for much longer periods of time and can do much more with that time. All of this means the market penetration of digital channels is growing rapidly. As the potential audience grows, so too does the allure of digital marketing. Marketers around the world are sitting up and taking notice, and big-name brands are starting to take the internet and other digital marketing channels seriously: loosening the purse strings and redistributing their advertising spend.

According to online market research specialist eMarketer, US online advertising spend for 2002 stood at US$6 billion, by 2005 it had more than doubled to US$12.5 billion, and their projections estimate it will grow to a massive US$36.5 billion by 2011. In 2004, 2005 and 2006, online advertising spend enjoyed unprecedented growth of over 30 per cent per annum.

'It's been a long time since any medium had three years in a row of 30 per cent plus ad spending increases', commented eMarketer senior analyst David Hallerman. 'With a 34 per cent gain in 2006, as new research from IAB/PwC shows, the internet now matches cable TV from 1983 to 1985 and broadcast TV from 1952 to 1954 for such strong, long-term spending increases.'

The growth looks set to continue, and although experts believe it is slowing, eMarketer's analysts predict that online ad spending in the United States will hit $36.5 billion by 2011. Across the Atlantic in the UK, the market is experiencing similar growth, with an online advertising spend of £2.02 billion for 2006, rising to £2.64 billion in 2007 – a rise of 31 per cent. Predictions by eMarketer suggest that the figure will reach £4.45 billion by 2011.

Perhaps more significant than the overall advertising spend, though, is the market share of digital advertising compared to other media. According to figures from the Internet Advertising Bureau (UK) for the first half of 2006 internet advertising accounted for 10.5 per cent of the total spend, eclipsing radio (3.5 per cent), consumer magazines (4.5 per cent) and outdoor advertising (5.1 per cent), and just behind national press advertising at 11.4 per cent. Television was still out in front with 22.7 per cent of the market. But that's about to change. Given its current rate of growth, internet advertising in the UK is predicted to usurp TV in the top spot during 2009 or 2010. The UK has a higher proportion of total spend online than any other country in the world. It looks set to be the first major economy to see internet ad spend overtake television – but it surely won't be the last.

Introducing Consumer 2.0

Unless you've been hiding under a rock in the outer Hebrides since about 2004 you'll be familiar with the Web 2.0 (pronounced two-point-oh) moniker. It's bandied about with alacrity by the web-savvy elite, but what exactly does it mean?

Let's start off with what Web 2.0 is not: it's not a new version of Web 1.0. Web 2.0 is not a revolution in technology; it's an evolution in the way people are using technology. It's about harnessing the distributed collaborative potential of the internet to connect and communicate with other like-minded people wherever they are: creating communities, and sharing knowledge, thoughts, ideas and dreams.

If you've ever shared photos on Flickr, read and commented on a blog, looked for friends on Facebook or MySpace, watched a video clip on YouTube, tried to find your house on Google Maps, video-called friends or family abroad using Skype or looked up an article on Wikipedia, then you've used Web 2.0 technologies.

Suddenly it seems we've been inundated with version 2.0 of anything and everything, as different sectors of society seek to demonstrate that they're current and progressive. We have Business 2.0, Government 2.0, Education 2.0, Careers 2.0 – and of course Marketing 2.0. Well, not to be outdone, we'd like to introduce you to the new, improved, Consumer 2.0.

Once upon a time consumers were quite happy to sit in front of passive broadcast media, accepting whatever was being peddled their way by editors and programme schedulers. Yes, there was an element of choice – you could buy a different newspaper, listen to a different station or choose a different channel – but the ultimate decision in terms of the content available to you rested with somebody else.

Then along came the web and changed all the rules. Now, with Web 2.0, broadband and rich media content, today's consumers are in control as never before. They can choose the content they want, when they want it, in the way that they want it. They can even create their own and share it with their friends, their peers and the world for free.

'Consumers are becoming better informed, better connected, more communicative, and more in control than ever', highlights Julian Smith, an analyst with Jupiter Research writing for the ClickZ network.

> They're better informed through the increased ability to access and sift an abundance of information any time, anywhere. They're better connected through the ability to instantaneously communicate with others across time zones and social strata. They're more communicative through the ability to publish and share their ideas and opinions. They're more in control through the ability not only to personalize their information and entertainment consumption, marketing messages, and the products and services they buy, but also to gain satisfaction on demand.

Analysts at Jupiter Research identified seven key ways in which the increasingly widespread adoption of technology is influencing consumer behaviour:

- *Interconnectivity:* Networked digital technology is enabling consumers to connect with each other more readily, be it through e-mail, instant messaging (IM), mobile messaging, or web-based social networking platforms such as Facebook, MySpace and LinkedIn – or more likely a combination of all of these platforms. Consumers are interacting with like-minded people around the world, paying scant regard to trifling concerns like time zones or geography. Peer-to-peer interaction is reinforcing social networks and building new virtual communities.

- *Technology is levelling the information playing field:* With digital technology content can be created, published, accessed and consumed quickly and easily. As a result the scope of news, opinion and information available to consumers is broader and deeper than ever. Consumers can conduct their own unbiased research, comparing and contrasting products and services before they buy. Knowledge is power, and digital technology is shifting the balance of power in favour of the consumer.

- *Relevance filtering is increasing:* With such a glut of information available to them, digital consumers are, through necessity, learning to filter out items relevant to them and to ignore anything they perceive as irrelevant. Increasingly digital consumers look to have their information aggregated, categorized and delivered (whether through e-mail or RSS feeds). They use personalization features to block out irrelevant content and increasingly employ software solutions to exclude unsolicited commercial messages.

- *Niche aggregation is growing:* The abundance and diversity of online content allow consumers to participate in and indulge their specialist interests and hobbies. Aggregations of like-minded individuals congregate online; the homogeneous mass consumer population is fragmenting into ever-smaller niche groups, with increasingly individual requirements.

- *Micropublishing of personal content is blossoming:* Digital media's inter-active and interconnected nature allows consumers to express them-selves online. Publishing your own content costs little more than a bit of time and imagination, whether through discussion forums, message boards, feedback forms, voting platforms, personal photo galleries, or blogs. Users are posting their opinions online for all to see and are consulting the opinion of their online peers before making purchasing decisions. How often do you check an online review before booking a table at an unknown restaurant or a weekend break at a hotel, or even buying a new car?

- *Rise of the 'prosumer':* Online consumers are getting increasingly involved in the creation of the products and services they purchase, shifting the balance of power from producer to consumer. They're letting producers know what they want in no uncertain terms: the level of interaction between producer and consumer is unprecedented. Individuals are more involved in specifying, creating and customizing products to suit their requirements, and are able to shape and mould the experiences and communications they receive from producers. Traditional mass-production and mass-marketing concepts are rapidly becoming a thing of the past.

- *On demand; any time, any place, anywhere:* As digital technology becomes more ubiquitous in people's lives, the corresponding acceleration of business processes means that consumers can satisfy their needs more quickly, more easily and with fewer barriers. In the digital economy, trifling concerns like time, geography, location and physical store space are becoming irrelevant. It's a world of almost instant gratification, and the more consumers get of it the more they want it – now, now, now!

For marketers this evolution of the marketplace, and the shift in consumer mindset that it heralds, presents a plethora of new challenges. As consumers increasingly embrace new ways of communicating, take greater ownership of the information and entertainment they consume, and aggregate in increasingly specialized niche online communities, marketers must shift their approach if they want to connect with them.

And that's what the rest of this book is all about.

2 Strategic thinking

The most dangerous strategy is to jump a chasm in two leaps.
(Benjamin Disraeli)

Perception is strong and sight weak. In strategy it is important to see distant things as if they were close and to take a distanced view of close things.

(Miyamoto Musashi)

Simplicity is the ultimate sophistication.

(Leonardo da Vinci)

Our chapter pledge to you

When you reach the end of this chapter you'll have answers to the following questions:

- What is a digital marketing strategy and why do I need one?
- How do I know if digital marketing is right for my business?
- How do I formulate a digital marketing strategy?
- How do I convince decision makers that now is the time to invest in digital marketing?
- Are my customers ready for digital marketing?

Why you need a digital marketing strategy

Why do you need a digital marketing strategy? The simple answer: because without one you'll miss opportunities and lose business. Formulating a digital marketing strategy will help you to make informed decisions about your foray into the digital marketing arena and ensure that your efforts are focused on the elements of digital marketing that are most relevant to your business. It's a crucial first step towards understanding how the constantly evolving digital marketplace relates to you and how it affects the relationship between your business or brand and your customers and prospects.

It doesn't matter what business you're in; it's a fairly safe bet that an increasing number of your target market rely on digital technology every day to research, evaluate and purchase the products and services they consume. Without a coherent strategy of engagement and retention through digital channels your business is at best missing a golden opportunity and at worst could be left behind, watching your competitors pull away across an ever-widening digital divide.

Unlike conventional forms of mass media marketing, the internet is unique in its capacity to both broaden the scope of your marketing reach and narrow its focus *at the same time.* Using digital channels you can transcend traditional constraints like geography and time zones to connect with a much wider audience. At the same time, digital technology allows you to hone your marketing message with laser-like precision to target very specific niche segments within that wider market. Implemented effectively, it can be an incredibly powerful combination.

It's often stated that the internet puts consumers in control as never before. But it's also important to remember that the internet also delivers an unprecedented suite of tools, techniques and tactics that allow marketers to reach out and engage with those same consumers. The marketing landscape has never been more challenging, dynamic and diverse.

And therein lies the crux of our need for a cohesive digital marketing strategy. If you're going to harness the power of digital marketing to drive your online business to dizzying new heights, you need a thorough understanding of your market, how your customers are using digital technology, and how your business can best utilize that same technology to build enduring and mutually rewarding relationships with them.

As digital channels continue to broaden the scope available to us as marketers, so they add to the potential complexity of any digital marketing campaign. Having a clearly defined strategy will help to keep you focused, ensure that your marketing activities are always aligned with your business goals and, crucially, ensure that you're targeting the right people.

Your business and digital marketing

Whether or not your business is suited to digital marketing depends very much on the nature of that business, where it is now, and where you want it to go in the future. If, for example, you're a dairy farmer in rural Ireland, have a fixed contract to supply milk to the local cooperative, and have little, if any, scope or ambition to diversify and grow your business year on year, then digital marketing probably isn't for you. Likewise, if you're a local butcher with an established client base in a thriving market town in the English Peak District, and simply want to maintain the status quo, then again you'll probably do just fine without digital marketing.

If however you're a Peak District butcher looking to diversify your product offering, broaden the scope of your business and start selling your quality organic produce to restaurants and hotels around the country, well, then, welcome to the world of digital marketing.

In truth there are very few businesses today that can't benefit from at least some degree of digital marketing – even if it's just providing a basic online brochure telling people what you do, and sending out the occasional update to existing customers via an e-mail newsletter or RSS (Really Simple Syndication – a way to retrieve updated posts or articles from a website automatically) feed.

Whether you are running a home-based 'lifestyle' business selling hand-embroidered cushion covers, are a small-scale artisan food producer or up-and-coming restaurateur, or managing a large multinational corporation, a growing proportion of your customer base is already online, with more joining them every day. Obviously, the more your target market comes to rely on these online channels for its information, research and purchasing needs, the more critical digital marketing will become to the ongoing success of your business.

Digital marketing – yes or no

There are really only two key questions you need to answer when it comes to deciding whether or not your business needs a digital marketing strategy.

Table 2.1   Are your customers online?

Demographic of internet users	

Below is the percentage of each group who use the internet, according to our October–December 2007 survey. As an example, 74% of adult women use the internet.

	Use the internet
Total adults	75%
Women	74
Men	76
Age	
18–29	92%
30–49	85
50–64	72
65+	37
Race/ethnicity	
White, non-Hispanic	76%
Black, non-Hispanic	56
English-speaking Hispanic	79
Geography	
Urban	77%
Suburban	77
Rural	64
Household income	
Less than $30,000/yr	61%
$30,000–$49,999	78
$50,000–$74,999	90
$75,000+	93
Educational attainment	
Less than high school	38%
High school	67
Some college	84
College +	93

N=2,054 adults, 18 and older. Margin of error is ±2% for results based on the full sample and ±3% for results based on internet users.
Source: Pew Internet and American Life Project, Tracking Survey, 24 October – 12 December 2007, showing the proportion of US adults online and their demographic make-up (www.pewinternet.org/trends.asp, accessed 5 June 2008).

First, *is my audience online or is it going to be online?* If your customers use digital technology to research and/or purchase *the products and services you provide,* then you absolutely need to embrace digital marketing now to engage with them and retain them. If they don't, then you don't. It really is that simple. Just bear in mind that, as the next generation of consumers start to become your new customers, they're likely to demand more digital interaction from your business. If you're not in a position to deliver that, they could well choose to spend their money elsewhere.

Second, *are my products, services or brands suited to digital marketing?* This can be a tricky one – but the answer is usually yes. Typically it doesn't matter what your product, service or brand is: as long as you've established that there's a viable online audience for it (see question 1), then you should be promoting it online. While some products and services are obviously more suited to online purchase and fulfilment than others (digital files, like e-books or music, spring to mind), you'll also find plenty of items being marketed effectively through digital channels that few people would ever dream of actually purchasing over the internet. Consumers go online to research, evaluate and compare their choices. They make purchasing decisions based on the quality of their online experience and then head to a bricks-and-mortar store to hand over their cash. Boats, cars, houses, apartments, horses, tractors – you name it, they're all being actively and successfully marketed online.

Defining your digital marketing strategy

Once you've decided that you do, in fact, need to pursue some form of digital marketing, the next step is actually to sit down and define your strategy. Unfortunately there is no 'one size fits all' strategic panacea here. We don't have a magic recipe to ensure your digital marketing success, and neither does anybody else (despite some of the online hyperbole you may read on the subject). Basically every business needs to 'bake' its own unique strategy based on its own particular set of circumstances. While the available ingredients are the same (and we'll cover the major ones later in the book), the resulting strategies can be radically different.

It's common sense really. If you sell apples to local grocers by the truckload, your strategy will bear little resemblance to that of a company selling downloadable e-books and reports on financial trading, which will in turn be very different to the strategy adopted by a sports clothing manufacturer who wants to cut out the retailer and sell directly to consumers over the web.

Different products, different markets, different needs – different solutions. What it ultimately boils down to is this: the best people to define your digital marketing strategy, curiously enough, are the people who best know your business.

Laying strong digital foundations

The good news is that you've almost certainly already started the process of defining your digital marketing strategy. Before even picking up this book you've probably been thinking about digital marketing in the context of your business, about what your competitors are doing online and why, about how your customers and prospects are integrating digital technology into their lives, and about how you can best exploit these new and exciting digital channels to foster longer, more productive relationships with them. These are the components that will form the foundation of your digital marketing strategy:

- *Know your business:* Is your business ready to embrace digital marketing? Are your products or services suited to online promotion? Do you have the right technology, skills and infrastructure in place? How will digital marketing fit into your existing business processes, do those processes need to change, and are you and your staff ready to accommodate those changes?
- *Know the competition:* Who are your main competitors in the digital marketplace? Are they the same as your offline competitors? What are they doing right (emulate them), what are they doing wrong (learn from them), what aren't they doing at all (is there an opportunity there for you?) and how can you differentiate your online offering from theirs? Remember, competition in the digital world can come from just around the corner or from right around the globe. The same technologies that allow you to reach out to a broader geographical market also allow others to reach into your local market. When you venture online you're entering a global game, so don't limit your analysis to local competition.
- *Know your customers:* Who are your customers and what do they want from you? Are you going to be servicing the same customer base online, or are you fishing for business from a completely new demographic? How do the customers you're targeting use digital technology, and how can you harness that knowledge to engage in a productive and ongoing relationship with them?
- *Know what you want to achieve:* If you don't know where you're going, there's a pretty fair chance you'll never get there. What do you

want to get out of digital marketing? Setting clear, measurable and achievable goals is a key part of your digital marketing strategy. Are you looking to generate online sales, create a source of targeted sales leads, improve your brand awareness among online communities, all of the above or perhaps something completely different? Your goals are the yardsticks against which you can measure the progress of your digital marketing campaigns.

● *Know how you're doing:* The beauty of digital marketing is that, compared to many forms of advertising, results are so much more measurable. You can track everything that happens online and compare your progress against predefined goals and key performance indicators (KPIs). How is your digital campaign progressing? Are certain digital channels delivering more traffic than others? Why is that? What about conversion rates? How much of that increased traffic results in tangible value to your business? Measure, tweak, refine, re-measure. Digital marketing is an ongoing and iterative process.

The process of formally defining your digital marketing strategy forces you to sit down and analyse the market in which you're operating with a critical eye, and to really think about the different components of your business and how digital marketing can help you to achieve your business goals.

Don't get too bogged down in the technical details – remember, digital marketing is about people communicating with other people; the technology is just the bit in the middle that helps it to happen. Your strategy should provide you with a high-level framework – a bird's-eye view of the digital marketing landscape with your business centre stage; the details will come later.

Understanding the digital consumer

There is a notion that pervades marketing circles today, a notion of mysterious ethereal creatures who exist in a hyper-connected, multifaceted cyber-world of their own. They are an enigma: they speak a different language, communicate in ways we don't understand, and they're turning the world of marketing on its head. These are the ephemeral, wraithlike 'digital consumers', who slip effortlessly through the marketer's grasp. Digital consumers are different, we're told – but are they really?

The digital consumer revealed

The first thing to realize about digital consumers is that there's basically no such thing. The customers and prospects you encounter online are the very same people who walk into your store every day, call you on the telephone, or order something from your mail-order catalogue. There's nothing dark, sinister or mysterious about them. They're people – like everybody else.

'There is no great mystery about how [digital consumers] think and what they want', maintains interactive marketing expert Giles Rhys Jones of Interactive Marketing Trends (http://interactivemarketingtrends. blogspot.com).

These consumers are doing exactly what people have been doing for thousands of years – communicating with each other. The fact that technology is enabling them to communicate with each other faster, over distance, over mobiles and in 3D worlds is being perceived as something dangerous, unique and extraordinary, something that needs to be controlled and pinned down. People talk to each other – they always have. They are talking the same language and saying the same things. They are just not necessarily sitting in the pub talking to one or five people but doing it online to 15 or 5,000.

Making the web their own

Consumers, whatever their 'flavour', don't care about the way marketers define what they do. Concepts like above the line, through the line, below the line, digital, traditional, experiential, linear, analogue, mobile, direct, indirect or any other 'box' we care to slip our marketing endeavours into are completely meaningless to them. All consumers care about is the experience – how the marketing available to them can enhance the experience and help them to make more informed decisions.

People are the single most important element in any form of marketing. That's just as true in the digital space as it is in any other sphere of the discipline. As a marketer you need to understand people and their behaviour – and here's where the notion of the digital consumer does carry some weight, because consumer behaviour is changing, and it's changing because of the pervasive, evocative and enabling nature of digital technology.

'The majority of today's consumers are actively personalizing their digital experiences and sampling niche content and video with increasing frequency', said Dave Friedman, president of the central region for Avenue

A | Razorfish, writing in an article for *Chief Marketer* (www.chiefmarketer. com).

In July 2007, Avenue A | Razorfish surveyed 475 US consumers across all demographics and geographies in an effort to understand their desires, frustrations and digital consumption habits. The results showed that US consumers are adopting digital technology across the board, and are harnessing its power to filter, organize and personalize the content they consume in an increasingly information intensive world.

'We've reached a collective digital tipping point as a majority of consumers are tapping into a variety of emerging technologies and social media to increasingly personalize their digital experiences', said Friedman. 'From recommendation engines, to blogs, to customized start pages, today's "connected consumer" navigates a landscape that is much more niche and personalized than we ever expected.'

The practice of broadcasting generic advertising messages to the mass market is rapidly being usurped by specifically targeted, narrowcast marketing, through digital channels, to an increasingly diverse and segmented marketplace, even, ultimately, to a target market of one. Digital marketing allows us to build uniquely tailored ongoing relationships with individual customers. This is a conversation, not a lecture. Marketing in the digital age has been transformed into a process of dialogue, as much about listening as it is about telling.

I don't know you and you don't know me

Perceived anonymity is another online trait that can have a profound effect on consumer behaviour. It liberates consumers from the social shackles that bind them in the real world; online they are free to do and say as they please with scant regard for the social propriety that holds sway in 'real life'. In a bricks-and-mortar store shoppers will wait patiently for service, and will often endure a less-than-flawless shopping experience to get what they want. Online they won't; they demand instant gratification and a flawless customer experience. You have to deliver, first time, every time. If you fail to engage, retain and fulfil their expectations on demand, they're gone, vanishing into the ether of cyberspace as quickly as they came, the only trace a fleeting, solitary record left on your web server's log file. And then they'll tell all their online friends.

Key traits of the online consumer

We're all familiar with the old road rage analogy of the congenial, neighbourly man or woman who suddenly becomes a raving speed demon when behind the wheel of a car. Well, there's something about the immediacy and anonymity of the digital experience that has a similar effect on people.

It's always risky to generalize and make assumptions about people – especially in a field as dynamic and fast moving as this one. The only real way to know your market intimately is to conduct original research within your particular target group. That said, a lot of research work has been done (and continues to be done) on the behavioural traits of online consumers, and a broad consensus has emerged around the key characteristics that epitomize digital consumers:

- *Digital consumers are increasingly comfortable with the medium:* Many on-line consumers have been using the internet for several years at this stage – and, while the user demographic is still skewed in favour of younger people, even older users are becoming increasingly web savvy. 'It's almost like a piano player who plays faster once they know the instrument. In the beginning people "pling, pling, pling" very carefully, and then they move on to playing symphonies', said web usability guru Jakob Nielsen in an interview with the BBC in 2006. As people become more comfortable with the medium they use it more efficiently and effectively, which means they don't hang around for long: your content needs to deliver what they want, and it needs to deliver quickly.
- *They want it all, and they want it now:* In the digital world, where every-thing happens at a million miles per hour, consumers have grown accustomed to getting their information on demand from multiple sources simultaneously. Their time is a precious commodity, so they want information in a format that they can scan for relevance before investing time in examining the detail. Designers and marketers need to accommodate this desire for 'scannability' and instant gratification when constructing their online offering.
- *They're in control:* The web is no passive medium. Users are in control – in the Web 2.0 world more than ever before. Fail to grasp that simple fact and your target audience won't just fail to engage with you, but they will actively disengage. We need to tailor our marketing to be user-centric, elective or permission based, and offer a real value proposition to the consumer to garner positive results.
- *They're fickle:* The transparency and immediacy of the internet don't eradicate the concept of brand or vendor loyalty, but they do erode it. Building trust in a brand is still a crucial element of digital marketing, but today's consumers have the power to compare and contrast competing brands literally at their fingertips. How does your value proposition stack up against the competition around the country and

across the globe? Your brand identity may be valuable, but if your *overall* value proposition doesn't stack up you'll lose out.

- *They're vocal:* Online consumers talk to each other – a lot. Through peer reviews, blogs, social networks, online forums and communities they're telling each other about their positive online experiences – and the negative ones. From a marketing perspective this is something of a double-edged sword – harness the positive aspects and you have incredible viral potential to propagate your message; get it wrong, and you could just as easily be on the receiving end of an uncomfortable online backlash.

The rise of the digital native

It's 7 am. Janet wakes up to the sound of her iPod, sitting in its cradle across the room, playing a random song from an album she set to download overnight. As she gets out of bed her mobile trills: a text has arrived from her college friend Simon. It's about last night's party.

Janet stabs at the mobile keypad with one hand, deftly firing off a reply, while her other hand opens up her laptop, logs her on to her various social networking accounts and fires up her e-mail. A cursory glance at the mini-feeds on her social network sites shows her that there's nothing major going on amongst her circle of friends, so she quickly checks her e-mail while simultaneously opening up her feed-reader and scanning what's new from her favourite news sites, blogs and other locations around the web. In the background her iPod picks another song at random from her music collection and continues to play.

As the 20 or so messages sent to her overnight jostle for space in her e-mail inbox, Janet's mobile trills again – it's Simon, replying to her message and arranging to meet her before lectures start. She checks the clock widget on her desktop sidebar and fires off a quick confirmation – she'll meet him outside the library in an hour and a half. A quick scan of her incoming mail reveals most of it to be spam that's slipped through the net, but one from her friend Amy catches her eye. She reads it, and is about to reply when she notices that Amy is signed in to her IM account. She sends her an instant message instead.

They chat for a few minutes, mainly about last night's party and what to do after college today. Janet checks the weather in another sidebar widget – there's rain forecast for later. They agree on the cinema. A quick visit to the cinema's website reveals what's on; they check out some online peer-reviews to see what's hot, agree on a film and pre-book the tickets. Job done. Janet glances at the clock – it's 7.15 am, time for a shower and then breakfast.

Welcome to the world of the digital native – a hyper-connected, high-octane world of instant access and gratification with digital technology at its core. To young people today these aren't merely digital tools; they are essential, seamlessly integrated elements of their daily lives. These are digital consumers, the net generation, generation Y – call them what you will. They are insistent, impatient, demanding, multi-tasking information junkies. They are the mass market of tomorrow – and it's absolutely imperative that we, as marketers, learn to speak their language today.

Using influencers to help spread the word

There is one particular category of users online that warrants a special mention when it comes to defining your digital marketing strategy. Dubbed 'influencers', these early adopters are the online opinion leaders. Through blogs, podcasts, forums and social networks they harness the power of the web to extol the virtues of products and brands that they like, and equally to denigrate those they find unsatisfactory.

Why are influencers important to you as a marketer? Because they have the virtual ear of the online masses. People read and listen to what they have to say; they value their opinion and trust their judgement. These online influencers have already won the pivotal battle for the hearts and minds of online consumers. Engage positively with them, and you essentially recruit a team of powerful online advocates who can have a potentially massive impact on a much wider group of consumers. This is the online equivalent of 'word-of-mouth' marketing, on steroids. Of course, give them a negative experience and, well, you can guess the rest.

But how exactly will you recognize these online influencers? A December 2006 report by DoubleClick ('Influencing the Influencers: how online advertising and media impact word of mouth') defined influencers as people who 'strongly agreed' to three or more of the following statements:

- They consider themselves expert in certain areas (such as their work, hobbies or interests).

- People often ask their advice about purchases in areas where they are knowledgeable.
- When they encounter a new product they like they tend to recommend it to friends.
- They have a large social circle and often refer people to one another based on their interests.
- They are active online, using blogs, social networking sites, e-mail, discussion groups, online community boards, etc to connect with their peers.

Identifying the influencers within your market sector, analysing their behaviour and tailoring part of your digital campaign to target this small but influential group can result in disproportionate knock-on benefits. Don't neglect your core market, of course – but certainly consider targeting influencers as part of your overall digital marketing strategy.

Mind your Ps

You might be asking yourself how all this newfangled digital 'stuff' fits into the traditional marketing mix: the venerable four Ps of **P**roduct, **P**rice, **P**romotion and **P**lace. Well, it breaks down something like this.

Place

Let's start with the obvious one: it's the internet. It's the one billion plus people around the world who have decided its better to be connected – whether it's accessed through a computer, a mobile device, IPTV or whatever else might come along. That's really it.

Price

Pricing is critical online. You have to be competitive: this is the internet, and pricing is transparent. You don't necessarily have to be the cheapest – but to compete you need to make sure your overall value proposition to the customer is compelling. Overprice your product and a host of price comparison sites will soon highlight the fact, as will the countless peer-review communities where consumers actively debate the relative merits (or otherwise) of everything from financial products to wedding stationery.

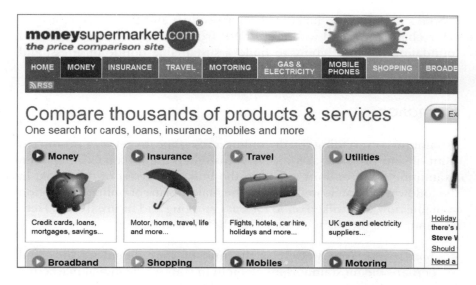

Figure 2.1 Moneysupermarket.com, billed as 'the UK's leading finance price comparison website and a leading UK travel price comparison website'

Product

This is what you have to offer – your unique value proposition to your customers. A good product, of course, is the cornerstone of all successful marketing, but it's particularly crucial in the digital arena. A product that delivers tangible benefits and fills a real need in the marketplace – something that leaves the customer with a genuine perception of value – gives marketers the scope they need to do their job effectively. When you're promoting something viable, it's much easier to engage with consumers and to convince them to buy.

Conversely, the best marketing minds in the world will struggle to promote a product that doesn't deliver the goods. And this is where the all-pervading, viral nature of the internet can really come back to bite you. If you promote a product online and that product doesn't deliver, you'd better be prepared for the backlash.

Digital consumers are no wallflowers – they are vociferous and well connected. They won't keep the shortcomings of your product or business to themselves – they'll shout about it from the tallest building in cyberspace, and others will quickly pick up the cry. Once that happens you can pretty much shelve your marketing ambitions and go back to the drawing board.

So it's important to make sure your product and the entire customer value chain associated with it are right from the start. You need a solid foundation if you're going to build a sustainable online business, and that all starts with a sound product.

Promotion

Promotion is everything you do, online and offline, to get your product in front of your prospects, acquire new customers and retain existing ones. Examining those options will form the bulk of the rest of this book: in the following chapters we'll discuss the major forms of online promotion available now, and will go on to look at emerging and future trends. Here we summarize the main elements to whet your appetite:

- *Your website:* Your website is the hub of your digital world – and perhaps the most important element in your whole digital marketing strategy. It's a vital piece of online real estate to which all of your other online activity will direct your prospects. A lot of the digital marketing techniques discussed in this book are about generating traffic to your website – but traffic in itself is worthless. To become valuable, traffic must be converted – and that's essentially what your website should be: a conversion engine for the traffic being directed to it.

- *Search engine optimization (SEO):* Part and parcel of the website is SEO, or the process of aligning content on your website to what your prospects are actively searching for, and presenting it in a manner that makes it accessible to both people and search engines. The organic or natural search results (the results in the middle of the search engine results page) are the place to be if you want to increase targeted traffic to your website.

- *Pay-per-click search advertising (PPC):* Pay-per-click advertising offers you a way to buy your way on to the search results pages for chosen keywords or key phrases. Depending on your business and what keywords you want to rank for, this can be an extremely effective way of generating search engine traffic quickly, although as the medium continues to gain in popularity more competitive keywords are becoming prohibitively expensive for smaller businesses.

- *Affiliate marketing and strategic partnerships:* how to partner with other organizations and websites in mutually beneficial relationships to promote your products or services.

- *Online public relations:* using online channels like press releases, article syndication and blogs to create a positive perception of your brand and/or position you as an authority in your particular field.

- *Social networking:* a relatively new marketing opportunity, but one that can potentially offer highly targeted advertising to niche social groups based on profile information they volunteer through sites like Bebo, Facebook, MySpace and others.
- *E-mail marketing:* the granddaddy of internet marketing, suffering something of a crisis in the wake of perpetual spam bombardment, but still an important tool in the digital marketer's arsenal, particularly when it comes to maintaining ongoing relationships with existing customers and prospects who've 'opted in' to receive information.
- *Customer relationship management:* Retaining existing customers and building mutually rewarding relationships with them are another important element of digital marketing. Digital technology makes developing an enduring connection with your customers more straightforward and effective than ever before.

Eyes on the prize

Another crucially important area of your digital marketing strategy is setting realistic goals. Your strategy should explicitly define the business goals you want your digital marketing efforts to help you achieve. As with any other journey, you can only plan an effective route if you have a clear, unambiguous destination in mind from the start. Or, to put it another way, you might be the world's best archer – but if nobody gives you a target to aim at what good will it do you?

To measure your progress towards those goals, you also need to set milestones along the way, consistently measuring your achievements, and steering your digital campaign towards your ultimate destination. Here again the digital realm offers a raft of tools and techniques to help marketers reap a better return from their investment.

We'll be examining the topic of web metrics and website intelligence in Chapter 5, but the crucial thing to remember here is that digital marketing is an iterative process of continuous improvement and refinement. You can monitor and analyse the effectiveness of your digital marketing campaigns in practically real time. You can measure everything and even run alternative ads and strategies side by side to see what works best before committing to a given course: test, refine, retest and then decide where to make your investment based on real data from real customers.

Tracking accountability

When a computer or mobile phone – in fact let's call it a digital media device – hits a site, a record is created in the web server's log file based on the unique IP address of that user, and the user's navigation through the site is tracked. Software on the web server also sends a small, unobtrusive file to the user's browser known as a 'cookie', which essentially allows the web server to recognize the same user when he or she comes back to the site again.

Based on information in the log file, marketers can tell a surprising amount about the user's activity on the site:

● We know the broad geographical location based on the digits in the IP address.
● We know when the user arrived and from where.
● We know what type of browser and operating system the person is using.

So far we know very little but we can already start to be more accountable. For example, we can now order our advertising and marketing messages to be delivered only to people with a Mac who live in Ireland and don't like working before lunchtime but are seriously interested in sports.

Now let's make things a little more interesting. By adding specific 'page tags' to our website (with the help of a website developer, webmaster and analytics partner) we can start to do some very clever things – following website visitors to the purchase point and beyond.

For example, say we choose to run a banner ad campaign. We can detect not only the people who click on the banner and go through the site to become purchasers, but also those people who do *not* click on the banner but then go ahead and buy the product anyway a few weeks later. This is really exciting stuff for marketers because ultimately it dispenses with our whole fascination with the value of the click-through.

Not long ago digital marketing metrics were all about clicks, clicks, clicks. Today, while clicks remain an important guideline, ultimately they are about as useful as saying 230 people noticed my ad today, isn't that great? Well, in a word, no. Today's online marketing investment is about tangible returns; it's about conversion and ROI; ultimately it is about the accountability of the brand, the price, the ad campaign and the job of the marketer.

Which scenario would you rather: a warm post-campaign glow when the research company pats you on the back and says well done for achieving a 10 per cent increase in brand recall among 18- to 24-year-olds, or 1,293 enquiries about your product and the names and addresses (e-mail, of course) of the 233 new customers who now own your product?

Online marketing is very like direct marketing in that regard. You invest, you sell, you weigh up your ROI, you learn, you adapt and you move on. Except that online the process is much accelerated. Yes, of course there's still value in brand-based advertising. The drum-playing gorilla who makes you want to eat Dairy Milk, or the girl on the bench who makes you want to whistle the Nokia tune and give her your Coca-Cola: it's all good brand-building stuff and the kind of advertising that's sure to remain with us. The big problem with it is its lack of accountability.

The truth is that digital is simply more accountable. You have far more control and can make far more informed decisions based on the feedback and information the technology provides. It's easy to control the pace and flow of your marketing budget, to turn it up or down and to channel it in different directions.

If you are selling holidays, for example, you already know enough about your customers to realize that certain times of the year (holiday season) are less effective for advertising than others (freezing winter days). But how cool would it be if you could target your holiday advertising so that your ads start to run when the temperature drops below 10 degrees in a particular region? What about being able to advertise your currency exchange services based on the performance of the markets? Well, in the digital world you can do that. The potential is boundless.

Bringing it all together

There's a lot to think about when defining your digital marketing strategy, but in the end the process is about researching, analysing and understanding three things that are crucial to your success: your business, your competition and your customers. Your strategy lays the foundation for everything you'll do as a digital marketer, and will guide the decisions you make as you implement some of the techniques outlined in the coming chapters – and choose not to implement others, precisely because they don't fit with your chosen strategy.

Effective digital marketing is about boxing clever. You pick and choose the elements that are specifically relevant to your business. Going through the process of defining a clear strategy, based on a thorough analysis of where your business is now and where you want digital marketing to take it, puts you in the ideal position to know what's likely to work for you and, just as importantly, what probably won't.

Case study: Dove Self-Esteem Fund 2006

Campaign brief

The focus of the campaign was to invite women in Canada to become involved in Dove's mission to foster positive self-esteem in the lives of young girls. The campaign was targeted at mums, mentors and educators as well as any other relevant agencies to reach as many women as possible with Dove's message of 'Real Beauty'. The ultimate goal was to effect change positively in the lives of 70,000 Canadian girls.

The specific online media objective was to provoke mothers to think about their daughters' self-esteem and inspire them to get involved in using the Dove Self-Esteem Fund resources and tools found on campaignforrealbeauty.ca.

Campaign concept

Two films were developed by Ogilvy & Mather, Canada to encourage attendance at Dove Self-Esteem Workshops and to engage with the Campaignforrealbeauty site. The first, 'Daughters', featured daughters talking about the pressures on young girls to be pretty and thin, and the overemphasis on external appearances. The film also featured mums talking about their empathy for their daughters struggling with these pressures. The film's message was 'Things won't change until we change them.'

The second film was 'Evolution'. This featured a young, pretty girl in front of a mirror whose image is 'modellized' by make-up artists, hairdressers, etc and then completely airbrushed so that the end result is completely different from the original shot of the girl. The core message of this film was 'No wonder our perception of beauty is distorted.'

Campaign strategy

The online media strategy was to develop a multi-layer online campaign that would:

1. Generate awareness of the Dove Self-Esteem tools and resources.
2. Launch a 'teaser' one-minute film. A 15-second viral 'film trailer' was streamed on mass and targeted women's websites in Canada. The trailers

exposed the need for the Dove Self-Esteem Fund and drove traffic to the Campaignforrealbeauty site to view the complete film.
3.   Develop a series of customized e-newsletters that were targeted at mothers and teachers to introduce Dove Self-Esteem Fund tools and resources.

Two viral films were produced, 'Daughters' and 'Evolution', with the aim of capturing attention and driving traffic to the Campaignforrealbeauty.ca website and encouraging viewers to sign up to the Real Beauty workshops to be held at 15 locations in Canada.

The campaign

In September 2006 the 'Daughters' video was posted on YouTube, and the viral version of the video was launched along with an e-mail and online banners campaign. The 'Evolution' video was posted on YouTube in October 2006, and again this was followed by the launch of the viral version of 'Evolution', the 'Evolution' e-mail campaign and online banners.

Results

During the fourth quarter of 2006 the average daily visits to the Campaign For Real Beauty site grew from 1,378 to 16,785, an increase of 1,118 per cent.
   Results from the 'Daughters' e-mail campaign:

● 220,942 e-mails delivered;
● 72,070 e-mails opened (33 per cent);
● 30,749 e-mails clicked (13 per cent).

Results from the 'Evolution' e-mail campaign:

● 224,174 e-mails delivered;
● 75,055 e-mails opened (33 per cent);
● 25,475 e-mails clicked (11 per cent).

The 'Evolution' film had compelling mass appeal online in its ideas and creative, while 'Daughters' was more targeted in its appeal to mothers and mentors:

● 'Evolution' video downloads: 115,212;
● 'Daughters' video downloads: 32,818;
● 'Evolution': Tell-a-Friend: 12,228;
● 'Daughters': Tell-a-Friend: 2,992.

Online media key findings:

● English-speaking and French-speaking Canadians responded differently to the creative messages. The English-speaking Canadians responded more to the 'Evolution' message, while the French-speaking Canadians responded more to 'Daughters'.

- There was a difference in the performance of different online advertising units: large 'Big Box'-type ads (sizeable ads appearing in the actual content of a web page) outperformed Leaderboard ads (large horizontal banners across the top of a web page). Consequently PHD, the agency responsible, shifted its focus from Leaderboard to Big Box format.
- Newsletter results were higher from niche sites, highlighting the higher degree of trust in niche sites and the greater interactivity by their visitors.
- Weekly campaign results enabled the campaign to be optimized effectively and adapted where necessary.
- The campaign had such an immediate and strong impact that it has been extended globally.

Credits

Brand: Dove, Unilever, Canada
Agencies: Ogilvy & Mather, Canada and PHD, Canada

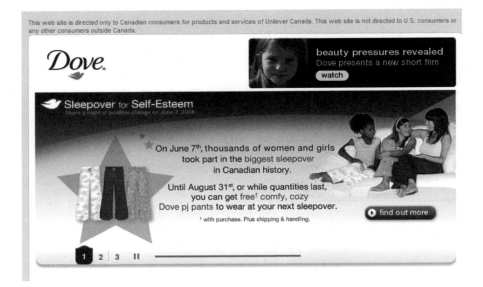

Figure 2.2 Dove Canada's 'Self Esteem Fund' and the 'Campaign for Real Beauty' website were so successful they were picked up and rolled out globally by the Unilever brand

3 Your window to the digital world

I feel I'm able to serve my customer by knowing what she or he wants. One of the ways I'm able to do this is through my website, and email: people give me great ideas, tell me what they want, what they don't want. It's really instrumental, and helps me stay in touch with people.

(Kathy Ireland)

If you do build a great experience, customers tell each other about that. Word of mouth is very powerful.

(Jeff Bezos)

Small opportunities are often the beginning of great enterprises.

(Demosthenes, 384–322 BC)

Our chapter pledge to you

When you reach the end of this chapter you'll have answers to the following questions:

- Why is my website so important?
- How do I build an effective website?
- How should I structure the information on my website?
- What is usability, and why should I care?

- Why are accessibility and web standards important?
- How do I create compelling web content?

Your website – the hub of your digital marketing world

If you are a digital marketer, your website is your place of business. You may have all sorts of campaigns out there, tapping the far-flung reaches of cyberspace for a rich vein of new customers, but ultimately everything will be channelled back through a single point: your website. That makes your website incredibly valuable. In fact, it's the single most valuable piece of digital real estate you'll ever own. Get your digital marketing strategy right and, who knows, it could well end up being the most valuable piece of real estate you own, period.

We can't stress this point enough. In an uncertain and constantly evolving digital world, your website is the one thing over which you have complete and explicit control. You can change anything and everything on your website; you can tweak it, tune it and manipulate it in any way you want; you can build in ways to track and measure *all* of the activity on your website. You own it, it's yours, and it's the yardstick by which your entire online business will be measured.

A conversion engine for traffic

All of the digital marketing techniques we'll discuss in the coming chapters have one thing in common: they're designed to drive targeted, pre-qualified traffic to your website. But traffic on its own does nothing but consume internet bandwidth. It's your website that converts that traffic into prospects and/or customers – taking the numbers and transforming them into something of tangible value to your business.

If you are a digital marketer your website is *not* just an online brochure to let people know who you are and what you do. Granted, some of the information you provide on your site will serve that purpose – but only in a peripheral capacity. Nor is it simply there to garner search engine 'mojo' and generate huge volumes of traffic. Think of your website primarily as a *conversion engine* for the traffic you garner through all of your other digital marketing endeavours.

Yes, you need to provide information about your business, products and services – but always with your conversion goals in mind. Everything on your website should be geared towards achieving those conversion goals, either directly (products and service information, online ordering and sales functionality, sales-focused copy and calls to action, enquiry forms, newsletter sign-up, etc) or indirectly (business and brand information that builds trust, and content that encourages repeat visits and/or establishes your authority or reputation in your field).

Your conversion goals could be anything from an actual online purchase (a sales transaction), to an online query (lead generation), to subscribing for your online newsletter (opt-in for future marketing) – or whatever else you decide is important for your business and appropriate for your customers. You can, of course, have multiple, tiered conversion goals. Your primary goal might be an online sale or booking, your secondary goal could be online lead generation and your tertiary goal could be to harvest e-mails for your opt-in mailing list.

It doesn't matter what your goals are or whether your website is a small information or brochure-type site or a huge online store; the important thing is that you keep them in mind when you design (or redesign) your website. Remember, conversion is the key to digital marketing success; your website, and the user experience you deliver through it, is what will ultimately drive that conversion.

Building an effective website

An effective website is essentially about the convergence of two things: your business goals and the needs of your target market. Build something that aligns the two and you'll end up with an effective website. Broken down like that it sounds simple, but achieving that convergence can be a tricky process – and a quick surf around the web will soon demonstrate that it's easier to get it wrong than to get it right.

You'll note we used the word 'effective' rather than 'successful'. For a website to be successful people need to be able to find it (which we'll cover in the next chapter on search), but if you build your site to cater for the right people's needs you significantly increase the chance that, once they arrive, they'll become more than just a passing statistic.

First, let's state here and now that this isn't a definitive guide to website development. This is a book about digital marketing. In this chapter we'll be exploring how to approach your website with digital marketing in mind. Our focus is to maximize the effectiveness of your website with a view to your digital marketing endeavours. What follows is a high-level overview of the important elements to consider when designing your website from a digital marketing perspective. It is not meant to be an exhaustive guide. Most of the topics we touch on here would warrant an entire book to themselves. In fact, if you surf on over to Amazon you'll find a swath of titles available in each category. You'll also find an avalanche of relevant (and of course irrelevant) information on the web.

Here, our aim is to arm you with the high-level knowledge you'll need to make informed decisions about your website design in a digital marketing context and to communicate exactly what you need to your web design partners when it's time to construct your digital hub.

The main steps of building your website

Different businesses will follow different processes involving different groups of people when designing, developing and implementing a website, but regardless of the approach you choose to take, how formal or informal the process, there are a number of key stages that generally form part of any web development project:

- *Planning:* Establish your goals for the site; analyse the competition; define who your target market is, how they'll find you online and what they're going to be looking for when they arrive; map out a schedule and decide who's going to do what and when.
- *Design:* Decide on the 'look and feel' of the site: colours, graphics, information architecture,[1] navigation, etc.
- *Development:* putting it all together, taking the agreed design and constructing the actual pages of the site, crafting the content, links and navigation hierarchy.
- *Testing:* making sure everything works the way it should before you let it out on to the big bad internet.
- *Deployment:* Your new site becomes live on the internet for the whole world to find – or not, as the case may be.

Before you start

Know why you're building a website

'What is my website for?' It's a simple enough question, yet you'd be amazed by how many businesses have never asked it. They have a website because everyone else has one and it seemed like a good idea at the time. The result is a site, invariably an isolated little island in the backwaters of cyberspace, that brings nothing to the business but the expense of annual hosting and maintenance.

Ideally you should have a clear idea of exactly what it is your organization wants to achieve from a website *before* you start to build it.

Know who your website is for

Knowing who exactly you're creating your website for is also crucial to its success. Yet, surprisingly, it's another thing that's often overlooked in the process. Far too many websites end up being designed to appeal to the committee of executives who ultimately sign off on the project, instead of the people who will actually be using them. Don't fall into that trap. For your website to succeed it needs to appeal to one group of people and one group of people only: your target market.

Think about how your users will access your website; what will they want to find when they get there, and how can your site fulfil those needs? Put yourself in their shoes or, better still, ask them directly what they'd like to see or do on your website. Try conducting some informal market research with people who would potentially use your website (online and/ or offline). The results may be illuminating, and could be the difference between a successful website and an expensive online experiment.

Build usability and accessibility into your website design

Usability and accessibility are central to good web design – and yet both are frequently ignored, or at least are not given the weighting they warrant when it comes to making design decisions. They are about making sure that your site content can be accessed by the widest-possible audience and delivering the information and functionality users want in a way they're comfortable and familiar with.

Usability

The theory behind web usability is straightforward enough: simple, elegant and functional design helps users to achieve what they want to achieve online more effectively. It's about taking the frustration out of the user experience, making sure things work intuitively, eliminating barriers so that users accomplish their goals almost effortlessly. Your goal is to help the users to do what they want to do in the most efficient and effective way possible. Everything else is just web clutter. Achieving a simple, elegant design that delivers what the user wants with a minimum of fuss isn't easy, but putting in the effort can pay huge dividends.

For a step-by-step guide to usability, and a comprehensive downloadable e-book of research-based web design and usability guidelines, check out the US government's usability website at www.usability.gov.

Accessibility

The term 'accessibility', in relation to the web, refers to the process of designing your website to be equally accessible to everyone. A well-designed website should allow all users equal access to the information and functionality the site delivers. By adhering to accessibility guidelines when designing your site you're basically making sure that it's useful to as broad a cross-section of your target audience as possible.

If your site complies with accessibility guidelines it will work seamlessly with hardware and software designed to make the internet more accessible to people with disabilities. For example, by making sure you include descriptive text alternatives to images and multimedia content on your website you can help visually impaired or even completely sightless visitors to access your site through special text-to-speech software and/or text-to-Braille hardware. How stringently you choose to adhere to these accessibility guidelines will depend on several factors, including the nature of your site, your target audience and, in some circumstances, the requirements of local accessibility legislation.

With both accessibility and usability very small and simple steps can make a big difference; even something as small as ensuring that the text on your website resizes according to the user's browser preferences can have a huge impact on some people's ability to use your site effectively.

You'll find a more detailed look at website accessibility, including all of the most current accessibility standards and guidelines, on the W3C website at www.w3.org/WAI/.

A word about the W3C and web standards

The World Wide Web Consortium (W3C, www.w3.org) is the gatekeeper of web standards. Its mission: 'to lead the World Wide Web to its full potential by developing protocols and guidelines that ensure long-term growth for the Web'.

Since its inception in 1994 the consortium has published more than 110 of these standards, which it calls W3C Recommendations. These open standards are primarily designed to ensure what the W3C calls the 'interoperability of the web' – or basically to make sure that all of the different computers, platforms and technologies that make up and access the web can work together seamlessly.

In practice it's a good idea to make sure that your website is designed and implemented to be web standard compliant. A standards-compliant website is much more likely to work consistently across the different browsers and operating systems used by your target market. It also future-proofs your site to some extent, reducing the need for maintenance. Standards-compliant sites should (in theory at least) continue to work consistently with new browser versions (which *should* be backward compatible with the standards), while a non-compliant site may not.

Maintaining a standards-compliant site is also more straightforward, because the code that makes up the pages is, you guessed it, *standard.* It makes it easier for a web developer to pick up and maintain somebody else's code – which could be important if you decide to change your web designer or to bring the entire process in-house in the future.

In general you should aim to make sure your site is as standards compliant as possible while still achieving what you need. Make sure your web designer knows you're aware of web standards and that you want your site to adhere to them. All of the standards are available on the W3C site, and there are online validators that will screen your pages for compliance. You can even download a little 'badge' to display in the footer of your standards-compliant website to prove to the world that your pages validate.

Words make your website tick

The world of the web is dominated by words. Audio, video, flash and animation may seem to be everywhere online but, even in an era where multimedia content seems to be taking over, at its core the web is still all about text and the connections between different words and phrases on and between websites. To a digital marketer, some of those words and phrases are more important than others, and knowing which words are relevant to your business is essential to building an effective website. These are your keywords or key phrases, and in the search-dominated world of the digital marketer they are, in a word, key. Exactly what they are will depend on your business, the digital marketing goals you defined as part of your overall strategy, and the online behaviour of your target market. But you need to know what they are.

Keywords are practically synonymous with search, so we cover the basics of keyword research and selection in the search chapter (Chapter 4). But it's a very good idea to have your list of target keywords in mind from the very beginning. It's much easier to optimize a site for search engines as you build it than it is to retro-fit search engine optimization after the fact. Your keywords will help to guide everything, from your site design to your information architecture and navigation, right down to the content you put on the individual pages of your website.

Know your competition

Identifying your competition, analysing what they're trying to achieve with their websites, where they're succeeding and where they're failing, can be a great way of getting ideas and looking at different ways you can compete online. Take the keyword phrases you've identified for your website and type them into leading search engines. The sites that rank highly for your keywords are your online competition.

What are they doing well, and how easy would it be for you to emulate and improve on those things? Put yourself in the user's shoes. What sort of user experience are the sites offering? How could it be improved upon? What about the content? A thorough analysis of your online competition can reveal a lot, not just about them and what they offer online, but about the direction you choose to take with your website in order to compete effectively with them.

Choosing your domain name

Every website on the internet has a unique address (a slight simplification, but we don't need to get into the complexities here). It's called an IP address, and it's not very interesting, informative or memorable to most humans. It consists of a series of numbers something like 64.233.167.99 (type that address into your browser and see where it takes you).

While that's fine for computers and the occasional numerically inclined tech-head, it's not much use to the rest of us. So back in the early days of the internet, the domain name system was developed to assign human-readable names to these numeric addresses. These domain names – things like digitalmarketingsuccess.com, google.com, wikipedia. org or harvard.edu – are naturally much more useful and memorable to your average human than the IP addresses they relate to.

You need your own domain name

If you don't have your own domain name, you're going to need to register one. As a business, if you want to be taken seriously online, piggybacking on someone else's domain is completely unacceptable. An address like www.mysite.someothersite.com or www.someothersite.com/mysite/ looks unprofessional, makes your web address difficult to remember, won't do you any favours with search engines and generally tarnishes your business image wherever you publicize it, online and off.

The good news is that registering a domain is cheap (less than US$10 per year, depending on the domain registrar you choose) and easy. It may be included as part of the package offered by your website developer, or you can easily register a domain yourself. You can check availability, select your domain and register it in minutes online (www.mydomain.com is the registrar we used to register the domain associated with this book; there are plenty more to choose from: just type 'domain registration' into your favourite search engine and you'll be presented with plenty of options).

NB: While most domains operate on a first-come-first-served basis, some country-specific domains (such as Ireland's .ie domains) have special eligibility conditions that need to be satisfied before the registration is confirmed. Check with the relevant country's domain name authority to see if any country-specific conditions apply to the domain(s) you're interested in.

Some things to bear in mind when choosing your domain name are:

- *Make it catchy, memorable and relevant:* Choose a catchy, easily identifiable domain name that's relevant to your business and *easy for people to remember.*
- *Use a country-specific top-level domain (TLD)[2] to appeal to a local audience:* If your market is local, it often pays to register the local version of the domain (.co.uk or .ie, for example) instead of (or as well as) the more generic .com, .net or .org. If you're appealing to an international audience, a generic TLD may serve you better. Of the generic TLDs, .com is by far the most universally accepted and popular – making it the most valuable one to secure.
- *You can buy multiple domain names:* There's nothing to stop you buying more than one domain to prevent others from registering them. You can then *redirect* the secondary domains to point to your main website. Another option is registering country-specific domains to give yourself an online 'presence' in each country you do business in. You can then deploy a regionally tailored version of your website to each of those domains (the preferable option) or redirect them to a localized section on your main website.
- *Keywords in a domain name can be beneficial:* You may decide to incorporate one of your keyword phrases into your domain name. Opinion varies on the significance of this in terms of its impact on your search engine ranking, but it may help both search engines and users to establish what your site is about right from the start.

Hosting – your website's home on the internet

The other bit of housekeeping you'll need to take care of before your site goes live is hosting. Your finished site will consist of files, applications and possibly a database, all of which sit on a computer that's permanently connected to the internet. This computer is your web server, and will be running special software that will accept requests from users' web browsers and deliver your web pages by return. It's a bit more complicated, but basically that's what it boils down to.

Unless you belong to a large organization with its own data centre that has a permanent connection to the internet backbone, it's highly unlikely that you'll host your site in-house. A much more likely scenario is that you'll arrange a hosting solution through a specialist hosting provider.

Different types of hosting

There are basically four different types of hosting offered by web hosting companies, all of which are perfectly acceptable for your business website. Which option you choose will depend largely on your budget, how busy you anticipate your website will be (in terms of visitor traffic), and the amount of control you want over the configuration of the server (whether you need to install your own custom software, change security settings, configure web server options, etc).

NB: A word of warning here: avoid 'free' hosting accounts. While they may be tempting for a small business site to begin with, they tend to be unreliable, often serve up annoying ads at the top of your site, don't offer the flexibility or functionality of a paid hosting account, may not support the use of your own domain name, offer limited (if any) support, and present a greater risk that you'll be sharing your server with some less-than-desirable neighbours – which can hurt your search engine rankings.

Shared hosting accounts

With shared hosting you are essentially renting space on a powerful server where your website(s) will sit alongside a number of other websites (typically hundreds, sometimes thousands, on a single server). Each hosting account has its own, secure virtual space on the server where you can upload your site's files. A dedicated control panel for account administration offers some degree of control over server configuration and usually provides access to a suite of additional software and tools to help you (or your webmaster) manage your website(s). All of the websites on a server typically share system resources like CPU, RAM, etc.

Shared hosting is the most common and cheapest form of hosting, and it's how the majority of websites – particularly for small to medium businesses – start out. Most shared hosting accounts have space restrictions and a monthly bandwidth cap. They are ideal for small to medium businesses and websites with average levels of traffic. In most instances this is the most cost-effective form of hosting.

Virtual dedicated hosting

With virtual dedicated hosting a single server is 'split' into a number of virtual servers. All the users feel as though they're on their own dedicated server, when in fact they're on the same physical machine. The users will typically have complete administrative control over their own virtual space. This is also known as a virtual private server or VPS. While virtual dedicated hosting offers complete flexibility in terms of the administration, software and configuration options available, you're still sharing server resources with other users and websites.

Dedicated hosting

Dedicated hosting solutions provide a dedicated, high-powered server for your website(s) and your website(s) alone. You don't share space or system resources with anybody else – which means you don't share the cost either, making dedicated hosting expensive.

Dedicated servers offer much more power and flexibility, because changes made to the server affect only your website(s). That means that you (or your webmaster or technical team) have pretty much complete control over server configuration, security, software and settings. Dedicated servers also typically offer much more capacity in terms of space and bandwidth than shared hosting – making them suitable for high-traffic sites.

Because of the flexibility and control offered by dedicated hosting solutions (complete control over the host computer), they tend to require more technical ability to administer than shared hosting environments.

Server co-location

Co-location is essentially the same as dedicated hosting except that, instead of the hosting company providing a pre-configured dedicated server for your website, you buy and configure your own server, which is then hosted in their dedicated hosting facility. This offers perhaps the ultimate in flexibility, because you have complete control not only over the software and setting on the server, but also over the hardware specification, operating system, software, security – everything. Co-location is essentially the same as hosting your own server in your own office – except that your server is plugged into a rack in a dedicated hosting facility with all of the bells and whistles you'd expect.

Choosing your hosting company

Your website developer will be able to help you decide which web hosting option is right for you, based on the size, design, functionality and configuration of your website, and your anticipated levels of traffic based on your business goals. The developer should also be able to recommend a reliable web hosting company that will serve your needs.

When choosing your web host bear the following in mind:

- *Choose a host in the country where your primary target market lives:* This is important, because search engines deliver local search results to users based on the geographical location of the server on which the web pages reside (which they can infer from the server IP address).
- *Make sure the host is reliable:* Do they offer guaranteed uptime and levels of service? Many hosts publish live server statistics that demonstrate the reliability of their services. You should expect a service level approaching 100 per cent from a high-quality hosting service.
- *Find out what sort of support they offer:* Make sure the hosting you choose includes efficient and effective support 24/7. If your website goes down you need to be confident you can call on your host for assistance whatever time of the day or night.
- *Back-up and disaster recovery:* If the worst happens and the server goes belly up, what sort of disaster recovery options does the host have in place? Ideally your host should take several daily snapshots of your entire account/server, allowing them to restore it and get your site back up and running as quickly as possible should the worst happen.
- *What others think:* Find out what other customers think. Read testimonials, and search for discussions on webmaster forums relating to the hosts you're considering. Are other people's experiences good or bad? Post a few questions.
- *Shop around:* Hosting is an incredibly competitive industry, so shop around for the best deal – but bear in mind that the cheapest option isn't always the best choice.

How to choose a web designer or developer

Unless you're a web designer yourself or have access to a dedicated in-house web development team, you'll need to bring in a professional web design firm to help you with your website project. You'll find a host of options out there, offering a range of services that will make your mind boggle. The good news is, if you've done your preliminary work, you should already have a fair idea what you want out of your website, who it's aimed at and the sort of features you'd like to include. Armed with that knowledge, you can start to whittle down the list of potential designers to something more manageable:

- *Look at their own website:* In trying to assess the relative merits of a web design company, the best place to start is with their own website. What's their site like? Examine it with a critical eye. Does it look professional? Is it functional? Think about what they're trying to achieve and how well the site addresses the needs of its target audience (you, in this case). Is it easy to find what you want? Does it meet or exceed your expectations? If not, do you really want the same people working on your website?
- *Examine their portfolio:* Practically every web design firm offers an online portfolio showing recent website projects they've worked on. Look at these – but go beyond the portfolio pages and click through to the actual websites themselves. Again, put your analytical hat on and ask what the sites are trying to achieve, who they're aimed at and how well the designers have achieved those goals.

That should give you enough of a steer to produce a reasonable shortlist of potential candidates. Now you can dig a little deeper:

- *Ask their customers for recommendations:* Go back to the best of the portfolio sites for your shortlisted designers. Go to the 'Contact us' page and drop them a line by e-mail or pick up the phone to ask for some honest feedback on their web design experience. Would they recommend the firm?
- *What's their online reputation like?* Web forums, online communities and peer-review sites are other good places to look for information about your shortlisted web design firms. Is the online vibe positive or negative? What are people saying about them?

- *Are they designing sites to be found?* Your website is only as good as the quality traffic it gets. Are your shortlisted designers search engine savvy? Go back to the portfolio sites you looked at and pick out some of the keyword phrases you'd expect them to rank for in a search engine. Now go to the search engines and type in those keyword phrases. Have those sites been indexed? Where do they rank on the search results page? Low ranking doesn't necessarily indicate a problem with their web design – there are many components that contribute to search engine ranking (see Chapter 4), but it may be something you should ask them to clarify before making your decision.
- *Do they adhere to web standards?* Go to the W3C website validation page (http://www.w3.org/QA/Tools/) and run the web addresses of your shortlisted web designers through the MarkUp Validator, Link Checker and CSS Validator. Do the sites validate as web standards compliant? You shouldn't necessarily discount your favourite designers because of this – but it is something else you should ask them about before making your final decision.

By now you should have whittled your shortlist down to a few competent and professional companies you'd like to quote or tender on your website project. The final decision is, of course, up to you.

Arranging your information

Your site structure – the way you arrange and group your information and how users navigate their way around it – can have a massive impact on its usability, its visibility to search engine spiders, its rank in search engine results pages (SERPs)[3] and its potential to convert the traffic once it arrives. Getting your information architecture right is absolutely critical to the success of your website.

It can be difficult to know where to start. You know what information you want on your site, but what's the best way of arranging it so that users can access it intuitively, at the level of granularity they desire, while also providing you with maximum exposure in the search engines for specific keywords? The answer, as is so often the case in digital marketing, is that it depends. It depends on the sort of business you're in, the type of site you're building, your target audience, your business goals and a whole host of other variables.

Start with your keywords

The keywords your potential users are searching on should give you a good indication of both the content they're looking for and the search terms you want your site to rank for in the SERPs. Take those keywords and arrange them into logical categories or themes. These themes, along with the staple 'Home page', 'About us' and 'Contact us' links, give you the primary navigation structure for your site.

Define your content structure

Look at your main themes, the keywords you've associated with each of them and the corresponding information or content you want to include beneath each. Now define a tiered hierarchy of sub-categories (your secondary, tertiary, etc navigation levels) within each theme as necessary until you have all of your targeted keywords covered. Arrange your content so that the most important information is summarized at

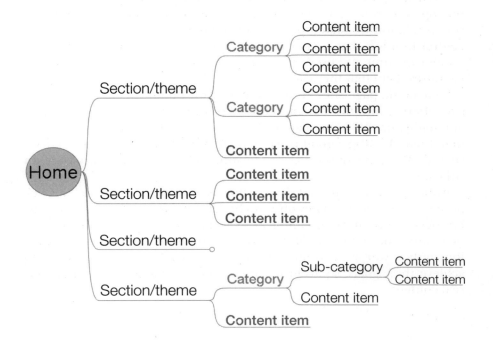

Figure 3.1 A simple website information hierarchy

the highest levels, allowing the user to drill down to more detailed but less important information on the specific topic as required. Try not to go too deep in terms of navigation sub-categories – it is rarely necessary to go beyond three, in exceptional cases four, levels deep from the home page.

Your home page

The home page is often perceived as one of the most important pages on your site, but is potentially one of the least useful, both to your business and to your site visitors. For a start, home pages tend, by necessity, to be relatively generic: too generic to answer a user's specific query or to entice instantly the conversion you crave. Indeed, many of your visitors – especially those arriving from a search engine or by clicking on a link from another website or an online advertisement – will tend to land on a much more focused internal page, one that deals with the specific topic that they've searched for or clicked on. This deeper page should be much better at satisfying their immediate requirements.

Where a home page comes into its own is as a central reference point for navigating your content. A breadcrumb trail or navigation path along the top of your site can tell users at a glance exactly where they are on your site in relation to a fixed point: your home page. It's also a convenient central location that users can easily return to. No matter where they wander on your site users are always only one click from home, which reassures them that they can't get lost.

Your home page should be a 'jumping-off point' for the rest of your site, offering intuitive navigation to all of your main sections or themes, and telling people immediately what your site is all about and how it can help them. It's also a good place to highlight new products and services, special offers, incentives, news or anything else you want to promote on your site.

Avoid splash screens that simply show your company logo and a 'Click here to enter' button. They offer no benefit at all to your users or to your business – they are web clutter at its worst. Likewise flash intros – the 'Skip intro' button is one of the most widely clicked buttons on the web. Remember, you want to make it as easy as possible for your visitors to achieve their goals, so avoid putting obstacles between them and your real content.

Writing effective web content

Now you've defined a structure for your information you're ready to put together your content. Stop! Don't make the mistake that often happens with new websites. You can't simply take your offline marketing collateral and paste the same copy into your web pages and expect it to work.

The golden rule of writing effectively in any medium is to know your audience – the more your writing is tailored to your audience, the more effective it is. It's exactly the same on the web. The difference between effective web writing and effective print writing reflects the core difference in the nature of the audience. Print is a linear medium; the web is random access. People read through printed material from beginning to end; on the web they scan and skip. Offline readers are patient; online readers want the information they're looking for now, now, now.

We already know a bit about the characteristics of online users from our look at online consumer behaviour in the last chapter – writing effective web content is about taking what we know about web users in general, and the target audience of our website in particular, and applying that knowledge to deliver our information in a format that meets those readers' needs:

- *Grab attention:* Web users are impatient. Forget flowery introductions and verbose descriptions; make your writing clear, concise and to the point from the start.
- *Make it scannable:* Avoid large blocks of uninterrupted text. Use headings, sub-headings and bullet points to break up the text into manageable, scannable stand-alone chunks.
- *Make it original:* Unique, original content is a great way to engage your users and establish your relevance and authority, and search engines love it.
- *Use the inverted pyramid:* The inverted-pyramid writing style often used for newspaper stories tends to work well on the web. Aim to deliver the most important points of your story first, going on to deliver supporting details in order of decreasing importance down the page. Ideally, the user should be able to stop reading at any point and still get the gist of the content.
- *Be consistent:* Use a simple, easy-to-read writing style, and keep things consistent across the site. If you have a number of people creating your content, consider developing a style guide or house style to help maintain consistency.
- *Engage with your reader:* Use a conversational style, and write as if you were talking to an *individual* rather than an audience. It will help your writing to engage with the reader on a much more personal level.

Top ten mistakes in web design

Jakob Nielsen

Since my first attempt in 1996, I have compiled many top-10 lists of the biggest mistakes in web design. This article presents the highlights: the very worst mistakes of web design.

1. Bad search

Overly literal search engines reduce usability in that they're unable to handle typos, plurals, hyphens, and other variants of the query terms. Such search engines are particularly difficult for elderly users, but they hurt everybody.

A related problem is when search engines prioritize results purely on the basis of how many query terms they contain, rather than on each document's importance. Much better if your search engine calls out 'best bets' at the top of the list – especially for important queries, such as the names of your products.

Search is the user's lifeline when navigation fails. Even though advanced search can sometimes help, simple search usually works best, and search should be presented as a simple box, since that's what users are looking for.

2. PDF files for online reading

Users hate coming across a PDF file while browsing, because it breaks their flow. Even simple things like printing or saving documents are difficult because standard browser commands don't work. Layouts are often optimized for a sheet of paper, which rarely matches the size of the user's browser window. Bye-bye smooth scrolling. Hello tiny fonts.

Worst of all, PDF is an undifferentiated blob of content that's hard to navigate.

PDF is great for printing and for distributing manuals and other big documents that need to be printed. Reserve it for this purpose and convert any information that needs to be browsed or read on the screen into real web pages.

3. Not changing the colour of visited links

A good grasp of past navigation helps you understand your current location, since it's the culmination of your journey. Knowing your past and present locations in turn makes it easier to decide where to go next. Links are a key factor in this navigation process. Users can exclude links that proved fruitless in their earlier visits. Conversely, they might revisit links they found helpful in the past.

Most important, knowing which pages they've already visited frees users from unintentionally revisiting the same pages over and over again.

These benefits only accrue under one important assumption: that users can tell the difference between visited and unvisited links because the site shows them in different colours. When visited links don't change colour, users exhibit more navigational disorientation in usability testing and unintentionally revisit the same pages repeatedly.

4. Non-scannable text

A wall of text is deadly for an interactive experience. Intimidating. Boring. Painful to read. Write for online, not print. To draw users into the text and support 'scannability', use well-documented tricks:

- subheads;
- bulleted lists;
- highlighted keywords;
- short paragraphs;
- the inverted pyramid;
- a simple writing style; and
- de-fluffed language devoid of marketese.

5. Fixed font size

CSS style sheets unfortunately give websites the power to disable a web browser's 'change font size' button and specify a fixed font size. About 95 per cent of the time, this fixed size is tiny, reducing readability significantly for most people over the age of 40.

Respect the user's preferences and let them resize text as needed. Also, specify font sizes in relative terms – not as an absolute number of pixels.

6. Page titles with low search engine visibility

Search is the most important way users discover websites. Search is also one of the most important ways users find their way around individual websites. The humble page title is your main tool to attract new visitors from search listings and to help your existing users to locate the specific pages that they need.

The page title is contained within the HTML <title> tag and is almost always used as the clickable headline for listings on search engine result pages (SERPs). Search engines typically show the first 66 characters or so of the title, so it's truly microcontent.

Page titles are also used as the default entry in the Favorites when users bookmark a site. For your home page, begin with the company name, followed by a brief description of the site. Don't start with words like 'The' or 'Welcome to' unless you want to be alphabetized under 'T' or 'W'.

For other pages than the home page, start the title with a few of the most salient information-carrying words that describe the specifics of what users will find on that page. Since the page title is used as the window title in the browser, it's also used as the label for that window in the taskbar under Windows, meaning that advanced users will move between multiple windows under the guidance of the first one or two words of each page title. If all your page titles start with the same words, you have severely reduced usability for your multi-windowing users.

Taglines on home pages are a related subject: they also need to be short and quickly communicate the purpose of the site.

7. Anything that looks like an advertisement

Selective attention is very powerful, and web users have learned to stop paying attention to any ads that get in the way of their goal-driven navigation. (The main exception being text-only search-engine ads.)

Unfortunately, users also ignore legitimate design elements that look like prevalent forms of advertising. After all, when you ignore something, you don't study it in detail to find out what it is.

Therefore, it is best to avoid any designs that look like advertisements. The exact implications of this guideline will vary with new forms of ads; currently follow these rules:

- banner blindness means that users never fixate their eyes on anything that looks like a banner ad due to shape or position on the page;
- animation avoidance makes users ignore areas with blinking or flashing text or other aggressive animations;
- pop-up purges mean that users close pop-up 'windoids' before they have even fully rendered, sometimes with great viciousness (a sort of getting-back-at-GeoCities triumph).

8. Violating design conventions

Consistency is one of the most powerful usability principles: when things always behave the same, users don't have to worry about what will happen. Instead, they know what will happen based on earlier experience. Every time you release an apple over Sir Isaac Newton, it will drop on his head. That's good.

The more users' expectations prove right, the more they will feel in control of the system and the more they will like it. And the more the system breaks users' expectations, the more they will feel insecure. Oops, maybe if I let go of this apple, it will turn into a tomato and jump a mile into the sky.

Jakob's Law of the Web User Experience states that 'users spend most of their time on other websites'.

This means that they form their expectations for your site based on what's commonly done on most other sites. If you deviate, your site will be harder to use and users will leave.

9. Opening new browser windows

Opening up new browser windows is like a vacuum cleaner sales person who starts a visit by emptying an ash tray on the customer's carpet. Don't pollute my screen with any more windows, thanks (particularly since current operating systems have miserable window management).

Designers open new browser windows on the theory that it keeps users on their site. But even disregarding the user-hostile message implied in taking over the user's machine, the strategy is self-defeating since it disables the Back button which is the normal way users return to previous sites. Users often don't notice that a new window has opened, especially if they are using a small monitor where the windows are maximized to fill up the screen. So a user who tries to return to the origin will be confused by a grayed out Back button.

Links that don't behave as expected undermine users' understanding of their own system. A link should be a simple hypertext reference that replaces the current page with new content. Users hate unwarranted pop-up windows. When they want the destination to appear in a new page, they can use their browser's 'open in new window' command – assuming, of course, that the link is not a piece of code that interferes with the browser's standard behaviour.

10. Not answering users' questions

Users are highly goal-driven on the web. They visit sites because there's something they want to accomplish – maybe even buy your product. The ultimate failure of a website is to fail to provide the information users are looking for.

Sometimes the answer is simply not there and you lose the sale because users have to assume that your product or service doesn't meet their needs if you don't tell them the specifics. Other times the specifics are buried under a thick layer of marketese and bland slogans. Since users don't have time to read everything, such hidden info might almost as well not be there.

The worst example of not answering users' questions is to avoid listing the price of products and services. No B2C ecommerce site would make this mistake, but it's rife in B2B, where most 'enterprise solutions' are presented so that you can't tell whether they are suited for 100 people or 100,000 people. Price is the most specific piece of info customers use to understand the nature of an offering, and not providing it makes people feel lost and reduces their understanding of a product line. We have miles of videotape of users asking 'Where's the price?' while tearing their hair out.

Even B2C sites often make the associated mistake of forgetting prices in product lists, such as category pages or search results. Knowing the price is key in both situations; it lets users differentiate among products and click through to the most relevant ones.

Updated 2007. Reproduced with permission.

Jakob Nielsen is one of the world's leading authorities on web usability and user interface design. You'll find more details and a host of web usability resources on his website www.useit.com.

Website design summary

- *Establish clear business goals for your website right from the start:* Remember the analogy in the strategy chapter: if you don't know where you're heading, you haven't a hope of getting there. What does your business want to achieve with this website? What is it for? We know your website's primary focus is taking the traffic you gain through digital marketing and turning it into something of tangible value to your organization. But what does that mean? Is it about building your brand, direct online selling, harvesting sales leads, building an online customer-centric community – what?

- *Know your target audience:* No surprises here. Like everything else in marketing, knowing what makes your target market tick will help you to design a website that will engage them. What are your potential customers looking for online? How do they look for it and what are the best ways to make sure your website delivers?
- *Know your competition:* What your competitors are doing online can provide real insight into what you should be doing. Don't copy them, but do emulate what they do well, enhance it and look for opportunities where you can differentiate your online offering.
- *Use a professional web designer:* Unless you're an accomplished web developer in your own right, or have a team of in-house web professionals at your disposal, it always pays to bring in a professional to design and implement your site. Anyone can build a website – but you want a good website, right?
- *Professional look and feel:* Your website needs to look professional and it needs to be functional. It doesn't have to look 'pretty' per se, as long as it doesn't look amateur and it gets the job done efficiently and effectively. On the web, function always outranks form, but if you can achieve both so much the better.
- *Follow standards:* Make sure your site is designed to comply with accepted web standards and, where relevant, accessibility standards. Your web designer should be familiar with these standards and should know how to implement them.
- *Keep it simple:* Relevant, efficient websites deliver what users want with a minimum of fuss and bother. The most successful websites are often those that do the simplest thing that works effectively to get the desired task done. Of course, achieving simplicity isn't easy, but it's almost always worth the additional effort.
- *Design to be found:* Make sure your site is search engine friendly as well as user friendly. Conversion is a function of usability, but getting traffic to convert in the first place is heavily dependent on your search engine rankings. Avoid search engine spider traps (see Chapter 4).
- *Content written for the web:* Use clear, concise, scannable, original and compelling content written specifically for your website and your target audience.
- *Test everything:* Nothing will erode your online credibility or your search engine ranking like a website that doesn't work. Before putting your site 'live', test it exhaustively to make sure everything works as it should and that it achieves your original goals. If possible test on different platforms (operating systems, browsers, etc) to ensure consistency.

- *Hold the initial marketing blitz:* Hold off on marketing your new site when it first goes live. Give yourself a few weeks to iron out any kinks – then officially launch it and promote the living daylights out of it!

That's it: your new site is ready, it's live online, it's there for all the world to see and it looks great. Now all you need is traffic, and in the chapters that follow we'll show you exactly how to get it!

Case study: IKEA

Brief

To inspire consumers using an interactive site focusing on Complete Kitchen Living, thereby confirming a leadership position in global kitchen markets. Several elements of the kitchen were to be presented: the essential kitchen (storage, appliances, counters, etc), cooking (pots, pans, etc) and eating and dining (tables, chairs, etc). The site needed to work in 23 different markets; therefore it was necessary to comply with a large range of different cultural requirements in order to communicate effectively with potential consumers.

Specific campaign requirements were:

- to inspire with IKEA's great kitchen and dining rooms;
- to convince about IKEA quality;
- to demonstrate smart storage solutions;
- to explain IKEA's easy buying process;
- to provide opportunities to highlight current special offers;
- to develop the site to work in 23 markets.

The campaign

The site was structured as a journey through kitchens and dining rooms in five different parts of the world. Exteriors were featured, giving the interiors a more geographic context. Intuitive navigation allowed the user to travel forwards and backwards, to turn around and travel through the site in opposite directions.

Each scene is linked to the next by a 'product universe', a kaleidoscopic 3D collage of IKEA products. These products are database driven and can easily be updated for each market with current offers in specific market locations. The site also features information about IKEA product quality, storage solutions and kitchen services.

The core message of the site is 'Dream kitchens for all – IKEA offers complete high-quality kitchens at prices everyone can afford', moving consumers along the purchase decision process and driving traffic to IKEA.com. Banner ads were also used to drive traffic to the 'Dream kitchens' site as well as IKEA.com.

Results

The quality of this website speaks for itself, but it has also been recognized by numerous prestigious awards such as a Webby award for its incredible navigation structure.

Client comment

Mattias Jöngard, Project Manager Advertising, IKEA:

'Around the world' was the third phase for our 'Dream kitchen' campaign.

When we started the whole campaign in phase 1 we moved away from the traditional TV media as the hub in our communication and turned to the web. It was a whole new way of presenting our products in a better and more interactive way. We had a couple of criteria: the website must be easy to navigate, enormously entertaining and inspirational, and at the same time give as much insight and knowledge about kitchens as possible.

At IKEA we know how complicated the process can be for consumers to remodel their kitchens. The buying process is both hard and takes a long time. The first step in this process is to take the decision to actually start thinking of remodelling the kitchen. That is a big step. Once you've mentally done that we know that the web is the preferred choice of media to search for inspiration and information.

That's why these activity sites became a success. People who started their buying process found our sites and were inspired. One other key factor that made this a success was the technique that was used. We created a whole new web navigation experience which was very user friendly.

Credits

Client: IKEA
Project Manager Advertising: Mattias Jöngard
Agency: Forsman & Bodenfors
Account Director: Philip Mascher
Web Director: Mathias Appelbad

Images

http://demo.fb.se/e/ikea/dreamkitchen3/en_US/rooms_ideas/ckl/default.html

Figure 3.2 IKEA's 'Dream Kitchens' campaign used an innovative navigation structure for this micro-site (a website specifically constructed to support an individual campaign) to whisk visitors on a journey through different IKEA kitchens around the world

Notes

1. Information architecture is the arrangement or structure of the information contained on a website. The way information is arranged can have a big impact on a site's usability and its perceived relevance and authority both for users and for search engines.
2. Top-level domain (TLD) is the element of an internet domain name that comes after the 'dot'. For instance, in the domain name digitalmarketingsuccess.com the top-level domain is com or COM (internet domain names are not case sensitive).
3. 'Search engine results pages' (SERPs) is a term in search engine marketing that refers to the results pages returned when a user submits a query to a search engine.

4 The search for success

If you make a product good enough, even though you live in the depths of the forest the public will make a path to your door, says the philosopher. But if you want the public in sufficient numbers, you would better construct a highway.

(William Randolph Hearst)

Learning is the beginning of wealth. Learning is the beginning of health. Learning is the beginning of spirituality. Searching and learning is where the miracle process all begins.

(Jim Rohn)

We've only achieved 2% of what we can do. The world of search will get much, much bigger.

(Marissa Mayer, Vice President, Search Products and User Experience, Google Inc, September 2007)

Our chapter pledge to you

In this chapter you'll discover answers to the following questions:

- Why is search important?
- What is a search engine, and how does it work?

- How big is search?
- How do I optimize my website for the search engines?
- What is paid search marketing?
- What is Black Hat SEO and why should I avoid it?

Search: the online marketer's holy grail

To an online marketer today there are few things in the digital world more significant than internet search.

We saw in the last chapter how your company's website is the hub of your digital world. It's more than just your shop window to a huge and growing global market: a well-designed and implemented website is a place where you can interact with your customers, a virtual meeting place where you can do real business, with real people, in real time. The commercial potential is, quite simply, unparalleled.

But if you're going to realize even a fraction of that potential then people need to be able to *find your site*. And, for the time being at least, the way that more than 80 per cent of internet users find new websites is by typing a query into one of the major search engines (Jupiter Research).

On the internet there's really no such thing as passing trade. The chances of a potential customer stumbling across your site while randomly browsing the web are practically negligible. That means your visitors have to learn about your site from somewhere else: by word of mouth, through conventional advertising and branding channels, by following a link from another website or, the current most likely scenario, by clicking on a link in a search engine results page (SERP).

Just think about the way you use the internet. Where do you go when you're looking for information, products or services online? Do you start typing random URLs into the address bar of your favourite browser and hope for the best – or do you head over to the home page of your favourite search engine and type in a query?

In fact, if you type something that's not a URL into the address bar of today's most popular browsers, you're automatically redirected to your default search engine, using the text you entered as your search string. While it's true that for a few class-leading online brands (such as Amazon.com for books, or eBay.com for online auctions) consumers are likely to know the URL they're looking for and access the site directly, for practically everything else people use search engines.

Search: still a new kid on the block

Can you even remember an internet before search – before Yahoo!, MSN, Ask and AltaVista – before Google?

Today, of course, it feels as though search engines have been with us for ever. But Google – the market leader in search by a country mile – was only established in late 1998. In 10 short years the search company has become a leading global brand to rival the biggest and the best out there. On 8 October 2007, Google's stock passed the US$600 threshold, putting the value of the company at a staggering US$190 billion, a figure that makes it more valuable than long-established global giants like FedEx, McDonald's, Coke, Intel, IBM and Wal-Mart. And it's still climbing.

Google's incredible growth, and the unprecedented rise of search in general, is testament to the practically ubiquitous appeal of online search, both to a constantly growing pool of internet users and as a marketing vehicle for businesses large and small.

To the user, search engines offer a window to the web – a convenient way for them to sift through the literally billions of pages out there to find valuable, relevant information on what they're interested in at any given time. For marketers, search engines offer a unique opportunity to get their products or services in front of online prospects at the exact moment they're looking for them. It is, perhaps, one of the ultimate forms of targeted, pre-qualified marketing.

The fact that the internet search industry is still in its infancy, and that it's growing and evolving so quickly, makes the whole area of search engine optimization (SEO) and paid search advertising an incredibly exciting and challenging one. Because things are changing constantly, you're always shooting at a moving target and have to tweak your aim accordingly. Search is a fluid and dynamic environment, and nobody has all the right answers, because the nature of the questions keeps changing.

That said, there are a number of widely accepted legitimate strategies (and some less ethical ones that we'll touch on later) that, if you implement them diligently and consistently, will help your site rise to a more prominent position in the SERPs. Equally there are plenty of SEO myths out there that won't help your search rankings but will waste your valuable time. We'll reveal some of the more common ones later in this chapter.

Looking forward

Both the increasingly widespread adoption of high-speed internet access in the home and the ever-increasing capability and market penetration of mobile digital devices are opening up a slew of new digital media opportunities for marketers the world over. The rise of social networking sites, and the word-of-mouth and viral marketing opportunities that they offer (see Chapter 7), may in time dilute the prominence of SEO and paid search advertising in the digital marketing mix. Likewise, as ever-increasing numbers of web users develop a 'feel' for where they need to go to find the things that they want online, and become comfortable with their favourite online brands, they are likely to access more and more sites directly and rely on search less and less.

While the significance of search may wane for a proportion of people over time, given its current level of importance for both internet users and digital marketers, the propensity of major search engines to innovate and adapt, and the fact that new people are going online and discovering the value of search engines every day, search looks certain to remain a cornerstone of digital marketing for some time to come.

About the engines

Why is search engine optimization so important?

In 2007, US businesses spent nearly US$1.3 billion on optimizing their web pages with the aim of improving their ranking in the 'natural' or 'organic' search results of major search engines (SEMPO Annual State of Search survey, 2007). Why do they spend so much?

Simple: it's because search engines give website owners a prime opportunity to put their products, services or brands in front of a vast and ever-growing market of prospective customers *at the precise time* those customers are looking for them. That's a pretty evocative marketing proposition – especially when you consider the volumes involved.

During the month of August 2007, in North America alone, the three leading search engines – Google, Yahoo! and Microsoft Live Search – fielded a mind-boggling 6.7 billion search queries. That's more than one search for every living person on the planet!

How do search engines work?

Before you start optimizing your site for the search engines, it makes sense to know how they work. Not the detailed, technical 'nuts and bolts' of it all – just a high-level understanding of what makes a search engine tick. Knowing what the search engines are trying to achieve and how they go about doing it is at the heart of good SEO.

The mission of search engines

It's important to understand at this point that search engines are interested, first and foremost, in delivering timely, relevant, high-quality search results to their users. You could say it's their prime objective – their reason for being. The search engines are constantly researching, developing, testing and refining ways to enhance the service that they provide – looking to optimize the relevance and quality of the results they serve back to the user on every single query.

The rationale is simple: the better the search experience for the user, the better the reputation of the search engine and the more users it will attract. The more users a search engine has, the more alluring it is to advertisers, and ergo the more ad revenue it can pull in. Putting users first makes search engines richer – and that makes search engine shareholders happy. QED.

In that respect the internet is no different to traditional marketing channels like commercial television, radio and print publications. It's the viewers, listeners and readers these channels look after first – because it's the audience that brings in the advertisers. Without an audience, they have no advertisers, and without advertisers they have no business.

From a marketer's perspective the search engines' constant quest to improve the search experience for users is something of a double-edged sword. Yes, it means that the best search engines have a bigger pool of potential prospects for your paid search advertising and your organic SEO efforts. But equally, the fact that things keep changing makes the process of optimization a continuous, uncertain and labour-intensive process.

Scouring the web

To deliver accurate, relevant, high-quality search results to their users search engines need to gather detailed information about the billions of web pages out there. They do this using automated programmes called 'bots' (short for 'robots') – also known as 'spiders' – which they send out to 'crawl' the web. Spiders follow hyperlinks and gather information about the pages that they find.

Once a page has been crawled by a spider, the search engine stores details about that page's contents and the links both into and out of it in a massive database called an index. This index is highly optimized so that results for any of the hundreds of millions of search requests received every day can be retrieved from it almost instantly.

It's a mammoth task. While nobody knows the real number of unique web pages out there (some estimates put it at more than 30 billion and climbing rapidly), and search engines typically don't publicize the size of their indexes, in August 2005 Yahoo! announced on its official blog that its index had grown to 19.2 billion web documents, 1.6 billion images and over 50 million audio and video files. Other leading search engines have since followed suit – Microsoft's Live Search reported a fourfold increase in its index to an estimated 20 billion documents in September 2007, while estimates put Google's index at around 24 billion documents and counting as of October 2007. Just how accurate these figures are is anybody's guess – but it is safe to assume that we're dealing with some very big numbers here.

The list of results, which can contain many millions of pages, is then run through the engine's ranking algorithms: special programs that use a variety of closely guarded proprietary formulas to 'score' a site's relevance to the user's original query. The output is then sorted in order of relevance and presented to the user in the SERPs.

Search engines process a huge volume of searches, scanning billions of items and delivering pages of relevant, ranked results in a fraction of a second. To the user the process seems quick, straightforward and seamless, but there's a lot going on behind the scenes. Google, Yahoo!, Microsoft Live and other search engines are running some of the most complex and demanding computer applications in the world.

Optimizing your site for the engines

To many, SEO appears to be something of an arcane art. It's a world that's shrouded in high-tech mystery, a complicated world full of secrets that mere mortals haven't a hope of understanding. But according to leading UK-based SEO expert Jason Duke, of Strange Logic, there are no real secrets in SEO. 'The web is a very open place', he says. 'If a site is riding high in the search engine listings, then you can, with enough persistence, get to see why it ranks so well. Replicate it, and you can join them – it really is as simple as that.'

Matt McGee, an SEO expert who specializes in advising small businesses (www.smallbusinesssem.com), concurs with Jason's sentiments. In an interview on the 'Your SEO Plan' (www.yourseoplan.com) blog in December 2006, Matt says:

> SEO is not rocket science. It's simple, but it's not easy. There's a difference! There's a small set of basic rules that apply to any web page or web site, whether you're a small business or not. Your site has to be crawlable, your content has to be good – and I'd include things like page titles, keyword use, etc., under the umbrella of 'content' – and you need quality, relevant inbound links. That applies to everyone.

One of the best places to start for tips on improving your site's ranking with the search engines is with the search engines' own guidelines, tips and resources for website owners (see Table 4.1).

Table 4.1   Links to webmaster resources for major search engines

Search Engine	Resource	URL for Webmasters
Google	Webmaster Central	http://www.google.com/webmasters
Yahoo!	Help for web publishers	http://help.yahoo.com/l/us/yahoo/search/webpublishers
Microsoft Live	Search help for webmasters	http://help.live.com/help.aspx?mkt=en-us&project=wl_webmasters

Make your site easy to crawl

If you're looking to attract search engine traffic, the last thing you want to do is make it difficult for search engines to index your website. Make sure your site design doesn't present unnecessary obstacles to search engine spiders.

Spiders are interested in text, text and more text. They don't see the graphics, clever animations and other flashy bells and whistles that web designers routinely use to make sites look pretty. In fact over-reliance on some of these things can even stop some spiders in their tracks, preventing them from indexing your pages at all.

While some of this 'window dressing' is obviously important to make your site appeal to real people when they arrive, to get enough of them to your site in the first place it's vital that your design doesn't unwittingly alienate search engine spiders. Make sure your site works for both, and

Table 4.2 Spider traps: web design features that hurt your search engine visibility

Website Feature	Why It's Bad for Your SEO
All-flash website	Difficult for spiders to crawl – many simply refuse to index all-flash sites.
JavaScript navigation	Unless you implement a workaround for the spiders, they may have trouble following script-based navigation to other pages on your site. Make sure you have a normal, text-only link to every page on your site.
Frames	Frames are notoriously difficult to implement effectively from a user-experience perspective, are really necessary in very few instances, and often cause indexing problems for search engine spiders.
Image map and other non-text navigation	Some spiders may have problems following these links. If you use image maps for navigation on your pages, make sure you have alternative text-based hyperlinks leading to the same pages.
Dynamically generated pages	These are less of a problem than they used to be, but some spiders can have trouble with dynamically generated URLs that contain too many parameters (?W=XYZ). Try to configure your site to use 'search engine-friendly' URLs, or at least restrict URL parameters to a maximum of three.
AJAX-generated text	See note for all-flash sites above.

that each page includes relevant text-based content; avoid flash-only sites and frames, which are difficult for spiders to crawl effectively; and make sure that every page on your site can be reached via a simple text-based hyperlink.

Words are the key to unlocking the power of search

The key to effective SEO is knowing what people looking for your products, services or information are typing into that little box on the search engine home page. Known as keywords or keyword phrases (which consist of two, three or more keywords), these form the foundation of your SEO efforts.

Find the optimum keywords, follow a few basic SEO guidelines, and when the spiders re-index your site you'll start to see it rise up the organic search rankings for those keywords and, with a bit of luck, you'll notice a corresponding increase in the level of targeted traffic arriving at your site. Choose the wrong keywords, however, and the best SEO in the world won't deliver the results you're looking for.

Choosing effective keywords

So how do you go about choosing the right keywords for site optimization? Well, a good place to start is with the people you're hoping to attract. Knowing your target audience is a critical component of any marketing campaign – and it's the same here. Put yourself in your prospect's shoes, sitting in front of your favourite search engine looking for information on the product or service you're selling. What would you type into the box?

These are your 'seed' keywords. They give you a starting point to work from. Take these keywords and play around with them. Imagine the various combinations of search terms your prospects might use to find your site. Type these into the engines and look at the results. Examine the sites that are ranking highly for your chosen keywords. Analyse them and try to work out how they're achieving those rankings.

You can also use a wide range of automated keyword suggestion tools, like the free tools provided by Google AdWords (http://tinyurl. com/qkfuh) and on the SEO Book website (http://tinyurl.com/ 22w6pa), or Wordtracker (www.wordtracker.com) and Trellian's (www. keyworddiscovery.com) keyword tools, both of which offer a free basic service with paid upgrades for a more comprehensive version. These tools typically provide insight into the search traffic volumes for the most popular phrases relating to keyword phrases you provide.

There are a lot of different keyword research tools and services available. Perhaps the best way to research your options is to use your preferred search engine to look for things like 'keyword research tool' or 'keyword suggestion'.

Analyse the competition

Other tools on the web can provide you with insight into how your leading competitors are doing in terms of search engine traffic for particular keywords. Services on sites like SEO ToolSet (www.seotoolset.com) and Compete (www.compete.com) can provide information on which keywords are driving traffic to your competitors' websites from the major search engines, and which of your competitors' sites are ranking for which keyword phrases – all of which can inform the choice of keywords you want to optimize for.

While automated tools are a good guide, don't underestimate the value of people as a source of inspiration for keyword selection. 'Use the automated tools to assist,' advises Jason Duke, 'but please remember that, although automated tools are brilliant, nothing is better at understanding the minds of people than people themselves.'

That's good advice. What you believe people will search for and what they actually type into the search box are often two very different things. Get a group of people together – if possible representative of your target market – and start brainstorming keywords. The results will probably surprise you.

I have my initial keyword list; now what?

After analysing your keywords and phrases and examining the competition, you've probably got a list of target keywords as long as your arm. What do you do with them all?

The first thing you'll want to do is narrow your initial list down to a more manageable size. What constitutes a manageable size will depend on your situation – on how much time, money and resources you have available for your SEO effort. Remember, there's nothing wrong with starting small: optimize a few pages for what you believe are your main keywords, and monitor the results on ranking, traffic and conversion for those pages. That will give you a solid foundation from which to build your optimization efforts and your SEO expertise.

To whittle your list down to size, start by eliminating all of the words or phrases that are much too general. Broad single-word terms like 'shoes', 'mortgages', 'bottles' or 'computers' tend to be both very difficult to rank for (because they're high-traffic terms that can apply equally to a huge number of sites across the net) and also far too generic to drive valuable targeted traffic to your site.

Suppose you're an independent mortgage consultant based in Killarney, County Kerry, Ireland. If you choose to optimize a page based on the keyword 'mortgages' you'll find yourself competing with a raft of mortgage providers, mortgage advisers, mortgage brokers, mortgage consultants, mortgage industry news sites, etc from all over the world. Even if (and it's a big if) your page does make it to those coveted elevated positions in the SERPs for that keyword, the chances that people searching for the term 'mortgages' will be looking for an independent consultant in Co Kerry are slim at best. Phrases like 'mortgages in Killarney' or 'mortgage consultant Kerry', on the other hand, are potentially much less competitive, and generate much lower search volumes, but are much more valuable to your business, because the people who search on those terms are far more likely to be interested in the products and services you offer.

In other words, the more general a keyword, the less likely it is that your site will contain what the searcher is trying to find. Effective SEO isn't just about generating traffic volume; it's about finding that elusive balance between keyword search volume and keyword specificity that drives the maximum volume of *targeted traffic* to your site.

'Your target keywords should always be at least two or more words long', explained search guru Danny Sullivan, in a 2007 article for Search Engine Watch (www.searchenginewatch.com). 'Usually, too many sites will be relevant for a single word, such as "stamps". This "competition" means your odds of success are lower. Don't waste your time fighting the odds. Pick phrases of two or more words, and you'll have a better shot at success.'

Single-keyword searches used to be the norm – but not any more. Search users are using more sophisticated search queries to narrow down the results they get back. These days two, three or even more words are becoming increasingly common. Exploiting that trend in your choice of optimization keywords can yield real dividends.

Long-tail versus short-tail keywords

Keywords in SEO fall into two broad categories. Short-tail keywords are simple one- or two-word phrases that are typically very general in nature and attract a large volume of individual search requests. Long-tail keywords, on the other hand, are more complex queries that contain more words and are much more specific in nature. Individually they attract a much lower volume of search traffic than their short-tail counterparts, but cumulatively these long-tail-type queries account for the lion's share of internet search traffic.

Martin Murray, CEO of specialist search marketing company Interactive Return (www.interactivereturn.com), sums it up like this:

> In any keyword domain there are a small number of highly trafficked keywords or phrases and a large number of low-trafficked keywords or phrases. Often, the keyword domain approximates to the right half of a normal curve with the tail of the curve extending to infinity. Low-trafficked keywords are therefore also known as 'long-tail keywords'.
>
> The highly trafficked [short-tail] keywords have the following characteristics: highly competitive, consist of one or two words, have a high cost per click and may have low conversion rates as they tend to be quite general. Examples from the accommodation sector might include 'hotel', 'London hotel' or 'cheap hotel'.

Low-trafficked [long-tail] keywords are not so competitive, often consist of four, five or more words, have a lower cost per click and can have a higher conversion rate as they are quite specific indicating that the searcher is further along the online purchasing cycle. Examples might include 'cheap city centre hotel Dublin', 'stags weekend hotel Temple Bar Dublin' or 'business hotel with gym and spa Wexford'.

Effective search marketing campaigns tend to put a lot of effort into discovering effective long-tail terms, particularly for use in sponsored listings (PPC) campaigns.

Typically it makes sense to take a balanced approach and work with a mixture of general short-tail keywords and more specific long-tail keywords as part of your organic SEO effort, while focusing on highly specific long-tail search terms is likely to yield a higher return on your investment for pay-per-click (PPC) campaigns (see page 90).

Focus on one page at a time

The list of keywords you're left with is very important. It essentially provides you with an SEO 'template' for your website.

One of the key things to remember when you're approaching SEO is that you'll be optimizing your site one page at a time. While you'll look at some site-wide factors as part of your SEO effort, SEO isn't a straightforward 'one-size-fits-all' operation, and each of the existing pages on your site will need to be optimized independently. It's also highly likely you'll want to create new pages to maximize your potential search engine exposure for as many of your chosen keyword phrases as possible.

Think about it: when a search engine presents results to a user, it's not presenting whole sites; it's presenting the individual pages that, according to its algorithms, best match a user's query. That means each individual page on your website gives you an explicit opportunity to optimize for specific keywords or phrases – and that's important.

'Each page in your website will have different target keywords that reflect the page's content', says Danny Sullivan. 'For example, say you have a page about the history of stamps. Then "stamp history" might be your keywords for that page.'

Jason Duke of Strange Logic also emphasizes the importance of optimizing individual pages for specific keywords: 'These [keywords] become the structure for your site, with a page for every topic. Laying these foundations and allowing them to grow according to what you, your team and your visitors think is the key to successful opportunities to rank.'

Your goal, then, is to isolate the important keywords and phrases in your particular market and then to ensure your site includes individual pages with unique, relevant content optimized for a small number of (ideally one or two, and no more than three) keyword phrases. The more individual pages you have, the more opportunities you have to get your business in front of your prospects in the SERPs – and at the end of the day that's what SEO is all about.

Choose your page <title>s carefully

There's a small but very important HTML tag that lives in the header section of the code on each of your web pages. It's called the 'title' tag, and the text it contains is what appears in the title bar at the top of your browser window when you visit a web page. It's also, crucially, the text that appears as the 'clickable' blue link for a page when it's presented to users in the SERPs.

That means that what you put in the title tag is incredibly important for the following reasons. First, the title tag is one of the most important on-page factors used by the search engines to rank your page. At this stage most, if not all, SEO experts agree that appropriate use of the title tag is a key factor in ranking well in the SERPs, and advise weaving your primary keyword(s) for a page into the title tag whenever possible. Just remember not to sacrifice readability for your human audience. Second, the title is the first glimpse of your content a search user will see. Giving your pages concise, compelling and informative titles will entice more users to click through to your page when it appears in search results.

Give each page a unique meta-description

Another HTML tag that used to be very important for SEO, but is now pretty much obsolete, is the meta-tag. Meta-tags contain information that is accessible to browsers, search engine spiders and other programs, but that doesn't appear on the rendered (visible) page for the user. Meta-data were once used extensively by search engines to gauge what a page was about – especially the ones obsessed over meta-keywords tags.

These days, however, the tag that was once the staple of SEO has become more or less redundant in terms of influencing a page's ranking in the major search engines. Engines rely principally on their increasingly comprehensive ability to analyse the *actual content* of the page – the words the user sees – and on incoming and outgoing links to help them determine a page's relevance to the submitted search query.

```html
<head>

<title>Copywriting, business writing, ghost writing and technical writing services in
Ireland - CJ Writing</title>
<meta name="author" content="Calvin Jones" />
<meta name="robots" content="index, follow" />
<meta name="description" content="CJ Writing -- business writing services, CJ Writing
provides freelance commercial writing services, helping businesses just like yours to
communicate more effectively online and off." />
<meta name="keywords" content="writing, freelance, writer, copywriter, blog writer,
copy, business writing, technical writing, marketing, ghost writing" />
<base href="http://www.cjwriting.com/" />
    <link rel="shortcut icon" href="http://www.cjwriting.com/images
/cjwriting.ico" />
```

Figure 4.1   HTML header section of a typical web page showing the <title> and <meta> description tags being put to
good use

There is, however, one HTML meta-tag that is still worth including as part of your SEO, and that's the meta-description tag. As with most things in search, the opinion of leading experts in the SEO community is divided as to just how valuable the meta-description tag is in terms of search engine optimization. While it is widely acknowledged that the tag does little, if anything, to improve your page ranking, it can help to boost your click-through rate (CTR) when your page does appear in the SERPs.

Depending on the query and the page content, leading search engines will sometimes use the contents of your meta-description tag as the descriptive 'snippet' of text that appears below your page title in the SERPs. A well-written description for each page can, in theory at least, entice more users to click through to your page when it's returned in search results.

Use of the meta-description text by search engines is inconsistent. The rules applied vary from engine to engine and even between different types of query on the same engine. However, having compelling, informative meta-description tags is something that search engines encourage, certainly won't hurt your rankings, is beneficial to users and may well boost traffic to your site.

Content – the most important thing on your site

Content is the single most important thing on your website, period. Unique, relevant, informative content is what sets your site apart from the competition. It's the reason users want to visit you, why other sites will want to link to you and, of course, why search engines will want to suggest your site to their users in search results.

The term 'content', if you take it literally, encompasses everything on your website. It includes all the visual elements on the site – the flashy graphics, animations, videos, banners, etc – that the search engine spiders can't see, and of course all of the text, which they can. In the context of SEO, though, when we talk about content we're really talking about the text on each of your web pages.

When writing content for your site the key thing to remember is that you're writing it, first and foremost, for a *human audience*, not for search engine spiders. Yes, your pages need to be 'search engine friendly', but the spiders should *always* be a secondary consideration: put your human audience first.

Frankly, if your copy doesn't engage real, live people when they arrive – address their needs right from the start – then investing time and resources to attract more search engine traffic is pointless. If your content doesn't deliver, visitors will leave as soon as they arrive. Remember, on the web you don't have a captive audience. Users are in control – one click and they're gone.

Your copy needs to be relevant, it has to be interesting, and above all it has to provide the answers the user is looking for. It needs to do all of this quickly, in a concise, easily scannable way (see the section 'Writing effective web content' in Chapter 3 for more on creating good web copy).

Content and the search engines

Search engines have evolved rapidly and are now in what's considered to be their third generation. Each generation has become much 'smarter' than the last at interpreting the actual visible content on a page and judging its relevance to the user. Today's generation of search engines, unlike their predecessors, don't rely on meta-data to judge the content of a page; they analyse and interpret the actual content presented to the user. And they're getting better at doing it all the time.

Ultimately all of the mysterious 'voodoo' behind search engine ranking algorithms is about analysing and prioritizing your content. There are all sorts of criteria that contribute to the process – some known, many guessed at and no doubt some that we'll never know. At the end of the day, though, they all combine to measure just two things: the relevance and authority of your page content in the context of what the user typed into the search box.

Search engine optimization for sustainable high ranking, therefore, hinges on the production of great original content that appeals to real, live people.

Keywords in content

The subject of keywords in content is something that generates a lot of debate in SEO circles: where to place them, when and how often they need to appear on the page and lots more besides. As with most things SEO, opinions tend to vary significantly on the subject.

Our advice: don't worry too much about it. If you're writing copy about a specific set of keyword phrases, there's a high probability you'll use those keyword phrases and related phrases organically in your writing and will achieve a natural balance. That's exactly what search engines are looking for. Focus on writing compelling copy that addresses the needs of your target audience while keeping your target keywords for that page in mind, and the search engines will do the rest.

'Just make sure that your chosen keyword or phrase is contained in the title tag and URL, and then simply make sure your content's on topic', advises Jason Duke.

Don't worry about any other 'on page' SEO such as keyword density, meta-tags, this trick or that trick, as it's all so 1999! Search engines are now more than intelligent enough to understand the semantic relationships between words and phrases, so trying to assist them with certain keyword densities is a fruitless effort. Leave them to their algorithms, and simply enjoy the rewards that their efforts can deliver to you and your website.

Jill Whalen, CEO and founder of search marketing firm High Rankings, and a regular columnist with the website Search Engine Land, emphasizes that there are no hard-and-fast rules to follow. 'Understand that there is no magical number of words per page or number of times to use your phrases in your copy', she says. 'The important thing is to use your keyword phrases only when and where it makes sense to do so for the real people reading your pages. Simply sticking keyword phrases at the top of the page for no apparent reason isn't going to cut it, and it just looks silly.'

Links – second only to content

The critical importance of links in securing a high page ranking is one of the few things that has universal consensus in the world of SEO. Popular opinion maintains that nothing, but nothing, is more important than high-quality inbound links from 'authority' websites in achieving high rankings in the search engine results.

But wait a minute – if nothing is more important than links, why did we just say in the heading that links are second only to content? Simple: because creating outstanding content is the most effective way of attracting high-quality inbound links from authoritative online sources. And there's no doubt that those are the links that have the biggest impact on your search engine rankings.

Why are links so important?

Search engines need to determine two things when they attempt to fulfil a user's search request – they need to decide which pages in their index are relevant to the user's query, and then they need to rank those pages in terms of quality and importance. And therein lies one of their biggest challenges, because a search engine algorithm can't read the content and assess its quality the way a human can – at least, not yet.

Instead the engines have to rely on other criteria, and one of the main things that indicates a page's perceived importance to a search engine's ranking algorithm is the quantity and quality of references – or links – to that page from other web pages.

Each link to a page is, if you like, a vote of confidence for that page. The more links that point to an individual page (and globally to the site as a whole), the higher the collective vote of confidence for that page (and/or site) becomes, and the more important the page is deemed to be by the search engines.

But of course it's not quite that simple. Votes from different pages carry more or less weight depending on the perceived importance or quality of the source page, the type of link, the anchor text used in the link and a host of other factors that are taken into account by the search engine ranking algorithms. When you consider the tangled skein of interconnecting links that make up the world wide web, you begin to appreciate the complexity inherent in assessing the relative importance or quality of all of those pages in relation to one another.

Fundamentally, though, what it boils down to is that incoming links in general are a good thing and play a critical role in determining your search engine rankings. The more links you have pointing to your site, the higher your perceived authority – but there's a caveat. For 'votes' to be counted, the incoming links have to pass certain search engine filtering criteria. Those that fall outside the engines' criteria (generally any link that is designed to hoodwink search engines into assigning higher rankings rather than to guide site users to a relevant page – check the search engine guidelines for more information) either are ignored (ie their votes aren't counted) or, more seriously, can have a negative impact on your ranking.

While all incoming links that satisfy the search engines' criteria will influence your ranking in a positive way, it makes sense to try to maximize the value of your incoming links by focusing your link-building efforts on quality links over quantity. Attracting high-quality, natural links from authority sites with subject matter that's aligned with the content on your site is the real key to high rankings. That's not easy, but the way to get those kinds of links is, of course, producing outstanding content that high-authority sites will want to point their users towards.

Links from authority sites are probably the single most significant factor in boosting your site's overall rankings in the SERPs. A single link from, say, the CNN.com or BBC.co.uk home page could be worth more to your site in terms of ranking and exposure than countless links from smaller, relatively unknown sites. Authority sites, by their very nature, also tend to be high-traffic sites, and you'll inevitably garner some direct traffic as people click through to your site via the link.

The flip side of this, of course, is that links from authority sites are notoriously difficult to secure, while links from smaller, less-well-known sites generally take less effort. It's a case of swings and roundabouts, but in practice your aim should be to get as many inbound links as possible from sites with as high a perceived authority level as possible.

The role of internal and external links

Internal links and external links are both important for boosting the ranking of individual pages within your site. First let's define exactly what we mean by internal and external links. *External links* are links that reside on pages that do not belong to your domain – in other words, links from other websites. *Internal links* are the links that reside on pages that belong to your domain or subdomains – in other words, links between pages on the same website, or pages that reside in subdomains of the primary domain.

All of these links are important. Links from reputable external sources boost your site's perceived authority with the search engines, which in turn helps your more popular pages to rank higher in the SERPs. Internal links give you a way of distributing the 'authority' accrued by your more popular pages (like your home page, for example) to other important pages that you want to rank for.

Getting good links

There are a huge number of ways that you can encourage people to link to your site. But building quality natural links isn't easy, and it takes time. It depends on creating high-quality content and building a reputation for excellence (or notoriety – which can work well for links, but might not project the right image to your customers) in your chosen field, which in turn encourages other website owners to link to you.

There are, of course, some quicker, easier ways to secure incoming links, but such links tend either to be of poor quality (hence of little SEO value) or to violate search engine guidelines. Search engines take a dim view of anybody trying to artificially manipulate search results. Remember, they're trying to deliver the most relevant, highest-quality results to their users and see any attempt to leapfrog a less relevant or lower-quality site up the rankings as 'search engine spam'.

Harvesting links purely for the purpose of boosting your site's rankings in the search engines is frowned upon and, while it may work in the short term, it's a risky strategy at best that will ultimately harm your rankings and may even result in your entire site being blacklisted and removed from the search engines' indexes altogether. If you're trying to build a sustainable, long-term online business it simply isn't worth the risk.

For sustainable, long-term rankings, focus instead on building high-quality links through ethical means, concentrate on your content, and build your site with your end user in mind. Exploiting search engine loopholes and 'clever' tricks to artificially boost your rankings isn't really search engine optimization; it's search engine manipulation, and it will ultimately backfire. It may take a lot longer to achieve the rank you're looking for working within search engine guidelines, but in the end it's generally worth it.

Link-building tips

- *Generate truly valuable content that other sites will want to link to:* These one-way unsolicited links are by far the most valuable kind. Search engines love them and see them as a genuine endorsement of one site by another. As your site becomes more visible, the content will organically attract more links, which in turn will improve your visibility, attracting even more links. When it works, this process is self-perpetuating, leaving you free to concentrate on quality content, while the links look after themselves.

- *Let people know your site is out there:* People can only link to your site if they know it's there. Promote your site at every opportunity, especially in places where you know there are other website owners. Use the medium to your advantage. Online communities, forums, social networking sites and e-mail lists all offer great opportunities to get your site URL out in front of people who can link to it. Blogs are another source of potential links – some blogs are incredibly popular, and bloggers are noted for their affinity to linking. Try submitting a few poignant comments to high-ranking blogs in your sector (do this responsibly; aim to add real value to the discussion rather than simply promoting your site – see Chapter 7 for more on using blogs to promote your site).

- *Create your own blog:* A blog can be an incredibly powerful promotional and link-building tool, if used wisely. If you have strong opinions, or a high level of knowledge in your industry, and you're happy to write regular posts, setting up a blog is easy and can be a great way to increase both visibility and incoming links.

- *Network, network, network:* Use your network of contacts both online and offline to promote your site and encourage people to link to it, and pass it on to their own network of contacts in turn. If people look at your site and like what they see they may well link to it.

- *Ask the people who link to your competitors to link to you:* Use Yahoo!'s Site Explorer to find out who's linking to your main competition for your selected search keywords. Approach those sites and ask them if they'd be willing to link to your site too. After all, if they link to your competitors, why wouldn't they?

- *Encourage links within content and with descriptive anchor text:* Links within content are preferable to links on a page that just lists links. Surrounding content helps to put a link in context, both for the user and for the search engines. You should also encourage descriptive anchor text that if possible and appropriate includes one or two of your chosen keywords.

- *Submit your site to high-quality directories:* Getting your site listed in high-quality, well-respected online directories like the Open Directory Project (www.dmoz.com, which is free) and Yahoo! Directory (dir. yahoo.com, which charges an annual fee for commercial listings) can be a great way to get your link building started. These links will help both search engine spiders and that all-important human traffic to find your site. As leading directories are considered 'authority' sites by the major search engines, links from these sites will also help boost your ranking.

- *Use link bait:* Link bait is anything that will entice incoming natural links from other websites or users. Link bait can be an interesting or controversial article, a downloadable document or report, a plug-in that improves the functionality of a piece of software or – the 'hot' link bait of the moment – widgets or gadgets (small applications that sit on the sidebars of either another website or your PC desktop) – or anything else that attracts incoming links. Be creative! Just stay within the search engines' published guidelines.

- *Offer to swap links with a select few relevant, high-quality sites:* These are called reciprocal links. Although they are less useful in terms of SEO value than they used to be, they can still be used effectively in moderation. While the power of reciprocal links to boost your rankings has been diluted, they do help to establish relevance and authority in your subject area – just be sure that you link to relevant, high-quality sites, and only swap links with a few of them. As a rule of thumb, you should *never* link to a site that you wouldn't genuinely recommend to your site visitors just for the sake of a reciprocal link.

Submitting your site URL and sitemap

Submitting your site URL, strictly speaking, isn't necessary any more. If you've followed the advice above and have managed to secure some inbound links, it won't be long before the spiders find you. That said, all of the major search engines offer a free submission process, and submitting your site won't hurt. If you want to kick-start the indexing process, by all means go ahead and manually submit your home page and one or two other important pages.

The other thing you can do that will help search engines to crawl all relevant pages on your website is to submit an XML sitemap that adheres to the sitemap protocol outlined on www.sitemaps.org, which defines a sitemap as follows:

> Sitemaps are an easy way for webmasters to inform search engines about pages on their sites that are available for crawling. In its simplest form, a Sitemap is an XML file that lists URLs for a site along with additional metadata about each URL (when it was last updated, how often it usually changes, and how important it is, relative to other URLs in the site) so that search engines can more intelligently crawl the site.
>
> Web crawlers usually discover pages from links within the site and from other sites. Sitemaps supplement this data to allow crawlers that support Sitemaps to pick up all URLs in the Sitemap and learn about those URLs using the associated metadata. Using the Sitemap protocol does not guarantee that web pages are included in search engines, but provides hints for web crawlers to do a better job of crawling your site.

The sitemap protocol was originally introduced by Google in June 2005 to allow web developers to publish lists of URLs for search engines to crawl. Google, MSN and Yahoo! announced joint support for the new protocol in November 2006.

Submitting a sitemap won't do anything to up your pages' rankings, but it will provide additional information that can help search engines to crawl your site more effectively. It's one more thing you can do to improve the odds, so ask your webmaster, web developer or SEO to include a sitemap for your site and either to manually submit it to the major search engines or to add an entry in your robots.txt file (a file that sits in the root directory of your web server that contains instructions for automated crawlers) that lets them pick it up automatically.

And start all over again...

Now you have your site optimized, it's time to sit back and start reaping the rewards, right? Unfortunately not! The ever-changing nature of the search environment means that there's no magic bullet in SEO. It's not a one-size-fits-all discipline, and it never ends. You have to work hard to find the right blend of targeted keywords for your particular business, operating within your particular market at the current point in time. You have to optimize your pages based on those keywords, and deliver compelling, high-impact content. You have to attract incoming links.

Then you have to measure, monitor and refine continuously, tweaking and tuning your optimization efforts based on changing conditions in the marketplace, the search engines and your customers. Take your foot off the gas and that high ranking you've worked so hard to achieve will gradually (and sometimes not so gradually) start to slip away.

Optimization is a dynamic and iterative process – and if you want sustained results it needs to be ongoing. In this section we've barely scratched the surface of the wonderfully dynamic, often frustrating but potentially incredibly rewarding world of search engine optimization.

To learn more, check out some of the links under SEO in the resources section on www.understandingdigitalmarketing.com – or, of course, you could just 'Google' it!

Top 10 organic SEO myths

Jill Whalen

SEO myths get crazier every year. Some are based partially in reality, and others have spread because it's often difficult to prove what particular SEO action caused a resulting search engine reaction.

For example, you might make a change to something on a page of your site and a few days later notice that your ranking in Google for a particular keyword phrase has changed. You might naturally assume that your page change is what caused the ranking change. But that's not necessarily so. There are numerous reasons why your ranking may have changed, and in many cases they actually have nothing to do with anything that you did.

Mixing up cause and effect is one of the most common things new SEOs do. If it were affecting only their own work, it wouldn't be so bad, but unfortunately the clueless often spread their misinformation to other unsuspecting newbies on forums and blogs, which in turn creates new myths. It's always interesting to see how people are so willing to believe anything they have read or heard without ever checking it out for themselves.

Here are 10 of the most common organic SEO myths:

- *Myth 1:* You should submit your URLs to search engines. This may have helped once upon a time, but it's been at least five or six years since that's been necessary.
- *Myth 2:* You need a Google sitemap. If your site was built correctly, ie it's crawler friendly, you certainly don't need a Google sitemap. It won't hurt you to have one, and you may be interested in Google's other Webmaster Central tools, but having a Google sitemap isn't going to get you ranked better.
- *Myth 3:* You need to update your site frequently. Frequent updates to your pages may increase the search engine crawl rate, but it won't increase your rankings. If your site doesn't need to change, don't change it just because you think the

search engines will like it better. They won't. In fact, some of the highest-ranking sites in Google haven't been touched in years.

- *Myth 4:* PPC ads will help/hurt rankings. This one is funny to me because about half the people who think that running Google AdWords will affect their organic rankings believe that they will bring them down; the other half believe they will bring them up. That alone should tell you that neither is true!
- *Myth 5:* Your site will be banned if you ignore Google's guidelines. There's nothing in Google's webmaster guidelines that isn't common sense. You can read them if you'd like, but it's not mandatory in order to be an SEO. Just don't do anything strictly for search engines that you wouldn't do anyway, and you'll be fine. That said, the Google guidelines are much better than they used to be and may even provide you with a few good titbits of advice.
- *Myth 6:* Your site will be banned if you buy links. This one does have some roots in reality, as Google (specifically Matt Cutts) likes to scare people about this. They rightly don't want to count paid links as votes for a page if they can figure out that they are paid, but they often can't. Even if they do figure it out, they simply won't count them. It would be foolish of them to ban entire sites because they buy advertising on other sites.
- *Myth 7:* H1 (or any header tags) must be used for high rankings. There's very little (if any) evidence to suggest that keywords in H tags actually affect rankings, yet this myth continues to proliferate. My own tests don't seem to show them making a difference, although it's difficult to know for sure. Use H tags if it works with your design or content management system, and don't if it doesn't. It's doubtful you'll find it makes a difference one way or the other.
- *Myth 8:* Words in your meta-keyword tag have to be used on the page. I used to spread this silly myth myself many years ago. The truth is that the meta-keyword tag was actually designed to be used for keywords that were *not* already on the page, not the opposite! Since this tag is ignored by Google and used only for uncommon words in Yahoo!, it makes little difference at this point anyway.
- *Myth 9:* SEO copy must be 250 words in length. This one is interesting to me because I am actually the one who made up the 250 number back in the late 1990s. However, I never said that 250 was the exact number of words you should use, nor did I say it was an optimal number. It's simply a good amount to be able to write a nice page of marketing copy that can be

optimized for three- to five-keyword phrases. Shorter copy ranks just as well, as does longer copy. Use as many or as few words as you need to use to say what you need to say.

- *Myth 10:* You need to optimize for the long tail. No, you don't. By their very nature, long-tail keyword phrases are uncompetitive, meaning that not many pages are using those words and not that many people are searching for them in the engines. Because of this, ranking for long-tail keywords is easy – simply include them somewhere in a blog post or an article and you'll rank for them. But that's not optimization.

Before you go spreading these myths or any other SEO info that you believe is true, test it many times on many sites. Even if it appears to work, keep in mind that it may not always work or that there could be other factors involved.

Jill Whalen, CEO and founder of High Rankings, a search marketing firm outside Boston, MA, and co-founder of SEMNE, a New England search marketing networking organization, has been performing SEO since 1995. Jill is the host of the High Rankings Advisor *search engine marketing newsletter. Her '100% Organic' column appears on Thursdays at Search Engine Land.*

Advertising on the search engines

Paid search marketing, paid placement, pay-per-click (PPC) advertising or search engine marketing (SEM), as it's also known, has in a very short space of time transformed search from what was essentially seen as a 'loss leader' activity into what's probably the digital world's biggest cash cow. PPC advertising is the principal way in which the search engines generate revenue – lots of revenue.

According to the Search Engine Marketing Professional Organization (SEMPO), in 2007 the PPC industry in North America alone was worth a staggering US$10.65 billion – or 87 per cent of the total spend on search marketing for that year. The organization predicts that the total North American search marketing spend will grow to a massive US$22.5 billion by 2011.

What is pay-per-click (PPC) search engine advertising?

Paid search marketing refers to the paid-for advertising that usually appears alongside, above and occasionally below the organic listings on the SERPs. These are usually labelled with something like 'sponsored links' or 'sponsored results' to make it clear to users that they are, in fact, paid-for ads and not part of the search engine's organic listing.

It's no surprise that the three biggest players in the pay-per-click arena are the top three search engines: Google with AdWords, Yahoo! with Search Marketing and Microsoft Live with Search Advertising. There are also a number of smaller PPC search programmes out there, which, for the time being at least, could offer better opportunities to reach local, industry-specific or specialized niche markets than the bigger players. For the most part, however, the big three are where the action is in terms of paid search marketing.

How does paid search advertising work?

When a user enters a search string into the search engine, the engine returns a list of organic search results. It also shows ads relevant to the search query adjacent to the organic listings. These ads tend to be small, unobtrusive text-based ads (remember the search engine's prime objective: to serve the users topical, relevant results).

While high ranking in the organic listing is the ideal that most webmasters are striving for (because it's 'free', and because users see organic results as impartial: they trust, and therefore click on, organic listings in preference to paid ads), optimizing pages to rank in organic search results can be difficult, and getting a consistently high and sustainable ranking takes a substantial amount of effort and a lot of time.

Time without traffic, of course, is a missed opportunity, and that's where paid search advertising comes in. By agreeing to pay the search engines a fee per click for your ads to show up as a sponsored result when a user types in your chosen keywords, you can put your site in front of your prospect in the SERPs almost immediately. When the user clicks on one of your ads, you get a new visitor, the search engine bills you for the click, and everybody's happy, at least in theory.

PPC keywords are bid on by advertisers in an auction-style system: generally the higher the bid per click, the higher the ad's placement in the SERPs. Some PPC systems also use a 'quality' quotient in their ad-placement rankings, based on the popularity of the ad (its click-through rate or CTR) and the perceived quality of the landing page it points to.

Why use paid search marketing?

There are a lot of reasons to use PPC search marketing. Here are just a few.

It generates traffic while you're waiting for your SEO to kick in: it can take months to get your site to the top half of the first page of organic search results through SEO. PPC ads can get your site in front of your audience almost immediately.

Highly targeted ads mean a better chance of conversion: you're not broadcasting your message to the masses as you would be with a display ad or banner ad – your search marketing ad will only appear in front of users who have pre-qualified themselves by typing your chosen keywords into the search engine in the geographical regions you've selected.

It can be an incredibly effective way to advertise. You only pay for your ad when a pre-qualified user clicks on it and is taken to your site. If users don't click, you don't pay. Providing your keywords are highly targeted and your landing pages convert well, it can generate a very healthy ROI. Some of the specific benefits of PPC advertising are:

- *Full financial control:* There's no minimum spend, you can set maximum monthly budgets on an account-wide basis or on individual campaigns, and you specify the maximum amount per click you're prepared to pay for each ad.
- *Full editorial control:* You're in complete control of every aspect of your campaign – from the title and ad copy, to the keywords and keyword matching option to apply, to the URL of the page you want users sent to.
- *Testing, tracking and tweaking on the fly:* There are tools that allow you to run real-time comparison tests to see how differences in your ads affect your click-through rate, and a host of reporting options that let you track your campaign and tweak it to achieve better results.
- *Improving your reach:* Target different keywords to those you rank for in the organic search, and broaden your reach for those more specific long-tail keywords that yield small volumes of high-value traffic.
- *Transcending the boundaries of the SERPs:* For even broader reach with some PPC offerings you get to select whether you want your ads to appear only on the search engine's own sites, on their advertising affiliate sites, or even on specific affiliate sites of your choosing.

Sounds great; how do I get started?

Unsurprisingly the search engines have made setting up PPC campaigns really easy. There are automated wizards to guide you through the sign-up process, and plenty of tools to help you establish, monitor and optimize your campaign. It's all very slick, and from a standing start you can have your first ad appearing next to search results and driving traffic to your site in under 15 minutes.

But hold your horses – just because you can doesn't necessarily mean that you should. Rushing headlong into your first PPC advertising campaign might yield great results for you 'out of the box', and then again it might not. As always it pays to do a bit of preparation first:

- *Choose your keywords wisely:* Look for longer keyword phrases that are likely to be less competitive and send highly targeted traffic to your site. Ideally you should aim for phrases that generate a healthy amount of search engine traffic without attracting a lot of bids from other advertisers.
- *Optimize your ads:* Your ads need to entice users to click on them if you're going to get traffic. Think carefully about your title and ad copy. Remember, you want targeted copy that will appeal to people who are *ready to buy* – so be specific. Generating clicks that don't convert is costing you money.
- *Converting clicks into customers:* Once you get the clicks, you need to turn your new prospects into paying customers as often as you can. It's your conversion rate that will make or break your PPC campaign. Don't direct traffic from your ad back to your home page. Send it instead to a page directly related to the text of the ad users have just clicked on – perhaps a product page or, better still, a special *landing page* designed specifically to reinforce your PPC campaign. Remember, if you fail to convert your traffic into revenue, all your PPC campaign will do is haemorrhage cash.
- *Measure everything and test, test, test:* The best way to learn is to start small, track your campaign carefully and study the metrics (see Chapter 5). Try out different ad combinations, different landing pages and different keyword combinations, and measure how the changes affect your CTR, your conversion rate, your cost per conversion and, ultimately, your bottom line.

Mastering the intricacies of PPC advertising could take a lifetime, but the basics are straightforward enough, and the best way to learn is to dive in and start using it. You'll also find plenty of resources to help you, both in the search engines' advertising sections and in the online marketing community. You'll find links to some of them in the resources section on www.understandingdigitalmarketing.com, but the best way of finding them online is – you guessed it – to use a search engine!

What are the downsides?

There are surprisingly few if you manage your campaign carefully and stay on top of your spending and conversion rates. The biggest one is that as bigger businesses are starting to wake up to the potential of search marketing they're beginning to funnel more of their advertising spend online – and that in turn is driving up the cost per click of more competitive pay-per-click keywords. However, there are still plenty of opportunities out there to reap real dividends from long-tail keywords.

The key thing to remember is that you have to pay for every click whether or not you convert, so it's important to keep track of the metrics and make sure you're getting value from your investment.

Black Hat, the darker side of search

The SEO methods explored earlier in this chapter are methods that adhere to the search engine's own guidelines (or at least they did at the time of writing – but guidelines can change, so it's important to keep up to date). Generally referred to as 'White Hat' SEO, these techniques are seen as legitimate optimization of a site to align it with the needs of the site visitor and simultaneously make the site content accessible and easy to index by the search engines.

But there is another side to SEO – an altogether darker and more sinister side, where less ethical practitioners attempt to exploit every trick and loophole they can find to 'game' the engines, increase their rankings and drive traffic to their sites. It is dubbed 'Black Hat' SEO, search engine spamming or spamdexing (spamming the indexes), and when discovered offending sites are quickly banned from the search engine index.

But the Black Hat SEO isn't worried by bans or penalties. For Black Hats, banishment from the search engines comes with the territory. They're not interested in building quality sites with sustainable high rankings – they're looking for short-term gains from high traffic to ad-laden sites. By the time one batch of sites has been banned they've already moved on to the next. Black Hatters typically have many sites running on many different domains across a variety of hosts, all exploiting loopholes in the system to artificially boost their rankings and generate advertising revenue.

Why should I care what colour hat these people wear?

On one level, you shouldn't need to. The battle that's raging over artificially inflated rankings in the SERPs is between the Black Hatters and the search engines. It's up to the Yahoos, Googles and Microsofts of this world to wage that war.

Wherever there is a system in place you'll find people – often some of the most clever and resourceful people out there – who will attempt to exploit that system for their own gain. You'll also have some equally clever and resourceful people trying to stop them. It's human nature, and it's not going to go away any time soon.

Essentially, Black Hatters are simply taking the principles of SEO that we discussed earlier in this chapter – creating a list of keywords, building pages, getting links – but they're pushing the boundaries to the extreme. Instead of a manageable selection of keywords for which they can create unique and engaging content, Black Hatters will create lists of hundreds or thousands of keywords and stuff their pages full of keyword-rich bunkum created by automated content generation tools. Instead of building links naturally, they'll use automated 'bots' to spam posts stuffed with links into blog comments, guestbooks, forums and wikis all over the web.

Black Hats typically aren't interested in you or your site – unless it's as a possible repository for link spam in your blog, guestbook, forum or wiki, and that can generally be avoided by implementing security features on your site that require human intervention to post. What's perhaps more significant is that by pushing their spammy sites up the SERPs they're artificially pushing down more legitimate sites like yours, making them less visible to searchers and potentially affecting your traffic.

Some common Black Hat SEO techniques

- *Keyword stuffing:* This is repeating keywords over and over again on a given web page. This is less successful now, as search engine algorithms are getting better at distinguishing copy that's constructed properly from gobbledegook.
- *Cloaking:* Cloaking is a technique that uses code to show one search-engine-friendly page to the spider and a completely different page

to a human visitor. The engines hate this as it makes it impossible for them to gauge the quality of the content a user is seeing. In early 2006 Google blacklisted car manufacturer BMW's German website www. bmw.de, dropping it from its index for employing a cloaking page.

- *Invisible text:* Invisible text is essentially text that is the same colour as the background of the page – result, humans can't see it but search engines can. This is like keyword stuffing – but with the cloaking element of showing the search engine bot and human visitor different content.
- *Doorway page:* This is a highly optimized web page whose sole purpose is to send traffic to other pages either through an automatic redirect or by simply being full of links.
- *Spam page:* This is a page with no meaningful content that is full of ads that the webmaster makes money from if someone clicks on them.
- *Interlinking:* This is the practice of setting up multiple websites on a given topic and linking backwards and forwards between them purely in an attempt to increase their rankings in the search engines.
- *Selling links to help ranking:* If you have a high-ranking website, you sell links from your site to another to boost its ranking.
- *Buying expired domains:* This is the practice of buying up expired domains that were once high-ranking pages to try to acquire some of the old site's inbound links.

That's just a small selection of the techniques Black Hat SEOs use to boost their rankings and drive traffic. There are many more. As a rule of thumb for your own site, if what you're doing *adds genuine value to the end user* you generally have nothing to worry about. If, on the other hand, you're implementing something to artificially manipulate your search engine rankings, you could be venturing into grey, or even Black Hat, territory. If you value your domain, be careful.

When you come across these sites while browsing the web they can be irritating, and having to deal with spam in any medium is infuriating, but for the most part you don't need to worry about the Black Hats who are doing their own thing to their own sites. But there is another, more sinister aspect...

Negative SEO

Far more worrying, potentially at least, is the concept of negative SEO. Some Black Hat SEOs have started peddling commercial services not to increase their clients' rankings in the SERPs, but to damage the ranking of their competitors – or even to get them banned altogether.

Dubbed negative SEO, it is still uncommon, but is certainly something that webmasters and online marketers need to be aware of. Google, the leading search engine, maintains that there's 'almost nothing a competitor can do to harm your ranking or have your site removed from our index'. But it's that 'almost' that has people worried.

In June 2007 *Forbes* magazine brought the subject of negative SEO out of the shadows of the search community and presented it to a mainstream audience. In the *Forbes* article two SEOs admitted to journalist Andy Greenberg that they use negative SEO, and revealed some of its implications. 'I understand the rules of search', SEO Brendon Scott said in the article. 'And once you understand the rules, you can use them not just constructively, but also destructively.' He went on to claim that he could reduce a competing site's visibility to searchers or even make it seem to disappear from search results altogether.

Negative SEO was spawned, ironically, from the efforts of Google, Yahoo! and other search engines to filter out the spam generated by Black Hat SEO and keep their search results relevant to their users. As part of the battle against spam, the search engine algorithms identify 'spammy' tactics and penalize the offending site's rankings accordingly. If there are enough, or severe enough, transgressions to the search engine's guidelines, the site could be thrown out of the index altogether.

Some of the negative SEO tactics that could have a negative impact on a site's rankings include, but are far from limited to:

- *DOS and 404 errors:* The attacker initiates a denial-of-service attack (DOS) to swamp the target domain. Once the target domain is down, the attacker then employs numerous methods to encourage search engine spiders to visit the site. If the spiders arrive and receive a 404 (not found) error, those pages will typically be de-indexed. Once the server recovers, the website is up and running, but is no longer appearing in the search results.
- *Redirection:* The attacker redirects to the targeted pages from 'bad neighbourhood' sites like porn sites, link farms, etc. The targeted pages can end up being removed from the search engine index through association with spammy domains.
- *Link bomb:* The attacker links to the targeted pages from blatant link farms or free-for-all link sites, using anchor text with irrelevant or spam-like keywords. They then submit those link-farm pages manually to the search engines and get as many spam sites as possible to link into it. Search engines flag the target site as spam and remove it from their index.
- *Duplicate content:* The attacker copies content from targeted pages and duplicates that content on disposable 'bad neighbourhood' domains,

embedding spammy keywords like 'porn', 'pills' or 'casinos', invisible text and other spam flags, which *may* result in both sets of pages being removed from the index.

* *Black social bookmarking:* The attacker sets up multiple accounts with social bookmarking sites, and tags targeted sites excessively with irrelevant and spammy terms like 'porn', 'gambling', 'pharmaceutical', etc. As a result the target site may be penalized heavily or even removed from the search engine's index once the social bookmark pages have been spidered.

(*Source:* Fantomaster, www.fantomaster.com)

NB: We in no way condone any of these tactics, and are listing them here merely to illustrate the potential real-world threat of negative SEO for digital marketers.

Negative SEO is potentially a very real threat – but for most websites not a very probable one. It pays to be aware of the possibility, and if you're concerned that your competitors might employ such tactics it at least gives you a heads up on the sort of things that you and your IT department or partners need to be looking out for. If you truly believe that your website is under attack through negative SEO, your best bet is to hire a specialist consultant to help you combat the threat in the short term. The consultant will typically help you to identify the nature of the attack and where it's coming from and to implement a security plan that will help shield against future attacks.

Bringing in the pros

While SEO and PPC campaigns can certainly be managed in-house, if you lack specialist search talent and want to fast-track traffic to your site then bringing in a professional search marketing consultant can pay real dividends.

If you decide to bring in an external consultancy to help with your search marketing, do your homework and choose wisely. There are many excellent SEOs out there who will do a great job of promoting your business online, but equally there are unscrupulous companies looking to exploit the uninitiated. Not all SEO companies are created equal, and it's an unfortunate fact that some of them will stray into less-than-ethical territory to secure high rankings quickly, making them and their services look good in the short term.

The good news is that, having read this chapter, you're now armed with the knowledge you need to engage positively with prospective search marketing partners, understand what they're telling you and discuss your SEO requirements with them in some detail.

Here are a few things to bear in mind when you engage with an SEO professional:

- Make sure you're dealing with a reputable company that has a strong track record to back up its claims.
- Ask to see case studies and get references from previous clients.
- Check the company's own site – has it been optimized and does it adhere to search engine guidelines?
- Look and listen for any hint of the Black Hat techniques listed above. If there's any doubt about the ethics and integrity of the company, walk away. It's your domain the company will be playing with, and it's not worth risking your reputation with the engines.
- Once you've engaged an SEO company don't just leave the company to it. You need to keep abreast of what your SEO company is doing on your behalf – after all, it's your site.

Universal search – more opportunities to rank

'Universal search' is a term coined by Google to describe a fundamental change in the way it presents its web search results. The search company introduced universal search in mid-2007 for Google.com users, and continued rolling it out to other Google domains (.co.uk, .ca, .ie, etc) through 2008. Billed by commentators as one of the most significant and radical developments in the history of the search industry, universal search (or blended search, as it's also known) takes results from Google's specialized (or vertical) search engines (Google News, Google Books, Google Local/Maps, Google Video, Google Image, Google Groups, etc) and slots them into standard web search results in order of relevance.

Google's Vice President of Search Products and User Experience, Marissa Mayer, explained it succinctly in a post on the official Google Blog (http://googleblog.blogspot.com) in May 2007: 'With universal search, we're attempting to break down the walls that traditionally separated our various search properties and integrate the vast amounts of information available into one simple set of search results.'

As you would expect, other major search engines weren't far behind, and both Yahoo! and Microsoft's Live Search introduced similar blended search results soon after Google. For users, this development is a huge boon. Instead of having to manage and navigate multiple specialized search tools, users can now enter their search query in one convenient location to find results across multiple platforms. But what does it mean to search marketers?

Essentially, there are two ways of looking at it. On one level it's a potential threat, in that for any given keyword phrase your pages now have

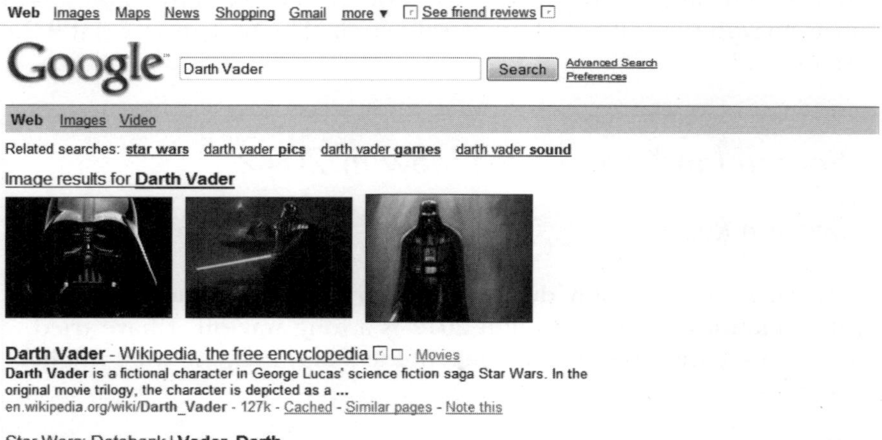

Figure 4.2 Universal search – also dubbed 'blended search' by some commentators – integrates search results from other specialized search engines (images, video, local/maps, etc). Here we see the SERPs for a search for 'Darth Vader' on Google.com

to compete with results for news, video, maps, discussion groups, images and a host of other sources to get those coveted top SERP rankings. On the other hand, if you produce the right sort of content and submit it to the relevant places, universal search offers additional opportunities to rank for your chosen keyword phrases.

Universal search doesn't change any of the SEO advice we provided earlier in the chapter – but it is something to be aware of as you optimize your pages, and offers additional avenues for you to get your content in front of your target audience. As the title of Marissa Mayer's blog post says, even with the roll-out of universal search 'The best answer is still the best answer.'

Search landscape – the view in 2012

Damian Ryan

Search is an incredibly dynamic industry that continues to evolve at a relentless pace. Although 2012 is a long way off, I have tried here to separate the various stakeholders and imagine what might be going on.

The consumer

As long as they are receiving quality customer service from their chosen suppliers, consumers may be less inclined to search for competitive offerings. Marketers will have to work harder to reach them and be more prepared to pay for their business.

Consumers are far more marketing savvy now than ever before and there is absolutely no reason to think this is going to become any less the case in five years' time, but their propensity to switch brands or suppliers (in the context of search) remains to be seen. If one takes a look at the top brands in the marketplace now and asks which new brands have broken into the rankings in the last 10 years I suspect the answer is only one or two.

Of course, consumers will still want to search for information and find answers to questions, but part of me feels they will already know where to go and may require the use of a search engine less than they used to. Ask yourself the questions – name an online provider of the following products:

- flights to London;
- supermarket deliveries;
- health insurance.

You shouldn't have had too much trouble filling the answers out there, so why do you need to use a search engine? I am watching the advance of price comparison and lead generation sites too – marketers should pay close attention to these developments.

The search engines

Search engines are going to have to work very hard to protect their space. I don't believe this sector has the same dynamics as, say, the publishing industry. There it was only ever a toss-up between, say, *Yellow Pages* and *Thomson Directories* – but the old phone directories never really had an issue with editorial credibility. It was always about being comprehensive, and the one that took out the biggest ad got the best position – which is fair enough!

But when I look at Google I sincerely believe that editorial credibility has to come into play at some stage. Yes, the algorithms are evident, but if the top-ranking site for say 'flights' is not delivering the best value then what is it doing there? And who are Google to say what is best for us? Won't there be a suspicion that some kind of transaction might have taken place? Do we even care?

One answer might be consensus. What do the rest of the planet think about the top-ranking 'flights' site rather than one organization? Representative of the populace it might be, but I don't think the net has ever been about anything other than freedom to choose and freedom of information. Personally I like what Amazon do, inviting people to review books. Maybe Google could, well, take a leaf out of theirs?

I fundamentally believe that search engines, like newspapers, magazines and other media, will, at least in part, become personality driven, with opinion formers and champions guiding us through their favourites. Doesn't this all sound spookily familiar? Celebrity endorsements, morphing of advertising and content – and all because you are worth it!

The marketers

I believe that marketers, following an intensive period of land grabbing and the pursuit of mind share, will demand a lot more creativity from search engines, and should be working with them now to push this forward. Marketers cannot afford to be priced out of the top page, and search engines will obviously be seeking new revenues, so it stands to reason that when an unstoppable force meets an immovable object something has to give!

Search engine optimization as we know it now will, I believe, become *less* relevant. Surely all the good rules and practices will be widely known by 2012 and will be bundled in with the latest web package at the time – so where will the focus points for marketers be?

Keyword buys – definitely, and maybe the engines will offer greater rotation and variation of brands. Possibly a new section on search engines listing 'brands you haven't heard about yet' or 'brands offering special deals today only'.

Whatever comes to light I am sure marketers' budgets for search will increase in the logical way – the more consumers using search, the more business through that channel, the more value it will hold for marketers, but as I mentioned above the major challenge for marketers will be protecting, retaining and defending their customers against competition and against competitive pressures.

Case study: GetTheGlass.com

The brief

The purpose of GetTheGlass.com was twofold: to create a website that made learning the benefits of milk fun and entertaining and to increase milk consumption in California. The target audience for this campaign was adults in California. The agency in charge of the campaign was Goodby, Silverstein & Partners (GSP), which developed the concept and implemented the strategy. The website was designed by North Kingdom according to GSP's instructions.

The concept

The GetTheGlass.com website was 'inhabited' by a family of characters called the Adachis, and each character suffered from ailments related to their lack of milk. On the site, visitors played a board game in which they helped the Adachi family get a glass of milk, which was a very challenging and engaging task. Players advanced in the game by rolling a pair of virtual dice and driving the Adachis' plumbing van through a series of milk-related challenges while trying to keep ahead of 'Fort Fridge' security and avoid being sent to 'Milkatraz'. If the players were sent to 'Milkatraz' they had an option to have a friend help them escape. This was a means of increasing the site traffic as well as creating the community aspects of the site. The successful players who completed the game were sent an actual 'GetTheGlass' souvenir glass.

The campaign

The website was the cornerstone of the campaign, which was supported by banner advertisements. Search marketing was used to drive traffic to the site. Given the unique concept of the website there was a large amount of press coverage, inclusions in blogs and referrals from friends. In effect the traffic was also driven by viral marketing.

The greatest challenge of the campaign was the creation of the characters. The 3D characters that were created had to be based on the talent that was selected for the TV spots. From concept to completing the campaign took six months.

The navigation structure of the site was contingent upon user behaviour in the style of traditional board games. GetTheGlass.com combined numerous video and 3D components. The game in itself was ground-breaking in terms of the style and execution. The details within each section of the game made it special and interesting. The greatest campaign challenge was the content development as well as the creation of the rules of game play.

The results

There had been over 3.4 million visits to the site worldwide as at April 2008. GSP's relationship with the California Milk Processor Board (CMPB) was further strengthened by the client's trust in the agency's brand strategy and creative development. The power and strength of the campaign are also evident from the industry recognition of its success. The campaign won a Gold Cyber Lion at Cannes 2007 and the Favourite Website Awards (FWA) Site of the Year and People's Choice Awards. GetTheGlass.com won awards at the Flashforward Conference, London International Advertising Awards and *HoWDesign* Magazine Awards.

Campaign comment

Quote from Goodby, Silverstein & Partners Creative Director (Interactive), Will McGinness:

> This was a huge team effort and possibly one of the most exciting projects we've worked on. The collaboration and breadth of thinking that went into GetTheGlass was nothing short of inspiring. Also, having an amazing client like CMPB was essential in creating a unique experience like this. Without their trust and enthusiasm it wouldn't have been possible.

Campaign credits

Client: California Milk Processor Board
Product: Milk
Advertising agency: Goodby, Silverstein & Partners, San Francisco
Creative Director: Pat McKay
Creative Director (Interactive): Will McGinness

5 Website intelligence and return on investment

Half of the money I spend on advertising is wasted; the trouble is, I don't know which half.

(William Hesketh Lever, the 1st Lord Leverhulme, 1851–1925. A similar quote expressing an identical sentiment has been attributed to John Wanamaker, the US department store entrepreneur and advertising pioneer, and also to Henry Ford)

What we call results are beginnings.

(Ralph Waldo Emerson)

I notice increasing reluctance on the part of marketing executives to use judgement; they are coming to rely too much on research, and they use it as a drunkard uses a lamp post: for support, rather than for illumination.

(David Ogilvy)

Our chapter pledge to you

When you reach the end of this chapter you'll have answers to the following questions:

- How will I know where to invest my digital marketing budget for maximum ROI?
- What information can I track on my website, how is it collected and how can I use it to inform my digital marketing investment?
- How can I track my online advertising that appears on other sites?
- What are key performance indicators (KPIs), and how can I use them to gain insight into my online marketing?
- Why is testing important, and what types of testing should I be doing?

Measuring your way to digital marketing success

So you have your search engine-optimized website up and running. You may even have set up pay-per-click or search advertising accounts with a few providers, and tried out a few ads, just to see what happens. Now what?

Well, that depends...

I know we keep saying this, but it really does depend. It depends on your business goals, your target market, the digital marketing strategy you've defined and the budget you have available. Digital marketing isn't a prescriptive medium. There are far too many variables involved. What works for you won't necessarily work for me, and what works for me probably won't work for A N Other Inc, even though we may all be operating superficially similar businesses catering to superficially similar consumers.

The long and the short of it is that nobody can tell you categorically what will or won't work for you online, not without an intimate knowledge of your business. You (and/or the specialist you bring in to help you) have to find out for yourself what works and what doesn't in your particular circumstances. That involves a bit more work than simply applying a prescriptive formula, but it's worth the effort, because defining your own customized digital marketing equation will give you much more insight into where the real online opportunities lie for your business, and will help you to differentiate yourself from your competition.

The great news is that, in the world of digital marketing, there are all sorts of tools available to show you *exactly* what's working for you and just as importantly what's not. The most successful marketing has always been about learning from your results: taking a finite budget and using it to do more of the stuff that is working and less of the stuff that's not. You test, you refine, you reinvest, and you test again.

Traditional marketing media threw up two major obstacles to this approach: buying advertising space to 'test' different advertising tactics was often prohibitively expensive, and measuring the results in any meaningful way was notoriously difficult. You were never quite sure which elements of your marketing mix were actually delivering the results. The internet has changed all that. With the migration towards performance-based advertising – pay-per-click and pay-per-acquisition models – you pay only for traffic or (even better) actual conversions gained through a particular advertising channel. That makes it easy and relatively cheap for you to test different ad combinations to see what works best for you, without your costs spiralling out of control. And because you can track and measure *everything* that's channelled back through your website you can build an accurate picture of how your prospects respond to these ads at a level of granularity that's simply unheard of in traditional advertising media.

Now, for the first time ever, you can capture the results of your advertising in practically real time, and adapt your digital campaigns on the fly to maximize return on your digital marketing investment. It's a level of control that's unprecedented in the history of advertising – and with that control comes a level of accountability for results that to date has been sorely lacking.

The rise of performance-based advertising

Brandt Dainow

The web is constantly evolving, as we all know. It's a changing environment because people are in the process of migrating from traditional media to online. This migration will not be total – people will still read books and watch TV – but the emphasis is changing. Print and broadcast media will become alternatives to the new mainstream – online.

We are passing significant markers in this migration right now. For example, people aged 17 to 25 now spend more time online than watching TV. I recently spoke to a friend whose son was starting university. He visited the student halls of residence and was surprised to see that none of the students had stereos (an essential of student life in his day) or TVs in their rooms. When he asked about this the students laughed at him – why would they need those when they had computers and internet connections? To this younger generation the idea of a device that can only handle a single medium, and that isn't connected to the web, is laughably archaic.

It's clear that we are evolving new ways of participating in society, new ways of communicating, and new ways of disseminating information. A key dynamic in this process is the transition of the print and broadcast advertising community on to the web. As this occurs, new models of advertising become possible.

Henry Ford once said 'I know only half of my advertising works. The problem is, I don't know which half.' The web solves this problem. The ability to record people's behaviour online means advertising can be assessed in terms of the behaviour people exhibit after being exposed to an ad. It then becomes possible to pay for the behaviour instead of the mere delivery of the ad. This is called performance-based advertising.

A shift from selling audience to selling behaviour

The dominating trend in the evolution of online advertising is the rise of performance-based advertising. Predictions are that there will be $40 billion in online ad sales in 2008 and that 50 per cent of this will involve performance-based payment. This represents a shift from selling audience to selling behaviour.

The traditional form of advertising involves selling audience. In print and broadcast, advertising rates are largely determined by the number of people who will be exposed to the ad. As traditional media employees moved online they took this model with them, selling 'impressions'. Banner advertising is traditionally sold this way.

Impression-based advertising simply consists of placing an ad somewhere on a reader's computer screen, in a manner similar to placing an ad somewhere on the page of a magazine. Performance-based advertising involves changing the emphasis from views to actions. Instead of paying the outlet to deliver my ad, I will pay it for delivering people.

The most common forms of performance-based advertising are PPC advertising and affiliate networks. Google's AdWords is a classic example of performance-based advertising. Advertisers pay not for exposure but for the people Google sends to the advertisers' sites.

Even where performance-based advertising is not the obvious basis upon which the advertising is being sold, it is often the way in which it is assessed. Mark Read is director of strategy at WPP UK, one of the world's leading marketing communication organizations. According to Read, many of WPP's clients, especially in finance and automotive, convert the metrics from their ad outlets back into performance metrics.

'It doesn't matter how people sell the ad space; it's bought on a performance basis whether they realize it or not', says Read.

Read is very much in favour of this shift to performance-based advertising. 'The advantage of performance-based advertising is that it converts ad spend from a line expense to a cost of goods sold. As such, the expenditure is potentially infinite... The secret of Google's success was to convert ad spend from line of business to cost of sale', Read says.

In other words, the potential income from an ad outlet is much greater than is possible with impression-based advertising. Performance-based advertising obviously represents better value for the advertiser, but it can also represent better value for the seller.

Ben Regensburger, president of DoubleClick Germany, agrees. 'If you know your audience and your inventory well you can make more money from performance-based ads than simple impressions, especially in finance', he says.

The drawbacks of performance-based metrics

Christoph Schuh is CMO of Tomorrow Focus AG, one of Germany's leading digital content providers. Tomorrow Focus is the largest supplier of German-language content on the web. As a media owner, someone whose income is based on selling advertising, Schuh can see issues with performance-based advertising.

'The danger in buying performance is that it ignores the value of repeated exposure and of time-delayed responses', he says. 'I think performance buying to a single-response dimension will become insufficient; we need to develop behavioural targeting.'

Notice that Schuh is not opposed to performance-based advertising. He simply wants to see performance assessment become more sophisticated.

One of the most common problems encountered when dealing with performance-based advertising is disagreement between the advertiser and the publisher over the numbers. Web metrics systems are still fairly primitive, and the web analytics community has yet to establish clear procedures for measurement. As a result, advertiser and publisher systems can often disagree about exactly how many people have been delivered.

'Currently, ad people don't understand the metrics', says Schuh. 'This makes resolving disputes extremely difficult.'

Addressing this issue requires training advertising salespeople in web analytics so they have a language in which to communicate and so they understand what it is their web analytics systems are telling them.

In addition, resolving discrepancies between the advertiser's and the publisher's numbers usually involves a technical conversation about how the data are processed on both systems. The field of web analytics lacks standards, and the few standards that do exist are rarely implemented consistently within analytics software. If both systems are measuring the same thing in the same way, the numbers will match to within a few percentage points.

But discrepancies occur because the two systems are measuring things differently or using the same terms for different things. If the respective technicians explain to each other what their systems are measuring, and how, it is usually possible to adjust the numbers to match. This requires that advertising and marketing people have access to their web analytics technicians, and have the training to be able to communicate with them.

Much of this can be avoided if the methodology for performance assessment is agreed upon before the deal is signed. Once again, this requires that sales staff have sufficient training to participate in such conversations, and that, where necessary, they can call on their technicians for assistance.

The publisher dilemma

For a publisher, performance-based advertising represents both an opportunity and a threat. As Christoph Schuh says, 'You have to understand your website better than your client... You have to understand the behaviour of your readers in the conversion funnel... You need an e-commerce unit within your editorial team.'

Once, the editorial focus was purely on producing content that would appeal to a large swath of the population – appeal to enough readers and the advertisers would follow. In the early days of the internet, we thought this was all we needed to do. Jim Barksdale, president and CEO of Netscape until the company merged with AOL, said in 1995: 'Don't worry about how to earn money online. Simply get a big enough audience and the money will come to you.'

This was true for a while, but advertisers are wising up. They're not interested in mere numbers; they want behaviour. This presents publishers with a dilemma. We all know you can't make money selling content to readers – they won't pay for it. The presence of huge quantities of free information on the web has devalued the perceived value of all information in the eyes of the online community.

The main way to make money as a content publisher at present, then, is via advertising. If advertisers become completely focused on performance, editors become confronted with the need to design content in order to get the acquisitions their advertisers want. Should editors, then, write to make sales, or do they write to gather audience and hope the sales just happen because they got the right audience?

In the long term, the future surely belongs to those who can develop content that attracts an audience and, at the same time, frame that content in a manner that encourages the behaviour advertisers want.

Brandt Dainow is CEO of ThinkMetrics, an independent web analytics and marketing consultant operating in the UK and Ireland. He works with client organizations' companies to design, manage and tune their online marketing and sales processes. For more details see Brandt's website www. thinkmetrics.com

Getting started

The ability to track, measure and refine your online marketing campaigns as they unfold is a huge boon, but it can't help to guide your investment decisions *before* you have anything to measure. So where do you start? Should you channel your budget into search engine pay-per-click campaigns, or would you be better off focusing more on long-term optimization for organic search results, coupled with a sprinkling of display ads on prominent, high-traffic industry websites? What about the explosion in vertical online advertising networks, or perhaps you should choose a more general ad network with broader scope?

Questions, questions, questions... when all you want is answers

While some of these questions may seem baffling, the truth is that you already have the answers you need. Remember all that research you did to define your strategy, create your website and optimize it for the search engines? At this point you know your target market; you know where they congregate online, what they're searching for, and the sort of things they like to find when they get there. You also know what your business is trying to achieve online and have a strategy for how you're going to go about it.

Take all of that information, apply a little business acumen and that stalwart of marketers everywhere – intuition – and you'll find you have a pretty good idea of where to focus your initial investment in order to reach your objectives. Don't worry about getting things perfect from the beginning; the most important thing is to *get started*. As long as you're aiming in roughly the right direction, get your initial campaign up and running and start collecting some real data. Bias your early investment towards the area(s) you instinctively feel will yield the best returns for your business – and then measure, refine and reinvest.

Online marketing is an iterative process of continuous improvement: you make a change, you try something new, you test, you refine and you track your results. Invest most of your budget in what you know to be working well at any given time, but never stop experimenting with new and different approaches. You could hit on something that works even better. As you accumulate real data about how your target market is responding to your campaigns you can start making really informed decisions that will have a positive and often dramatic impact on your ROI.

How information is measured

Imagine if you could tell not just how many people were visiting your website (your traffic) but for all individual visitors where they came from (both on the internet and geographically), what browser and operating system they were using at the time, what keywords they used to find your site and on which search engine, the page they arrived at, how long they stayed for, what pages they visited while they were there, which page they ultimately left from and whether or not they came back again.

That would be really useful information, right? It would let you analyse how your users were finding your site, whether you were giving them what they wanted when they arrived, where they were leaving from, whether your site was optimized for the right search keywords, how effective your different forms of advertising were at driving traffic to your site and what proportion of that traffic was ultimately being converted into sales, leads or whatever other conversion goals you'd defined. In other words, marketing gold dust.

Well, the good news is that with modern website analytics software you can track all of that information and more. Like everything else on the internet, web analytics has gone all '2.0', so you can get all of the data you want, presented to you when you want and in the way that you want.

Website analytics uses information your visitors volunteer

It's important to note here that there's nothing underhanded about tracking and analysing website statistics. All we're doing is looking at the information that's readily volunteered by the user or the user's browser. There's no magic 'voodoo' or (as a rule, at least) underhanded cyber-espionage going on here. We're simply collecting the information that's routinely recorded when a visitor comes to our website and then using analytics software to aggregate it and present it in a format that lets us view trends and make informed decisions.

There are two main ways of collecting information about your website visitors. You can analyse the web access logs created by your own web server or you can embed some code (called a page tag) in every page on your website that sends similar information to your chosen analytics service provider.

Web server log files

Every time your web server receives a request for a resource (a file) on your website it stores details of that request in its server access logs. What exactly is recorded depends on a variety of factors, including the way the server itself is set up, the format of the log files it produces and the settings of the user's browser.

That said, a server log file will typically contain the following kind of information for every browser request it receives:

- the unique IP address of the user's computer;
- a time stamp showing the date and time of the request;
- the URI of the requested resource;
- a status code confirming the result of the request;
- the file size of the returned resource;
- the URL of the referring page;
- other information supplied by the 'user agent' (typically browser type/version, language and operating system).

From this information, website analytics software can derive a host of useful information. For example, from the IP address it can determine where in the world the user is browsing from; the referring URL can tell it whether the user entered the site directly, was referred from a link on another site or came from a search engine and, if so, what search query string the user entered to reach your site. The IP address *may* also help track an individual user's path through the site during the user's visit (although using the IP address to track this can be unreliable and is typically augmented by the use of cookies).

Log file analysis software comes in all shapes, sizes and flavours. Some merely read raw log file data, aggregate it and spit out the results as crude tables for you to trawl through manually. Others format the information to make it more readable and present it in easy-to-comprehend graphs and tables. The most sophisticated let you define your own summary reports, segment your audience, define and track conversion goals and analyse conversion 'funnels' (the navigation steps a user follows to complete a 'conversion' goal), and will integrate data from other sources to give you a complete picture of your website's overall performance.

Most web hosts provide some form of basic log file analysis software as part of their hosting package, so it's worth looking at this first to get a basic idea of the kind of information that's available in your log files. There is a wide range of software options available, ranging from free open source offerings (like Webalizer, AWStats and Analog) to costly enterprise-level solutions from leading industry players like WebTrends and Omniture, and a host of other options in between.

Page tagging and hosted solutions

The second method is a process known as page tagging. This involves putting a small piece of code on every page of your site that you want to track. Whenever a visitor requests the page the code sends information (gleaned in much the same way as that recorded in the server log file) and sends it to your chosen provider. This form of tracking has become very much in vogue with the rising popularity of the software-as-a-service (SAAS) concept, and has been fuelled by the introduction of free, powerful and highly configurable analytics services like StatCounter (www.statcounter.com) and the very popular Google Analytics (www. google.com/analytics).

Once the code is installed on your pages these services will start collecting data and can provide you with a wealth of easily accessible and highly configurable information. You just have to make sure the tracking code is included on every page of your site that you want to track (including new pages you may add over time) and your service provider will look after the rest.

Augmenting information using cookies

Using a user's IP address to uniquely identify visitors is inconsistent and inaccurate for a variety of reasons, no matter which of the tracking methods above you choose to use. For instance, a large number of internet users (AOL users being the primary example) may share a single IP address assigned by their internet service provider (ISP). That means that, if your analytics solution relies purely on IP address to identify unique visitors, it will count these multiple users as the same visitor, skewing your metrics. Similarly, users are often assigned a dynamic IP address that changes each time they log on to their ISP, so a person returning to your site may be counted as a new visitor rather than a returning one.

To get around these limitations and to remember site settings that help to improve the user experience, many sites and third-party tracking services employ HTTP cookies to identify individual users. Cookies are small files that are sent to users' browsers and stored on their local hard drives. Typically they store a unique ID that allows the site (or tracking service) to identify a returning visitor, store site preference and personalization settings that enhance the user experience, and help you to track that visitor's navigation around your website.

Cookies get a bad press because of the potential privacy issues associated with what are called *persistent third-party cookies*, or cookies that are set by a domain other than the one you're visiting and that persist beyond the scope of your existing browser session. In theory these cookies could be used to track visitor behaviour across multiple websites on different domains, building up a picture of users' behaviour as they surf the web. That's perceived as a bad thing, because large ad-serving and tracking companies can potentially use cookies to build up profiles of user behaviour across all the websites that they serve without explicit consent from the user.

In practice, though, cookies tend to be largely harmless, enable websites to deliver a better user experience to their customers, and allow more accurate tracking of website statistics. The vast majority of internet users' browsers are set to accept cookies by default, but it's important to note that some choose to reject cookies out of hand, others accept them only for the duration of their current browser session and then delete them, while others choose to accept first-party cookies (cookies originated by the domain they're visiting) but reject third-party cookies (originated by any other domain). All of these factors can affect the accuracy of your statistics – by how much will depend on the profile of your target audience and their acceptance of HTTP cookies.

As a rule of thumb, if you use cookies it's best practice to include an entry in your site's privacy policy explicitly stating what you use cookies for, what information they contain, and who (if anyone) that information is shared with.

The pros and the cons

Advantages of log file analysis

- Your server will generally already be producing log files, so the raw data are already available for analysis. Collecting data using page tags requires changes to the website, and tracking can only begin once the changes have been made.
- Every transaction your web server makes is recorded in the log file. Page tagging relies on settings in the visitors' browsers (such as JavaScript being enabled), so a certain (small) proportion of visitors may go undetected.
- The data collected in your log files are *your data*, and are in a standard format that makes it easy for you to migrate to analytics software from a different vendor, use more than one package to give you a broader view of your data, and analyse historical data using any log file analysis program you choose. Page tagging solutions usually mean you're locked in to the relationship with your chosen provider – if you change providers you typically have to start collecting data again from scratch.
- Your log files capture visits by search engine spiders and other automated bots as well as human users. Although it's important that your analytics software can differentiate these from your human visitors, knowing which spiders have crawled your site and when can be important for search engine optimization. Page tagging solutions typically overlook non-human visitors.
- Server logs record information on failed requests, giving you insight into potential problems with your website; page tagging, on the other hand, only records an event when a page is successfully viewed.

Advantages of page tagging

- The tagging code (typically JavaScript) is automatically run every time the page is loaded, so even viewing a cached page will generate a visit. Because viewing a page from a cache doesn't require communication with the server, log files contain no records of cached page views.
- It is easier for developers to add customized information to page tagging code to be collected by the remote server (eg information

about a visitor's screen resolution, or about the goods the visitor purchased). With log file analysis, custom information that's not routinely collected by the web server can only be recorded by appending information to the URL.

- Page tagging can collect data based on events that don't involve sending a request to the web server, such as interactions with Flash, AJAX and other rich media content.
- Cookies are assigned and handled by the page tagging service; with log file analysis your server has to be specially configured to use cookies.
- Page tagging will work even if you can't access your web server logs.

Bear in mind here that you're not restricted to using one type of analytics solution or the other – you're free to use both as necessary, extracting the best information from each to suit your particular needs.

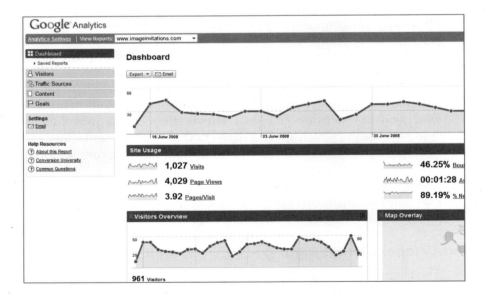

Figure 5.1 Google Analytics is a very capable, free, hosted analytics service from Google. The service uses JavaScript page tags to collect information about visitors and allows webmasters to track a wide range of metrics to evaluate the performance of their websites

Hybrid analytics solutions: the best of both worlds

A number of analytics solutions on the market, particularly at the enterprise level, have the ability to combine log file analysis and page tagging methods within the same analytics suite. These hybrid systems analyse all of the data, and consolidate the information to present a seamless reporting solution to the analyst. While these may offer the most comprehensive analytics solutions, with each data collection method compensating in part for the inadequacies of the other, it's important to remember that *no analytics solution is 100 per cent accurate*. Most, however, are near enough to the mark to allow you to spot trends and make informed decisions about your online investment.

Other sources of traffic

With log files and page tagging you can track pretty much everything that happens on your website – but what about the ads you place on other sites, your affiliate or ad-network campaigns, e-mail newsletters, or pay-per-click advertising? The good news is that the new generation of analytics software (even the 'free' Google Analytics) allows you to 'tag' incoming links from all of your external advertising campaigns so that you can isolate and track visitors who are directed to your site from those campaigns.

All you have to do is add the appropriate parameters to the end of the linking URL, and the analytics software will do the rest. Some will even generate the 'tagged' URL for you – you just fill in the parameters and then cut and paste the resulting code into your ad. Some tracking solutions, with the help of cookies and page tags, even allow you to recognize visitors who saw your ad on another site, didn't click on it, but some time later decided to visit your website anyway. Powerful stuff.

Hit me, baby, one more time: the evolution of web metrics

Back in the early days of the web, webmasters would get excited about how many 'hits' their sites were getting. Before long 'hit counters' – small bits of code that displayed the number of 'hits' a site was getting – were rife on pages across the rapidly growing web, with webmasters eager to show off how popular their little corner of cyberspace had become. Their aim, of course, was to raise the profile of their sites and perhaps to attract the brave pioneers of online advertising to buy space on their site (flashing banner ad, anyone?).

The trouble with 'hits' as a unit of measuring page popularity was that it was completely unrepresentative of the number of unique visitors to a site. A 'hit' represents a single resource request from a user's browser (or other user agent) to a web server. For a basic web page containing 10 images, the browser initiates one request for the page itself and 10 separate requests for each of the image files on that page, or a minimum of 11 'hits' in all – more if there are other design elements being pulled from other files on the web server. Different pages therefore generate a different number of 'hits' depending on their make-up, which means the whole concept of using 'hits' as a comparative unit of measure of page popularity is inherently flawed.

Thankfully, while 'hits' are still recorded in web server log files (and you'll see the individual records if you browse through the raw text of a server log file), modern web analytics software aggregates the data into far more useful metrics. Today you're far more likely to hear about 'page views' or 'page impressions' (which mean pretty much what they say – a complete page delivered to a user's browser), or 'visits'.

With modern software you can automatically collect, collate and compile the information being volunteered by your users' browsers and then use sophisticated graphical interfaces to analyse trends, present the data in a range of different ways, and conduct comparative analysis that can help inform your digital marketing investment. 'Hits' may well be dead as a unit of measuring website success, but take the information revealed by your web analytics solution, use it to understand your online market, and take action based on what you've learned, and your website itself is sure to be a big hit!

Measuring what's important to you

While web analytics allows you to have your finger on the pulse of your website, to monitor the beating heart of your online audience, you can easily get overwhelmed by the sheer volume of information available to you. You want to spend your time focusing on what's important to your business, not wading through reams and reams of information that may offer interesting insight but does little to further your strategic goals.

You need to determine what exactly you need to measure. What metrics are important to your business? What will help you extract maximum value from the visitor information available? If you can't answer those questions, how can you make the strategic decisions that will drive your online business forward?

The concept of key performance indicators (or KPIs) is nothing new, and has been common in the world of business analysis for many years. KPIs are used to distil key trends from complex, often disparate pools of data and to present them as a series of clear, unequivocal indices – a snapshot of how your organization (or website, in our case) is performing at any given time. KPIs do 'exactly what it says on the tin': they *indicate* progress (or lack of it) in areas that are *key* to your website's *performance.*

Why KPIs are important

The real value of KPIs is that they let you extract meaning from your website data at a glance. Without them, it's all too easy to drown in the proliferation of data your web analytics solution churns out. It's a classic case of not seeing the wood for the trees.

By defining and measuring your KPIs you're creating a regular snapshot that allows you to monitor your website's performance over time. You know that if this KPI is going up it means one thing, if that one's going down it means another, and so on. Your KPIs not only give you an immediate sense of the overall health of your website, but also help to highlight potential problems and point you in the right direction before you delve deeper into your data looking for solutions.

Choosing effective KPIs

The main difference between the metrics you select as your KPIs and all the other metrics you can get out of your web analytics software is that the KPIs should be the ones most critical in measuring your site's success.

In their document *Web Analytics: Key metrics and KPIs* (G Creese and J Burby, Washington, DC, 2005), the Web Analytics Association (WAA) defines a KPI in the context of web analytics as:

> *KPI (Key Performance Indicator):* while a KPI can be either a count or a ratio, it is frequently a ratio. While basic counts and ratios can be used by all Web site types, a KPI is infused with business strategy — hence the term, 'Key' — and therefore the set of appropriate KPIs typically differs between site and process types.

Another thing to note is that the terms 'KPI' and 'metric' are often used interchangeably. This is misleading because, although a KPI is *always* a metric, a metric is not necessarily a KPI. So how do you tell the difference?

- *KPIs are always clearly aligned to strategic business goals.*
- *KPIs are defined by management:* Decision makers have to identify, define and take ownership of the key drivers of their organization's success.
- *KPIs are tied to value drivers critical to achieving key business goals:* They should represent the 'deal breakers' in the pursuit of your organizational goals.
- *KPIs need to be based on valid data:* You only get out what you put in.
- *KPIs need to be quantifiable:* You have to be able to measure your KPIs in a consistent and meaningful way over time.
- *KPIs need to be easy to understand:* They should be a barometer of your site's performance – a quick glance at your KPIs should tell anyone in your organization, from management to trainee, how well your website is performing.
- *KPIs can be influenced by, and used as triggers for, positive action:* One of the main values of KPIs is that they immediately highlight where your organization 'could do better' and highlight areas where action is required to get things back on track.

From a digital marketing perspective choosing the right KPIs is crucial to monitoring your site's performance effectively and allowing you to make informed decisions for continuous improvement. But with a bewildering array of different metrics to choose from, it's also notoriously difficult to pin down exactly what represents a KPI for your site.

If you find yourself struggling with this, it's an area where a session or two with a professional web analytics consultant could be money well spent. Don't let the consultant take over – you know your own business better than the consultant ever will; rather, leverage the consultant's expertise with web metrics to help you define your own KPIs.

The important thing is that you end up with a manageable suite of KPIs (usually numbering in the single figures) that together encapsulate the performance of your website.

Some generic web-based KPIs you may find useful

- *Conversion rate:* This is the proportion of visitors to your site who go on to perform a predefined action – such as complete a purchase, subscribe to your online newsletter, register on the forum, fill in an enquiry form or any other conversion factor you've defined. Naturally the higher your conversion rate, the more of your visitors are carrying out the actions you want them to perform on the site, and the better your site's performance (to get an idea of some average conversion rates across a variety of online business categories see http://index.fireclick.com).

- *Page views:* Simple and straightforward, this is the number of pages viewed by your visitors over a given period.

- *Absolute unique visitors:* The number of individuals who visited your site over a given period (as opposed to visitors, where each returning visitor is counted again).

- *New vs returning visitors:* The proportion of your visitors who have been to your site before, assuming the analytics package can recognize them (ie they accept and haven't deleted cookies).

- *Bounce rate:* The bounce rate is the number of people who arrive on your site, scan the landing page and then leave immediately. This is an important metric, because it can highlight either that your traffic isn't targeted enough (your keyword choices might be too generic) or that your landing page design and content aren't delivering what the visitor expects.

- *Abandonment rate:* Abandonment rate comes in a variety of flavours – it basically highlights the proportion of your visitors who start down a predefined conversion funnel (a series of pages leading to a target action, or conversion) but bail out before committing to the desired action. The classic example is visitors dumping an e-commerce shopping cart before checking out, or abandoning the checkout process.

- *Cost per conversion (CPC):* This is basically a calculation of the total cost of advertising (or of a particular advertising campaign where you've tagged the ads so that your analytics software can differentiate resulting traffic) divided by the total number of conversions generated as a result.

There are plenty more. A look at the 'dashboard' or overview page of your web analytics package of choice will offer plenty more, and you'll find literally hundreds of suggested KPIs online. In the end, picking the metrics that are relevant as KPIs for your website is down to you.

Thinking outside the online box

One last thing to bear in mind: you don't necessarily have to limit your KPIs to the data being churned out by your web analytics software. In fact it might be better not to. There are plenty of tools (starting with the humble spreadsheet, right through to sophisticated customizable enterprise KPI dashboard applications) that allow you to aggregate and report on data from multiple sources. You may want to pull data from your web analytics, your back-office financial database, your call centre records, etc to build a more complete profile of your business and how your website fits into the bigger picture.

Testing, investing, tweaking, reinvesting

While collecting and analysing statistics through web analytics is incredibly powerful, it's also inherently limited. It can tell you only *what's* been happening on your site; it can never tell you *why* it happened. That's where the human element come into play: the ability to analyse the what and infer the why. There is almost always more than one explanation for why your users are behaving in a certain way on your site.

Suppose, for example, you notice that the bounce rate for visitors from a particular PPC campaign seems unusually high. That could mean there's a problem with the ad itself (copy appealing to an audience that's too generic) or the choice of keyword you're bidding on (keyword choice too generic to drive targeted traffic), or that the value proposition on your landing page isn't compelling enough.

The beauty of the web is that we can try 'fixing' these things one by one and measure the results to pinpoint exactly where the problem lies. Because we can measure everything, we can literally test each possible variation, and use real data from actual visitors to our site to identify which change delivers optimum results.

The role of testing in online marketing really can't be overstated. When you can measure, you can test, and when you can test you can make changes based on actual visitor behaviour. You eliminate the guesswork, which in turn eliminates much of the risk.

A/B split testing

The A/B split test is a familiar tool in the marketer's arsenal. It basically means running two different versions of an ad or a page and measuring the results to identify which version produces the best results. If you conduct PPC campaigns you're probably already familiar with A/B split tests. The functionality to conduct this kind of testing is integrated into the control panel of most, if not all, of the major PPC service providers. You can also split-test your online display advertising on other sites, ad networks and affiliate sites, and of course you can split-test landing pages on your own website to see what works best.

The main problem with A/B split testing is that you can use it effectively only to test variances in the impact of a single page element at a time. Change more than one element, and you can't be sure which change was responsible for the change you see in the results. It's very difficult to conduct accurate tests that measure the impact of varying different components on the same landing page and how the changes combine to affect your visitor behaviour. Or, at least, it was until recently.

Multivariate testing – the 'suck it and see' approach to landing page optimization

Enter multivariate testing, a process that enables website owners to test multiple components on a web page simultaneously in a live environment. Think of it as conducting tens, hundreds or even thousands of A/B split tests simultaneously, and being able to ascertain, based on real data from real visitors to your site, which combination of the variables produces the best results.

Multivariate testing is rapidly becoming the conversion optimization method of choice among digital marketers, largely because it allows for far more complex testing options than simple A/B split tests, delivers results in a short space of time and can have a dramatic impact on conversion rates.

For example, let's say you had a landing page that was underperforming, and you wanted to optimize it. To keep things simple, let's say you wanted to try out two different headlines, two different images, and whether to use a text link or a 'buy-now' button as a call to action.

That's $2 \times 2 \times 2$ variation – or eight possible combinations to test. With multivariate testing tools you simply set up a straightforward experiment that will dynamically serve different variations of your page to your visitors and record the corresponding conversions. At the end of the experiment you're presented with data showing how each of the different combinations performed, allowing you to choose the most effective of them and implement it permanently on your site.

There are numerous commercial tools available for conducting multivariate testing, including a tool called Website Optimizer from Google, which like its other products is absolutely free, making it an ideal place to start. You'll find it at www.google.com/websiteoptimizer, where you'll also find a wealth of tutorials, articles, online seminars and documentation to help you get to grips with testing. If you'd prefer to recruit professional help for your foray into multivariate testing, a quick search should turn up web professionals in your area offering the service.

Action stations

Action! It's a relatively small word that can have a huge impact. Without action all of that theorizing, data collection and testing will yield insight – but not results. Pretty graphs, trends, spreadsheets and experimentation are all very well, but unless you translate what you learn into tangible, measurable (that word again) action that will make a real difference to your online ROI then it's all just a theory.

Putting theory into practice means taking decisive action. That means getting real commitment from all the stakeholders in your website: commitment to take the intelligence gleaned through your analytics and testing and use it to implement real changes to your website, to your online and offline advertising creative, to when and where you buy your online advertising – everything.

Change your site

When your tests reveal that something is working well, implement changes to echo that success in other areas. Likewise, if your data point to problems with your site, use that information to analyse and inform your refinement of the user experience. Your data offer insight into what your users want – give it to them, and you'll see your site's performance soar.

Change your advertising

Your analytics can give you powerful insight into what advertising is working best for you online (and offline, if you use unique landing page URLs in your offline ad campaigns). Use that information to inform your investment decisions: the advertising creative you develop and where you choose to place your online advertising media. Build tags into your online creative so that your analytics can track individual ad performance, and use the data to inform future online marketing investment.

Harness the power of online data, and watch your ROI take off

Time spent getting to grips with your web analytics, learning to use the data to hone your understanding of your online consumers, is always time well spent. Use the insight you gain to take decisive action, implement a process of continuous improvement, and test before you invest, and you can be confident your ROI is going to head in only one direction.

Measuring the internet

Richard Foan, Managing Director of ABCe

In order to measure something it is a good start to understand what you are looking at. However, the internet is far from a tangible, predictable entity. It has rapidly developed into an endless, living, breathing organism that constantly extends under new guises.

Gone are the days of the internet being a collection of static web pages. Now the internet extends across almost every platform and is intertwined with nearly every medium. TV, radio and mobile are now directly connected, literally, with the internet. Such is the change that the terms 'TV' and 'radio' are fast becoming redundant in exchange for the terms 'video' and 'audio' as the English language evolves to keep up.

The fragmentation of media has created more niche audiences than ever before. And they are constantly dividing and subdividing and regrouping in many different forms at different levels on a national, even global, scale. Citizen publishers have created a new source of content. Publishers and broadcasters are now media companies with a mixed content offering.

The effects of the fragmentation of media and emergence of Web 2.0, amongst other things, have made it increasingly challenging for sample-based research to measure these fragmented audiences accurately. For instance, there might be 1,000 people a month who are regularly visiting a blog on gardening. These people have distinct interests and needs and may well be a very valuable audience. However, in a country of approximately 70 million these people are simply not being picked up.

That is not to say that progress isn't being made. Over the past two years nearly all the national newspaper brands have committed to publishing their monthly web traffic figures to industry agreed standards. For the month of March 2008, the *Mail, Financial Times, Guardian, Mirror, Sun, Times* and *Telegraph* all reported their web traffic as audited by ABCe – an unprecedented number.

The *Guardian* recorded over 18 million unique users/browsers for March with, interestingly, nearly 8 million coming from the UK and almost 11 million from the rest of the world. National newspaper brands are leading the field with the frequency of reporting their online properties. The men's publishing sector is another keen to demonstrate its digital reach. Titles including *FHM, Loaded, Monkey, NME, Nuts,* the *Sun Online,* and *Zoo* all report their web traffic through ABCe. *Zoo,* for instance, commanded 807,059 unique users/browsers in January 2008 in addition to its total average print circulation of 179,006 for the second part of 2007.

Clearly, multi-platform extensions for magazine brands are tapping into new audiences, offering advertisers exciting cross-platform options and opening up new revenue streams. Other sectors tapping into the benefits from regular web traffic reporting include the recruitment, business publishing, sport, automotive, lifestyle, travel, consumer publishing, property and gaming sectors.

Publishers reporting their online traffic through ABCe to industry agreed standards is a step forward, as greater transparency will better inform advertiser and media agencies in their decisions when allocating advertising budgets.

However, Web 2.0 and the natural development of the internet have brought a host of new opportunities and challenges for measuring the internet in the shape of blogs, video, audio, RSS feeds, podcasts, and so the list goes on.

For many years the Joint Industry Committee for Web Standards in the UK and Ireland (JICWEBS) has worked to ensure independent development and ownership of standards for measuring site-centric, transactional web data. The body, whose members include the Internet Advertising Bureau (IAB), the Institute of Practitioners in Advertising (IPA), the Incorporated Society of British Advertisers (ISBA), the Newspaper Publishers' Association (NPA), the Newspaper Society (NS) and the Association of Online Publishers (AOP), has moved fast to agree and evolve measurement standards for developing media against which ABCe can audit.

Right now the TV, radio and mobile industry sectors are making positive steps to establish industry-backed measurement standards to help quantify online audiences. Broadcasters have been swift to make moves to measure video delivered over the internet. In 2007 the major broadcasters came together to form the Broadband

Measurement Working Group (BMWG) to develop a common approach for measuring online video content viewing to deliver accountability to rights holders. The group, chaired by Ron Coomber, is made up from the BBC, BSkyB, BT Vision, Channel 4, Five, ITV, Virgin Media and industry body the IPA, as well as ABCe. The UK TV audience measurement body the Broadcasters' Audience Research Board (BARB) also joins the meetings as an observer. The group has tasked ABCe to develop a rights metric for measuring content delivered over IPTV, including simulcast, streams and downloads. The rights metric will enable broadcasters to measure and report video content to a consistent and agreed standard for those rights holders.

Broadcasters clearly feel that video over the internet has reached a point where a reliable measurement tool is needed. This is particularly important for commercial broadcasters who are investing a great deal in developing a variety of video-on-demand services and will need to generate revenue from video advertising to sustain their businesses.

Whilst BARB is investigating other techniques to be able to assess the people side (who is watching), the BMWG project could provide granular information on the screen side (what the equipment is being used for). A common goal would be to connect these two types of information when an appropriate means is agreed upon.

Industry agreed standards for measuring simulcast, streams and downloads over the internet will add the vital element of trust in the medium, enabling advertisers, broadcasters and rights holders to use them with the professionalism and confidence of traditional TV advertising.

Another sector keen to measure its online presence is the mobile industry. This year the GSM Association (GSMA), the global mobile operators association, charged ABCe to develop and deliver industry agreed standards for the reporting of all web traffic over mobile. The move to establish industry-backed mobile metrics has been initiated by the demand from operators and advertisers for effective reporting and accountability in order to secure investment and to justify driving media budgets to mobile.

ABCe will make its recommendations on the project to the UK industry standards body, JICWEBS, which will ratify that the measures meet the industry agreed needs. Clearly mobile has a tremendous capacity to deliver as a marketing channel, but this is dependent on the mobile industry's ability to provide reliable usage data to justify the interest. It is hoped that this project will help deliver the missing link.

Whilst the project will focus on the UK market, the GSMA is a global association and has the ambitions to deliver standards in other countries, so the scale of the project is potentially very large indeed. ABCe champions the phrase 'global standards for local markets' as a mantra for internet measurement with localized reporting rules. Obviously the internet is a global medium and so the international implications can't be ignored. In fact, global measurement structures are helpful. The International Federation of Audit Bureaux of Circulations (IFABC) draws together ABCe's sister organizations across the globe to implement constructive international measurement initiatives.

However, advertising budgets, for which internet measurement is largely required, are still determined in local markets and so require measurement for individual territories. Furthermore, different countries often have dissimilar methods of measuring traditional media, which has shaped the practices for measurement of digital media to allow a level of comparison. Whilst an international focus is essential, localized standards are paramount.

Another sector heavily affected by the growth of the internet is the radio industry. Increasing numbers of people are listening online, and sooner or later these people will have to be accounted for. Radio Joint Audience Research (RAJAR) has recently announced that it is turning to an online diary system to record listener numbers, and it will be interesting to see what proportion of listeners consume content online.

However, a sample-based approach can go only so far on its own. Nothing makes this point more patently clear than comparing sample- and transaction-based data for supposedly the same websites. The most recent figures for arsenal.com are a case in point. ABCe recorded 2,504,308 unique users/browsers (ie devices connecting to that site), comScore recorded 1,774,000 unique visitors and Nielsen/NetRatings reported a unique audience of 311,485 for user traffic on the football club's website in the same one-month period.

One option is to tie transaction data to sample-based data – potentially securing the best of both worlds. Nielsen Online, Survey Interactive, Stir in Holland, Agof in Germany, CIM in Belgium and Gemius in Poland and Israel are already fusing transaction data with sample-based data, in addition to following the total activity through websites in the territories. With modelling, these organizations are creating an impressive, bigger picture of online activity.

The UK market, however, is considerably trickier to ring-fence. The sheer number of media and their international focus present a number of challenges. With English the common language in business, online and across most of the Western world, traffic on English-speaking websites can have a considerable international following. For instance, millions upon millions of US-based web users visit UK-based websites and vice versa. Again, Spanish-speaking South American countries may have difficulty separating web users along political boundaries, owing to the shared language facilitating internet activity on an international basis.

With audience and channel fragmentation rife, the one thing that can shed light on users is IP addresses for a single visit. Whether someone is using instant messaging, looking at a blog or website, receiving an RSS feed, or watching streaming video content (to name a few of the multiple options) the one thing that identifies a machine and tracks activity is IP addresses. Tracking online behaviour based on IP addresses could potentially make online the best measured medium out there. However, the major challenge here is that IP addresses aren't permanently fixed to a specific computer.

The current industry agreed approach of using IP and user agent data to underpin the unique user/browser metric helps get closer to the number of devices used. The important principle is to be transparent in the definitions used and encourage compatibility through standards.

Taking measurement of the internet to its ultimate, and arguably too far, would be for humans to have a specific unique IP address, so every time people logged on to the internet they would input their code, possibly by iris recognition. Obviously there are a host of privacy issues and social factors that make this '1984'-style solution unlikely ever to be realized. The furore around the debate of whether UK citizens should carry ID cards just goes to show the likely level of resistance.

In truth, measurement of the media has always had to compromise, and it probably always will. This applies to online measurement as well as offline.

The immediate challenge is for ABCe and the media industry to continue to build a critical mass of online media reporting its traffic data to industry agreed standards. In recent years a host of new and traditional media owners have opened up to reporting their digital audience data to industry agreed standards through ABCe, and the momentum continues to build.

The more media owners that report their online audience data, the better the result will be for everyone. Improved standards of online measurement will result in better insight and an increase in confidence in the medium.

With considerable budgets being invested online from advertisers and media owners, the commercial interest around the internet has never been so great. The best agencies have grasped the opportunities for brands in Web 2.0, and media owners are increasingly relying on online as a central business pillar. Online is no longer an add-on or a testing ground. Instead it has become a central part of business plans.

The media industry has now truly recognized the benefits of trusted industry approved data as part of the process of monetizing online media, and 2008 is set to be the year when this approach comes into its own.

Case study: MINI – the White Rabbit

In August 2006 Profero launched a teaser campaign for the new MINI. The campaign demonstrates a unique and innovative concept that pushes the boundaries of online advertising and blurs the separation between a creative and a media idea.

Enticing users to break from their daily surfing habits, the campaign encourages users to join MINI for a random adventure into the world wide web. Inspired by Alice in Wonderland, 'White Rabbit' takes every user on an unexpected journey to a range of eccentric British websites, from one dedicated to the best roundabouts of Britain to one for a handlebar moustache appreciation society.

The campaign was targeted to an adventurous audience who enjoy discovering new content on the web. The first execution shows a White MINI emerging from the ad, spinning around on the site and taunting the user as it sits there, revving when the user rolls over the execution, with simple copy stating 'This is not the way to the MINI site.' Instead of taking the conventional route to the MINI site, users are taken through a virtual porthole by the MINI, which lands on to the homepage of one of the many carefully selected sites. Users can choose either to browse the site or be taken through a second porthole to continue the MINI adventure. With four destinations within one journey and three unique journeys created, the user is always taken on a new adventure.

On the day the campaign launched, 33 blogs raved about this new adventure that MINI had produced and commented on the excitement that the campaign had injected back into what had become the mundane habit of surfing the internet.

Results

This campaign was a perfect match between the online experience and the MINI experience. Its success can be measured by the fact that it won eight prestigious awards, among them a Gold Cyber Lion, November 2006 BIMA Winner Best Interactive Campaign, December 2006 Epica Awards Best Campaign, and March 2007 Future Marketing Awards Winner for both Best Internet Campaign and Best Internet Innovation.

Agency quote

Jamie Coomber, Account Director/Digital Strategist: 'We wanted to bring spontaneity and a sense of excitement through discovery back to the internet, and MINI was the perfect brand to bring that to life. The end result was an idea that was fun, simple and allowed the users to experience the true values of MINI.'

Client quote

Ysabel Vazquez, National Communications Manager: 'This totally fresh idea really captured the thought that every journey in a MINI feels like an adventure and translated it perfectly by exploiting the online media channel. It's a big idea that could only have been created online.'

Campaign URL

http://www.profero.com/whiterabbit

Campaign credits

MINI National Communications Manager: Ysabel Vazquez
Profero Account Director/Digital Strategist: Jamie Coomber

Figure 5.2 MINI's 'White Rabbit' teaser campaign invited visitors to follow the new MINI on a whistle stop tour of a selection of unique British websites

6 E-mail marketing

The new information technology, internet and e-mail, have practically eliminated the physical costs of communications.

(Peter Drucker)

E-mail marketing has been called the original social networking tool and I could not agree more. If you think about social networks in general, email plays a large role in them.

(Simms Jenkins, author of The Truth about Email Marketing*)*

We forget that the RSS-centric world we live in isn't the one many (and probably most) of our customers live in. That's why the old-fashioned occasional email update – which gives people the juiciest bits and leaves out the rest – still has so much power.

(Matt Linderman, Signal vs. Noise)

Our chapter pledge to you

When you reach the end of this chapter you'll have answers to the following questions:

- What is e-mail marketing and how can it benefit my business?
- How can I make sure my e-mail marketing campaign won't be seen as spam?
- How can e-mail marketing tools help me?
- How can I use technology to manage my customers?

- How can I write effective copy for my e-mail marketing campaign?
- What are the main design considerations when crafting an e-mail?
- How can I test a campaign's success?

The new direct mail

E-mail marketing is one of the most powerful elements in your digital marketing toolbox. It lets you communicate easily with your customers on a personal level through a universally accepted digital medium. Choosing the right approach for your e-mail marketing communications is, of course, key. Unsophisticated mass-marketing techniques, or anything that smacks of e-mail spam, are likely to be ignored, that's if they make it to your prospect's inbox at all.

Think of the junk mail that arrives through your letterbox every day. Most of that gets thrown out, unread, and in many cases unopened. A scene in the 1991 Steve Martin comedy *LA Story* depicts the main character, Harris Telemacher, watching a never-ending barrage of junk mail pouring through his letterbox. He nonchalantly kicks a wastepaper basket under the unwanted stream of promotional bunkum and continues eating his breakfast. While exaggerated, it's a scenario many of us can empathize with – and an apt analogy for what's happening with electronic mail today.

Naturally, as e-mail started to become integrated into our business and personal lives, so the mass marketers turned their attention to the new medium. Junk paper mail became junk virtual mail. But whether it's online or in the 'real world', if your business becomes associated with streams of junk mail (or spam) it will destroy your credibility. People will either ignore your electronic missives or filter them out before they even arrive.

Despite the proliferation of spam and the fact that most people's inboxes today are bursting with irrelevant and unsolicited messages, e-mail can still be used as a *beneficial and effective* marketing tool that delivers real value, both to your customers and to your business.

Customers will still open your e-mail

The truth is, many customers will welcome regular e-mail communications from your business, in the same way as they may welcome the occasional traditional or 'snail' mail offering a money-off voucher for their favourite store. They'll open an e-mail containing a newsletter or promotion from you, *as long as they recognize your brand, are expecting to receive communication from you, and are confident it will contain something of value to them.* The key is to make these messages *relevant and interesting* for your chosen audience; fail in that, and unfortunately your message is destined for the virtual recycling bin.

E-mail marketing can be a tricky field to navigate effectively. You have to simultaneously respect your customers' right to privacy, protect your brand, and ultimately maintain your value proposition over time. It's very easy for your carefully cultivated e-mail prospects to unsubscribe from your mailing list, and once you've lost them they're probably gone for good.

What exactly is e-mail marketing?

E-mail marketing is a fusion of marketing savvy and imaginative copy. In its simplest form, it's an e-mail sent to a customer list that usually contains a sales pitch and a 'call to action'. This could be as simple as encouraging the customer to click on a web link embedded in the e-mail. Some examples of e-mail marketing campaigns are:

- a hotel promoting a special summer discount;
- a recruitment company informing business clients about a free seminar;
- a gadget store offering a money-off code to be used at its online checkout;
- a fitness centre offering members a special printout voucher that entitles the bearer to bring a friend along for free;
- a beverage company encouraging people to download a game that integrates into the user's Facebook or MySpace profile.

You can also use e-mail when you don't have anything specific to market, as a mechanism to maintain consumer engagement, strengthen your brand and add credibility to your business. In fact, even in the Web 2.0 world of blogs, social networks and RSS feeds, e-mail newsletters are still incredibly popular and offer a very effective way to get your brand out in front of your list of prospects on a regular basis. Examples might include:

- an accountancy firm keeping in touch with its clients by informing them about changes in tax legislation;

- a weekly newsletter from a public relations company that contains interesting snippets of industry news and web links to longer articles;
- a daily digest or breaking-news alert from an online newspaper;
- a young-adult book publisher using e-mail marketing to promote free and exclusive screensavers, ring tones and wallpapers to its young readers.

Because e-mail is an incredibly cost-effective communications medium, when used effectively it can deliver an excellent return on investment (ROI).

E-mail marketing tools

When it comes to managing and sending your marketing e-mail, you probably won't want to rely on your standard desktop e-mail client to do the job. While it's a perfectly feasible approach for very small lists, as more people subscribe to your e-mail offering it will quickly become cumbersome and unmanageable.

What you need instead is one of the many customized e-mail marketing systems out there. These can be software you install on your local machine, software you run on your own server, or a software-as-a-service (SAAS) offering hosted by an online service provider. These systems let you manage your e-mail list and craft your design templates for your messages and, most importantly, help you to track your e-mail campaigns.

Some of the functions e-mail marketing tools can provide (and this is not an exhaustive list) include:

- easy-to-use tools that let you create and work from e-mail templates without having to be a technical expert;
- testing tools that allow you to check that your message will make it past major spam filters;
- tracking tools that show how many people have ignored, opened or responded to your e-mail (more about this is mentioned in detail towards the end of the chapter);
- personalization tools that let you modify the content dynamically to individuals or specific target profiles on your list.

Customer relationship management

It's no good using e-mail marketing tools if you don't know who you're sending your e-mails to. Customer relationship management (CRM) is a

Figure 6.1 E-mail marketing specialists like EmailLabs (www.emaillabs. com) offer hosted solutions to manage every aspect of your e-mail marketing campaigns

business concept that has been around for about 25 years. It's the art, if you will, of keeping your customers happy and maintaining an ongoing personal relationship with them. Let's say you run a small grocery shop in an equally small neighbourhood. Over time you'll get to know your regular customers, their likes and dislikes, and what other products they might be interested in trying, etc. Larger businesses struggle to maintain that sort of personal connection with consumers, and that's where CRM comes in.

For instance, if you keep a record of the products or services customers have bought from you in the past, what they've looked at on your website and how often they've contacted you, you can merge that information with the relevant demographic details and then, using CRM technology, you can track and anticipate what those customers are likely to be interested in. The result? Relevant, targeted marketing that is much more likely to convert.

When it comes to e-mail marketing, CRM can help you segment your list, allowing you to focus highly targeted campaigns to the customers most likely to respond. You can fine-tune your e-mail offering and align it with your customers' purchase history. The possibilities are virtually endless.

If your business already uses CRM systems for more traditional marketing, then you should be able to incorporate that information into your e-mail marketing strategy. Some CRM systems cater for e-mail campaigns as part of their feature set, while others integrate with your chosen e-mail marketing solution.

We'll talk about technology where appropriate as we progress through the chapter, but ultimately e-mail marketing tools will prove effective only if you, as a digital marketer, spend time developing the right e-mail strategy for your business and execute it in the right way.

Before you start

Before you begin planning your e-mail marketing campaign, there are a number of things you need to consider from practical and legal perspectives.

Gathering your e-mail list

As we mentioned earlier, people won't respond to seemingly random e-mail communications: they won't even open them. So before you can do any e-mail marketing you're going to need to build up a list of customers who are willing to receive e-mail communications from your business. The best way to do that is to encourage them to *opt in* to receiving your e-mails at every opportunity.

In Chapter 3, we mentioned that your website is the hub of your digital marketing world. It's also the ideal place to capture e-mail addresses for your opt-in mailing list. You can place a simple, prominent form on your website encouraging visitors to sign up for regular e-mail updates, the latest special offers or any other value proposition that will resonate with your audience.

You can *rent* e-mail lists to try to recruit new customers, but make sure that the organization providing you with the list is a member of your country's direct marketing association or similar, and ensure that its anti-spam and privacy policy is clearly outlined. Anyone on these lists should have opted in to receiving third-party e-mails from companies like yours. You'll also need to check whether anyone on that list has previously asked to be taken off your own mailing list.

Another way to attract opt-in is when a customer completes some kind of transaction on your website, like purchasing a product, downloading a whitepaper or requesting additional information. By making an e-mail address a mandatory component of the transaction you can add to your e-mail list. Legalities vary here, but in many cases, including in the UK, it's fine to send marketing e-mails to people once they've completed a transaction with you – as long as you've given them the option to decline. This is referred to as a 'soft opt-in'. And remember, *every* marketing e-mail you send out must provide the recipient with a straightforward way to *unsubscribe* from your mailing list – an opt-out, if you like.

Legal requirements

Another crucial factor is, of course, to be familiar with the law in your jurisdiction. Sending unsolicited e-mail out to random consumers will breach spam legislation in most Western countries. Anti-spam laws are there to enforce ethical e-mail marketing practices that respect customer data and privacy. Legitimate businesses will follow the laws, but spammers are hard to trace. They will typically use underhanded techniques to harvest e-mail addresses and send large volumes of unsolicited e-mails.

Astonishingly, about 80 to 95 per cent of e-mail traffic today is spam (News.com, 12 December 2007, http://tinyurl.com/5veq4w). The practice continues because: 1) it costs practically nothing to send a marketing e-mail to millions of people on a list; 2) even the tiniest conversion rate turns a profit for the spammers; and 3) most spam can't be traced, and originates outside the relevant jurisdictions.

Just in case you hadn't picked up the vibe, we'll spell it out: *spam is bad.* It's against the law, and what's more it annoys the very people you're hoping to connect with – your future customers. When you're just starting out and don't have much of an opt-in list, it can be tempting. Don't do it!

Anti-spam legislation in the United States

In the United States, the CAN-SPAM Act (Controlling the Assault of Non-Solicited Pornography and Marketing Act) came into effect on 1 January 2004. The Federal Trade Commission has a fact sheet, accessible at www.

ftc.gov/spam, outlining legal requirements for businesses sending e-mails. The main points include:

- Recipients must be able to opt out of receiving future e-mails, and such actions must be processed within 10 business days.
- The source of the e-mail must be traceable.
- Subject lines must not be deceptive.
- Your full postal address must be included.

Apart from fines of up to $11,000 for violation of any of these terms, there are additional fines for using spammers' techniques including automatically generating e-mail addresses or harvesting them from the web.

Anti-spam legislation in Europe

The Privacy and Electronic Communications (EC Directive) Regulations 2003 are the overriding anti-spam legislation. You'll find that individual countries will interpret the law in their own ways, and you'll need to take data protection legislation into account too.

In the UK, you can download a fact sheet for marketers from the Information Commissioner's Office website at www.ico.gov.uk. This clearly outlines, in Q&A form, what digital marketers can and can't do with e-mail. As we've mentioned, having the recipient opt in to marketing messages is crucial (but don't forget the 'soft opt-in', which means that once you've collected contact details from people who've bought a product or service from you or expressed an interest then you can go ahead and market to them as long as they've been given an easy way to opt out).

Logistical problems

Sometimes the mail doesn't get through. There is a variety of reasons why your e-mails may not arrive in your customers' inboxes. They may have been inadvertently or incorrectly categorized as spam by the internet service provider (ISP) or filtered into a junk mail folder by a web-based or desktop e-mail client. Spam filters are so aggressive these days that people may not even see much spam in their inbox, but an overzealous spam filter can sometimes intercept legitimate mail too.

For customers this seems great, but it does mean that they're missing out on potentially useful and informative e-mails – like your latest missive! In internet lingo, whenever a legitimate e-mail is blocked it's referred to as a 'false positive'. For your e-mail marketing campaign these false positives can be a real setback. Even discovering that your bona fide opt-in marketing e-mail is being blocked can be tricky, and resolving the problem can be difficult, especially when you've followed the rules to the letter.

Your best bet is to avoid the spam trap problem from the start by making sure your e-mails don't look and read like spam. If your e-mail software has an option to test how well your message will fare with spam filters, use it, and change anything that it flags as suspect. You should also make sure that all of your e-mail can be traced back to a valid IP address from a reputable host. If you do that, there's no real reason for your e-mails to be blocked.

An organization called the Spamhaus Project (www.spamhaus.org) works to track and block spammers, and you'll find more information on why legitimate e-mails can sometimes be blacklisted on their website.

E-mail formats

Another reason your e-mails may not be seen is that you're sending them out in a format that your recipients' e-mail clients – the software or website used to read and reply to e-mails – don't recognize. This isn't as much of a problem as it used to be, because the adoption of internet standards has improved significantly, and almost all mail clients today will handle rich text or HTML e-mail *unless the user has specified otherwise.*

When you send out your marketing e-mail, you can normally choose to send it in its most basic *plain text* form (with no formatting). You can then be pretty certain that all clients can read it. One step up from plain text is *rich text format*, which allows you to format the text with font sizes, colours, bold and italics, and allows recipients to click on web links. This looks better than plain text and can be very effective for simple informational newsletters.

The most sophisticated e-mails are built using HTML (the same code that developers use to build web pages). This essentially means that your e-mail can look exactly like a regular web page, complete with images, web links and all the rest. Images aren't sent with the e-mail, but are usually pulled in from a web server when the e-mail is viewed. HTML e-mails can tie in with the look and feel of your website, which is great news if you're looking for brand continuity and a seamless user experience when your prospects click through to a landing page!

Some e-mail clients (and web-based e-mail like Hotmail and Gmail fall into this category) automatically block external images for security reasons, but allow recipients to override the setting for mail from people that they trust. Even so, you'll probably want to make sure that your message is clear without images, just in case. Use images to augment the main message of your e-mail, but make sure your value proposition and call to action are clearly outlined in text form.

Generally you won't need to worry about sending different versions of your e-mails to different customers. A standard called Multipurpose Internet Mail Extensions (MIME) allows you to send messages out in 'multipart' format. This means your recipient's e-mail client will be able to view the message in the best way it can, and if recipients prefer to receive text-only e-mails then that's what they'll see.

Planning your campaign

As we've covered in the strategy chapter (Chapter 2), you need to know what you want out of your overall digital marketing campaign. Specifically, when it comes to your e-mail campaign, you'll need to *define* who you are targeting, why, and what you want out of it. Do you want to generate more sales? Or are you looking to maintain a relationship with your customers by keeping them up to date with the business? It's important to be specific here and to make sure that your e-mail marketing strategy feeds into your overall business goals.

Digital CRM can help you to segment your customers and to target a specific group of them with a certain offer if that makes sense. You can also deliver personalized content to them, and you should endeavour to personalize all of your e-mail marketing as much as you can. At its most basic, this involves using the customer's name at the start of the e-mail, but more sophisticated software will allow you to pull in tailored dynamic content based on a particular user's profile. For example, an e-mail from an airline could highlight the number of frequent flyer points a particular customer has left to spend before they expire, or an online bookshop could recommend new books based on what a customer has recently purchased.

Good *e-mail design* is also important here. It makes sense to establish some brand continuity between your e-mail templates and your website design, so that every aspect of your digital marketing campaign works together seamlessly. Remember though that the content is paramount, and while your design should look good it should complement rather than compete with your content for the readers' attention. Make your content punchy, scannable and engaging, and don't forget the all-important call to action.

You should also take the *frequency* of the e-mails you send out as part of a campaign into account. People don't want to be bombarded with marketing e-mails – even ones they've opted in for. Sometimes it can be hard to predict exactly how often you should send out marketing e-mails and when, in fact, is the best day or time to send them, which is why it's so vital to track and analyse how your campaign is progressing. If you notice people suddenly starting to unsubscribe from your mailing lists, ask yourself what's gone wrong. Perhaps you've been sending out too many e-mails or have changed their format. Whatever it is, keep a close eye on your e-mail campaigns and try to rectify any problems quickly. If you don't, your marketing e-mail may be perceived as spam, and that's damaging not just for your e-mail marketing but for the broader online reputation of your business.

Dos and don'ts of an e-mail marketing campaign

Take a look in your own inbox; look at the array of newsletters and marketing e-mails you've signed up to receive. Do any of them jump out at you and scream 'Read me'? Why? What was it about that particular message that made you want to open it? Are there any e-mails you've signed up for that you actively look forward to receiving? Analyse the marketing e-mails in your own inbox, deconstruct them, and apply what your learn to your own e-mail marketing campaign.

There are some best-practice guidelines, many of them based on common-sense principles and, of course, putting the consumer first. The ones we're listing cover design, copy and delivery of your e-mails. This certainly isn't a definitive list; and of course, as with everything else in digital marketing, some of these 'rules' are more relevant in some circumstances than in others – so feel free to interpret these as they apply in your particular case. As your e-mail marketing campaigns evolve, you'll naturally start to find what works best for you. After all, nobody knows your business or your customers like you do.

E-mail design

Many of the same usability principles that apply in website design will relate to e-mail template design, particularly if you're using HTML to construct your e-mails. You will want your message to display consistently and effectively across as many computers and e-mail clients as possible.

People will be viewing their e-mails using different screen widths, and they'll be using e-mail clients that display messages in different forms. Test your templates on as many different platforms as possible to make sure they work.

Of course, a strong design is only one part of the story, but it is an important one and works to make a positive first impression. Keep things simple and follow the dos and don'ts below to enhance your message:

- *Do* think in terms of 'above the fold': just like a newspaper folded in half, the top of your e-mail needs to capture the recipients' attention immediately. You don't want to force them to scroll through a page of text before they reach your once-in-a-lifetime offer announcement. Make sure you get to the good stuff early. Remember, too, that some e-mail clients will show a 'preview' of the message below the subject line. Where possible you need to engage your prospects in the first couple of lines.

- *Don't* clutter your e-mail message with images, because a lot of e-mail clients will block images by default. Your recipient should be able to read your message and call to action without relying on images. Images are there to support and *enhance* your message; they shouldn't *be* the message. Don't simply scan in the company brochure and plonk it into the e-mail – it's a recipe for disaster!

- *Do* think of your corporate identity and how this should extend into the design of your e-mail. Your business should have a consistent brand identity. Your e-mail marketing message should complement your brand image perfectly. This is especially true if the reader clicks through from your e-mail to your website. You want the experience to flow seamlessly between the two.

- *Do* work out the most popular e-mail clients among your target audience, and design your mails accordingly. Doing so will ensure that the vast majority of them will see your e-mail correctly. Remember to test your e-mail by sending it to a variety of different web-based e-mail accounts, and use a number of common clients like AOL, Apple Mail, Mozilla Thunderbird, Windows Mail and Microsoft Outlook to view your e-mail before sending it to your list.

- *Do* remember mobile users. More people are using Blackberrys, iPhones and other mobile digital devices to access their e-mail while on the road. They may not be able to view the entire subject line of your e-mail and may also be limited by small screen size when they click through to the mail. It's vital for mobile users that your message works in text form and that you 'hook' them with killer content really early.

- *Don't* put fancy videos, music and Flash animation in your e-mails. For a start they're distracting, and because of the inherent security threat of active content they can be blocked by firewalls (software that helps to shield your computer from internet nasties). If you want to promote using rich media content, use your e-mail as a vehicle to encourage recipients to click through to it on your website rather than embedding it in the mail itself.
- *Do* remember that if you sketch out (on paper or in Photoshop) what your e-mail message should look like, it needs to be converted into HTML. Your web designer should be working with you to ensure that the design will work as a functional e-mail.
- *Do* be consistent. Make sure your template maintains some consistency between e-mails. Most e-mail marketing tools let you create templates that you can use to format your e-mail consistently over and over again.
- *Don't* send attachments, like PDFs or word documents, in your e-mails. People are naturally suspicious of e-mail attachments sent out to lots of people, and with good reason. It's also not a good idea to 'push' content out to people. If you have a file you want to make available (perhaps a new brochure or whitepaper) it's much better to provide a link in the e-mail to a web page where your prospects can *choose to download it if they so wish.*
- *Do* provide a link for the person to unsubscribe. This is a legal requirement. If the person can't click the link, make sure it's clearly spelled out so that they can copy and paste it into their browser. Some people will automatically respond to the e-mail and use the word 'unsubscribe' in the subject line or e-mail body, so try to incorporate a way to pick those up, if you can.
- *Don't* forget to link to your website's privacy policy. If you are tracking stuff in your e-mail (such as how many people are actually opening it, etc), then you'll need to point that out in your privacy policy and reassure your readers you won't be using the data for nefarious means.

E-mail copy

While the design and look of your e-mail are important, it's the copy that's going to galvanize people into action. Beneath the gloss and the sheen, you'll need to write compelling, engaging copy to get results. Our top things for writing great e-mail content are:

- *Do* think of a catchy subject line that *clearly outlines what the e-mail is about* and encourages the recipient to open it. Don't try to be too clever – clever headlines can be ambiguous, and ambiguous e-mails don't get read. Your headline should be descriptive, yet compelling, which can be a tricky combination to pull off – but if you manage it you'll see your e-mail open rates soar. Also remember that some e-mail clients (including Gmail) let people preview the first sentence or two of their e-mail before they open it – giving you another opportunity to grab their attention.

- *Don't* assume people know what you're talking about. Your customers aren't stupid, and you shouldn't treat them as such, but they're busy and will tend to scan through your e-mail quickly. You need to make sure your value proposition and call to action are crystal clear and that key elements of your message (including links back to your website) stand out from the body of your e-mail.

- *Do* get someone else to proofread the e-mail before you send it out. Read it in its final, HTML form. Then proofread it again. Make sure as many other people as possible in the business read your e-mail to ensure that it's accurate not only in terms of spelling and punctuation but also in terms of the content. Check prices, dates and contact details. Then check them again!

- *Don't* go crazy. Multiple exclamation marks, overuse of capitals (seen in the internet world as shouting!) and desperate pleas will turn people off and may also flag your message as spam, which means it won't reach your prospects at all. Avoid overzealous use of punctuation and formatting, not just in the body but in the subject line too.

- *Do* mention your company name in the 'From' field.

- *Do* follow through. It's not worth enticing people to your website with a killer e-mail offer only for them to discover all sorts of terms, conditions and caveats when they arrive. Make your offers genuine, and follow through with them when people respond; otherwise there'll be no second time.

- *Don't* use long paragraphs. Keep text short and punchy. Long paragraphs can be unwieldy unless they're exceptionally well written. They're difficult to write well, and when written poorly they're difficult to read, so people don't read them. Keep your paragraphs and sentences short and punchy. It will give your content life and energy and will zip people through your e-mail quickly.

- *Do* think about tone. Be approachable. E-mail is a business tool, but messages tend to be on the informal side. That informality can be even more important in a marketing e-mail. Be personal and approachable. Write as if addressing an individual rather than an audience. You may be sending it out to thousands of people, but each person is reading it as an individual. Use a conversational style, as if you're interacting with the other person face to face.

- *Do* provide as many details about where the e-mail has come from as possible. Always use your company's domain name to send the e-mail, and provide full contact details for your business within the body of your message.
- *Don't* use scare tactics. Never flag e-mails as 'high priority' or 'urgent' if they're not. It can alarm people, and they won't appreciate it when they open your message to find just another 'one-time-only' offer.

E-mail delivery

- *Do* keep your e-mail list 'clean'. Unsubscribe notifications need to be applied to your mailing list regularly – automatically where possible, but you should also monitor for unsubscribe requests that fall through the automatic list-management net. If you discover that an address on your list is *bouncing regularly* (ie the messages are undeliverable), then investigate why, and if the address is dead prune it from your list (don't remove it immediately, as e-mail downtime is more common than you might think).
- *Do* be prepared for an onslaught of replies when you launch your campaign, such as 'out of office' autoresponders and 'unsubscribe' requests, as soon as your e-mail starts hitting people's inboxes.
- *Do* investigate any irregularities. Make sure your e-mail definitely got out OK by sending it to a few 'test' or 'seed' e-mail addresses of your own. If a lot of mail bounces, check that an ISP or webmail provider isn't blocking your e-mail. If it is, contact your e-mail service provider immediately to get the situation resolved.
- *Do* remember to use the BCC (blind carbon copy) field if you choose to use a regular e-mail client to send e-mail to small lists. You don't want people seeing everyone else's e-mail address!

Measuring your success

Analysing the success of your first campaign can provide you with valuable data that can shed light on how you progress and evolve future campaigns. You can use your e-mail marketing tools to analyse:

1. approximately how many people opened the e-mail (called the open rate);
2. *when* people typically opened your e-mail;
3. what links people tended to click on (the *click-through rate*);

4. the percentage of people who opened the e-mail who then went on to click through to the website (the *click-to-open rate*);
5. who *never opens* e-mails;
6. the types of e-mails with the best *conversion rates*;
7. e-mails that regularly *bounce*;
8. how many people *unsubscribed* to your message;
9. which e-mail clients or providers *blocked* your messages;
10. how *frequently* a series of e-mails is opened by a particular sub-scriber.

Target your campaigns

The more data you have on your subscribers, the more you can split and segment them into niche groups that you can target with more specific campaigns, as long as your set-up can support it.

If you have a complex business with a wide array of different customers, investing in a sophisticated CRM system will let you build an even more detailed profile of your customer base and of their purchasing behaviour. By linking your customers' accounts (if they have registered on your website) to other databases within your business and 'mining' customer data from a variety of sources, you can get an increasingly granular view and can target ever more relevant messages to particular subsections of your e-mail list.

Test your techniques

To gauge the success of a potential e-mail campaign, you can also run A/B split tests with a small group of subscribers. Have two (or more) versions of the e-mail that communicate the same message in different ways (a different subject line, for example), and see which one is more effective. Then analyse the results and send the one with the best result to the entire list.

Still a vital component of digital marketing

The beauty of e-mail marketing is that it lets you deliver your message directly to an individual who actually wants to hear from you. Compare this to your website, which is necessarily more generic (to appeal to a broader audience) and needs to work harder to attract and retain a visitor's attention.

While e-mail marketing is just one of the many ways of connecting and maintaining a relationship with your customers, and is perhaps getting a bit long in the tooth compared to the young and dynamic social media channels that are emerging, it nevertheless remains a stalwart of internet marketing and when executed properly can be incredibly effective.

Case study: Iwanttoseeaghost

The brief

Before starting the campaign three clear objectives were established:

1. to create expectation before the premiere of the movie *Pulse* in the cinema;
2. to get audience involvement to be both receiver and spreader of action;
3. to create synergies between different parts to make it easier to remember them.

The aim was to ensure that audiences of multi-screen cinemas would choose *Pulse* as its best leisure option. The plot of *Pulse* dealt with a deadly virus spreading on the internet.

The concept

This was to bring the *Pulse* plot to real life by creating a fake blog that is possessed by ghosts and allowing users to become main characters of the movie and spreaders of the action by using a high-level personalization tool that allows text, audio and real-time webcam recording video in order to scare friends.

The campaign

The terror begins with a simple e-mail that was sent to the whole internal database of BBDO. The seed of the virus was sown: the e-mail invited recipients to open Google and write 'Iwanttoseeaghost' and push the 'I am feeling lucky' button. They were then brought to a blog featuring an entry only 10 minutes old stating that there was a strange wave of suicide among bloggers around the world. The information included a strange video related to these incidents in effect conveying the impression that the computer is possessed by ghosts.

It then becomes clear that the false blog is actually a promotional tool for the cult movie *Pulse*. The campaign did not end there. Recipients of the e-mail discovered the real potential of the site on clicking the 'Scare your friends' button. This action launched a powerful and unprecedented viral tool providing extreme customization of the site, personalized text and real-time audio and video recording.

The recipients of the e-mail could now add a friend's name to be broadcast in the video and forward the e-mail to the friend. The cycle now started again but with greater intensity.

On opening up the video the friend sees that one of the characters among the suicidal bloggers is the person who has sent them the link, the video viewer's own name then appears in the text on the screen and even more terrifying the ghost utters the viewer's name before the final fright.

The results

The first day after the internal e-mail was sent there were 518 visits to the site. Seven days later there were 35,576 visits. Before the premiere of *Pulse* there were more than 1 million visits. Almost two months after the premiere the daily average was around 4,000 visits.

There were 175,000 viral e-mails sent, and over 18,000 references on blogs, forums and websites.

The campaign was picked up on numerous blogs, portals, discussion groups and TV programmes. The campaign won many awards, including a prestigious Gold Cyber Lion in the viral category at Cannes 2007. The most significant result was that an unknown movie achieved third place in box office rankings competing against Hollywood blockbusters such as *The Pursuit of Happyness* and *Apocalypto*.

See http://www.canneslionslive.com/cyber/win_2_1_01090.htm.

Campaign credits

Client: DeAPlaneta
Product: the movie *Pulse*
Advertising agency: CP Proximity, Barcelona
Executive Creative Director: Enric Nel-lo
Art Director: Jaume Leis

7 Social media and online consumer engagement

Informal conversation is probably the oldest mechanism by which opinions on products and brands are developed, expressed, and spread.

(Johan Arndt)

Why does listening to your customers sound like a Web 2.0 idea? It should be a business 1.0 necessity.

(Jeff Jarvis)

We have technology, finally, that for the first time in human history allows people to really maintain rich connections with much larger numbers of people.

(Pierre Omidyar, founder of eBay)

Facebook is silly.

(Damian's Dad)

Our chapter pledge to you

When you reach the end of this chapter you'll have answers to the following questions:

- What does the term 'social media' really mean?
- How is it changing the digital marketing landscape?
- Why should I get involved?
- How can I harness the power of social media to reach and engage with my target audience?
- How can consumer input help me do business more effectively and refine my products and services?
- What are the social media rules of engagement?

Join the conversation

Do you listen to consumers – really listen to them? Do you take their opinions, ideas and criticisms on board and allow them to inform your business decisions? If you do, you're ahead of the game. Historically marketers have focused on delivering a particular message, to a predefined target audience, with the aim of eliciting a specific response. Consumers were sometimes consulted in the process, of course – through market research, consumer surveys, focus groups and the like – but by and large the marketing tended to be 'show and tell' in nature, the consumer's role that of a passive recipient of information peddled by the marketer.

Now, thanks to the increasingly interactive nature of the internet and a shift in the way people are consuming media, all of that is changing. Consumers are talking, just as they always have, only now they're talking online to more extensive groups of their peers. The conversations they're having seamlessly transcend geographical, temporal and cultural boundaries. The web is abuzz with a billion conversations, and that presents exciting opportunities for marketers who are brave enough to engage.

Marketing too is evolving rapidly to become more of a conversation than a lecture. Progressive marketers realize that, to be heard in today's interactive world, they need to participate in that conversation – and, of course, if you want to get the most out of any conversation, you have to spend part of your time *listening*.

Listening isn't a trait marketers are traditionally renowned for, but to truly embrace the opportunity presented by Web 2.0 and beyond we need to sit up and take notice of what our online customers and prospects are telling us about our brand, our industry and the world in general.

Through blogs, wikis, social bookmarking, online discussions, social networks, peer review sites and other online media, we have the potential to foster a much more productive and meaningful relationship with our customers, to gain powerful insight into their perceptions of our products, services and brand, and allow them to contribute and collaborate in our businesses in ways that were never possible before.

Understanding social media demands a paradigm shift for the marketer. We have to realize that our target audience is, in fact, no longer an audience at all. They are now active participants in a constantly evolving debate; it's a debate in which we, as online marketers, can't afford to sit on the sidelines.

What is social media?

'Social media' is the umbrella term for web-based software and services that allow users to come together online and exchange, discuss, communicate and participate in any form of social interaction. That interaction can encompass text, audio, images, video and other media, individually or in any combination. It can involve the generation of new content; the recommendation of and sharing of existing content; reviewing and rating products, services and brands; discussing the hot topics of the day; pursuing hobbies, interests and passions; sharing experience and expertise – in fact, almost anything that can be distributed and shared through digital channels is fair game.

In a webcast for Search Marketing Now (www.searchmarketingnow. com), Google alumnus and leading social media commentator Vanessa Fox described it as follows: 'There are all kinds of ways that people talk online, and Social Networking really is anywhere people are talking online. From a corporate perspective what you're most interested in is where people are talking about you, talking about your products, and talking about the topics that you care about.'

A huge range of websites now leverage elements of social media to engage with their audience, and some, including a number of the highest-profile sites to emerge in recent years (the Facebooks, MySpaces and YouTubes of this world), base their entire business model around the burgeoning popularity of online social media, user participation and user-generated content (UGC).

Social media is nothing new

One of the biggest misconceptions about social media is that it is a new phenomenon. Online social interaction has been around from the beginning. Pre-dating the web by some two decades, bulletin board services (BBSs) and online services like CompuServe and Prodigy allowed

Figure 7.1 The proliferation of social media sites on the internet today is making it incredibly easy for like-minded consumers to connect with each other. They're talking about everything – things that are important to you and your business. It's time to join the conversation!

users to post messages online for other members to read and respond to, Usenet newsgroups (early internet discussion groups) allowed like-minded participants to exchange views about all sorts of topics ranging from brain surgery to budgerigars, e-mail discussion lists did the same, Internet Relay Chat (IRC) introduced real-time chat into the mix, and browser-based forums and chat rooms brought the discussion on to the web. Social media, one and all.

What has changed over recent years is the reach and penetration of these social media technologies, their adoption into the everyday lives of a mainstream audience, and the proliferation of user-generated content and peer-to-peer interaction that's resulting from it. In the past online discussion was generally restricted to early adopters: technologists who felt comfortable interacting over the net and who had the technical skills to fathom clunky, often unwieldy user interfaces to accomplish their goals. Today though, anyone can participate through slick, well-designed, browser-based user interfaces that adopt conventions that everyone is comfortable with. It's easy, it's convenient and it's incredibly powerful, not because of the technology, but because of how that technology nurtures the connections between people.

Social media is naturally compelling

The proliferation of social media is a natural extension of increasing levels of internet usage and the penetration of always-on broadband access. As more people head online and start weaving the internet seamlessly into the fabric of their daily lives, it's only natural that they bring the very human need to interact and belong with them. We're biologically programmed to be social and gregarious creatures. The need to interact with other people is hard-coded into our DNA; it's part of who and what we are, and that's as true online as it is off. That's one of the main reasons so many of us find social media incredibly compelling.

Social media is nothing to be afraid of

Compelling it may be, but for many marketers the thought of venturing into this openly interactive, anything-goes, consumer-championed world can be daunting, even scary. The rules here aren't dictated by marketers, but by consumers – media-savvy consumers who can spot marketing hype a mile away and want nothing to do with it. It's a dynamic, unpredictable world, and if you get things wrong you risk the very real prospect of a backlash that will travel throughout the network in the blink of an eye.

Worrying? Possibly, but at the end of the day you have to remember that social media is just about people talking, connecting and sharing with other people. Marketing as an industry is (or at least should be) also all about people: understanding them and communicating with them. Is the prospect of talking with the very people you, as a marketer, want to connect with really such a frightening prospect?

With or without you – why it's good to get involved

But, we hear you cry, how can I hope to control this open conversation? You can't – so don't even try. What you can do, however, is choose to participate in that conversation and strive to have a positive influence on its direction. That's fundamentally what social media marketing (SMM) is all about.

One thing is certain: your customers are already talking to each other online; they're talking about your industry, your competition, your company, your brand and other topics that are relevant to what you do. The conversation is happening, regardless of whether you choose to get involved or not. Surely it's better to be aware of what's being said, to listen, engage and foster relationships with these communities, rather than wondering from the periphery.

Effective social media marketing is about leaving the sledgehammer approach to product promotion at home. Stop beating your prospects over the head with the cudgel of marketing hyperbole and instead work to develop your skills in the subtler art of consumer engagement. Find out what people are interested in and what they're talking about, and then provide useful information, advice and content for them. Talk to them, not at them, and above all *listen to them*. If you manage to do that effectively, then social media can have an incredibly positive impact on your organization's online profile.

Why get involved?

- Deeper engagement with customers
- Get insights not available any other way
- Your customers are online already

Figure 7.2 Why it's important for your business to get involved in social media

Source: Slide courtesy of search marketing and social media specialist Vanessa Fox – www.vanessafoxnude.com – sourced from a presentation on social media delivered at Search Marketing World, Dublin, in April 2008. © 2008 Vanessa Fox

Just how deep you choose to steep yourself in the social media marketing game will depend a lot on your business, your customers, your goals and your overall digital marketing strategy. But there really is something out there for everyone. Here are just some of the potential benefits of engaging with your customers through online social channels:

- *Stay informed:* Find out what your customers really think. Get invaluable insight into their perception of your products, services, brands, industry and more general topics of interest. Knowing your customers is the key to effective digital marketing – and engaging with them on a social platform can be incredibly revealing, without being intrusive.
- *Raise your profile:* By engaging proactively through social media you appear responsive and can build your reputation as an authoritative and helpful player in your field of expertise.
- *Level the playing field:* Focus groups, market research surveys and other offline methods of gauging consumer sentiment are expensive and can be well beyond the means of smaller businesses. Now any organization can immerse itself in the social web to discover what consumers are talking about and how they feel, with little or no financial outlay.
- *Influence the influencers:* Often the people who are most active in social media circles will be the element of your target market who can be classified as *influencers*. While small in number compared to the market as a whole, these influential individuals have already gained the trust and respect of their online peers, and fostering their good opinion can have a disproportionate impact on your broader online reputation.
- *Nurture brand advocacy:* By engaging positively with people who already have a positive attitude to your brand, you can nurture passionate brand evangelists who will voluntarily advocate your organization through online social media.
- *Pass it on:* One of the most powerful aspects of social media is its capacity for viral propagation. It's the online equivalent of word-of-mouth marketing, except that online the word can travel further, faster. Whether it's a video on YouTube, a high-profile news story about your company or a post on your blog that's picked up and distributed by your readers, if it hits the right note, suddenly it's everywhere, and your profile soars. If you get it right, there's no more effective way to promote your business.
- *The wisdom of the crowd:* You know what they say: two heads are better than one. Well, hundreds, or even thousands, of heads are better still. Smart companies realize that by harnessing the collective intelligence of online communities they can find answers to some of

their most challenging business problems. Getting input from online communities using social media is affordable and effective. As well as helping to solve real business dilemmas it can also help you to make more informed research, design and development decisions based on what customers actually want. Now there's a radical concept!

The different forms of social media

Social media websites come in a wide variety of 'flavours', which are all broadly based around the premise of personal interaction, creating, exchanging and sharing content, rating it and discussing its relative merits as a community. The content can be links to other websites, news articles or blog posts, photographs, audio, video, questions posed by other users – anything, in fact, that can be distributed in digital form.

Most social media websites don't sit neatly into a single category; they tend to mix a range of social components that transcend the discrete boundaries people try to define for them. Still, given our human propensity for filing things into nice, neat boxes, there are several generally accepted groupings into which most social media sites sit with relative comfort based on their primary function. The following list is a taster and is far from exhaustive. Start looking, and you'll find plenty of social media sites or components out there that don't fall neatly into any of the categories we outline below, some that span multiple categories and others that defy categorization altogether, all of which demonstrates the dynamic, constantly evolving nature of the space. As the saying goes, we live in interesting times.

Social bookmarking

Social bookmarking sites, like delicious (www.delicious.com), Ma.gnolia (www.ma.gnolia.com), StumbleUpon (www.stumbleupon.com) and others allow users to 'save' bookmarks to their favourite web resources (pages, audio, video, whatever) and categorize them using tags (labels that help you to identify and filter the content you want later). The concept is much the same as adding a page to your browser favourites, just taken to the next level.

Now, instead of having your bookmarks stuck on the hard drive of a single computer, they're up in 'the cloud' (the fashionable umbrella term for the amorphous mass of software and services that run in the ether of cyberspace), which means you can access them from anywhere. That also makes them easy to share with friends, colleagues or the world at large, and the tag-based organization means no more cumbersome hierarchical folder systems to remember. Just choose a 'tag' and you'll be presented with a list of all the bookmarks labelled with that tag. Simple.

Behind the scenes these sites anonymously aggregate the data submitted by all of their users, allowing them to sort and rank sites according to their user-defined tags and popularity.

What's in it for marketers

- *Amplify your exposure and traffic:* By creating compelling, useful content and making it easy for visitors to bookmark your pages (by providing 'Share this' links or icons encouraging them to do just that) you can harness the social element of these sites to improve your reach, and get valuable, targeted traffic in return.
- *Increase your perceived relevancy and authority:* The tags applied to your pages by people who add them to social bookmarking sites can help search engines and visitors to gauge what your site is about more effectively. This can boost its perceived relevance and authority for particular keywords, which can in turn help your search visibility.

Social media submission sites

Social media submission sites, like Digg (www.digg.com) and Reddit (www.reddit.com), and niche sites like Sphinn (www.sphinn.com), a site for submission and discussion of articles about online marketing, are rather like social bookmarking sites (see above), only instead of saving personal bookmarks users submit articles, videos, podcasts and other pieces of content they think the broader community would appreciate. The more people who 'vote' for a particular content item, the higher up the rankings it rises. Submissions that get enough votes end up on the site's home page, which can drive significant traffic.

As well as the votes, of course, there also tends to be a lot of discussion and debate on these sites, which means they can offer tremendous insight into the way people think and react.

What's in it for marketers

- *Find out what people are interested in:* You can use social media submission sites to gauge what type of content in your particular field people find compelling. Look at the content that's floating to the top. Ask yourself why it's so popular. What's appealing about it, and how can you draw on that to make your own content more compelling?

- *What's the buzz?* As well as what's 'hot' on the sites, there's a lot of discussion going on around popular content items. The more popular an entry gets, the more people see it and the more debate there is. Examine what people are saying – look at reviews, comments and discussions; find out what people like and what they don't like, and use that insight to inject that elusive 'buzz' quotient into your own content.
- *Amplify your exposure, traffic and online reputation:* As with social book-marking, having articles and other content ranking highly on these sites can give you a tremendous boost in traffic. However, they also give you the opportunity to raise your profile and perceived authority within your online community. By contributing constructively, sub-mitting relevant and interesting content, and joining the debate sur-rounding on-topic content you can boost the community's overall perception of your brand.

Forums and discussion sites

Online forums and discussion sites have been around since the early days of the internet. Broad, general discussion groups like Yahoo Groups (http://groups.yahoo.com) and Google Groups (http://groups.google. com), where anyone can sign up and start their own online or e-mail discussion community on any topic under the sun, are still popular, and you'll find a mass of other discussion sites focusing on general, industry-specific (vertical) and niche communities covering every topic imaginable.

What's in it for marketers

- *Get closer to your customers:* Checking out what consumers are talking about in forums is a great way to find out what makes them tick. The more you can learn about your customers, the better prepared you will be to engage with them in a meaningful way.
- *Raise your profile:* Contribute to the discussion, offer help and advice, and demonstrate your expertise. Pretty soon people will start to respect and trust your contribution to the community – and that can do wonders for your online reputation and profile.
- *Nip bad things in the bud:* By participating in forums you will be able to spot potentially negative comments or conversations relating to your business or brand and be proactive in resolving them before they escalate (more about this in the next chapter). What's more, if you're already participating as a valued member of the community, you may well find others jumping to your defence.

- *Targeted traffic:* Traffic shouldn't be your main reason for joining a discussion forum – blatant off-topic promotion and linking to your own sites for the sake of it are frowned upon, but most forums allow (even encourage) one or two links in your signature (a short snippet, usually a few lines, that is appended to the bottom of every post you submit to a forum). Make sure you follow the forum rules on this, but by including links in your signature you give other people on the forum a convenient way to find your site(s) and to discover more about you and your company. Many will click through for a closer look, particularly if you make regular, valuable and relevant contributions to the forum.

Media sharing sites

Media sharing sites are incredibly popular. Sites like Flickr (www.flickr.com) and Picasa Web Albums (www.picasaweb.google.com) allow communities of members to upload, share, comment on and discuss their photographs. YouTube (www.youtube.com), Y! Video (video.yahoo.com), MSN Video Soapbox (video.msn.com/) and others do the same for video content. A host of other social media sites support alternative media types: Slideshare (www.slideshare.com), for example, is a site that allows people to upload, share and discuss their presentation slides with the world.

The sites typically allow you to make content publicly available or restrict access to the people you specify, to send content to your 'friends', and even to 'embed' (seamlessly integrate) the content in your blog post or website for others to find it, distribute it and discuss it.

What's in it for marketers

- *Find out what turns your target market on:* By analysing the popularity of items on content submission sites and reading the user comments, you can gain insight into your target market's likes and dislikes and can incorporate that into your own content creation.
- *A ready-made vehicle for content distribution:* These sites are the ideal vehicle for rapid distribution of your own digital media content. In fact, a whole micro-discipline of digital marketing has evolved around YouTube and viral video content. Hit the right buttons with your audience and, who knows, maybe your video clip will become the next 'Dove Evolution' (http://tinyurl.com/ylzku6) – 6,694,180 views and counting.

Reviews and ratings sites

Reviews and ratings sites do exactly what the name says: they allow users to review and rate companies, products, services, books, music, hotels, restaurants – anything they like. They can be stand-alone review sites, like Epinions.com (www.epinions.com), Reviewcentre.com (www.review centre.com) or LouderVoice (www.loudervoice.com), or a review component added to a broader site, such as the product rating and review facilities on e-commerce sites like Amazon (www.amazon.com).

You'll also find specialist industry-specific review sites covering many industry-specific or vertical markets, like TripAdvisor (www.tripadvisor. com), for example, which focuses on consumer reviews of travel destinations, accommodation and transport options, or RateMyTeachers (www. ratemyteachers.com), which allows pupils and parents to rate and comment on their educators.

Figure 7.3 LouderVoice (www.loudervoice.com) – one of a new breed of peer review websites that lets people share their opinions about products, brands and services either directly on the site or via their blogs, micro-blogs or SMS

What's in it for marketers

- *Advertising:* Most review sites rely on advertising to generate revenue and therefore offer advertising opportunities for businesses either directly or through advertising and affiliate networks.
- *Insight into what's good and what's bad:* Even if people aren't rating your business directly, you can still get valuable information on these sites on what's working for consumers and what's not within your particular industry. If you run a hotel, for example, you can see what people's main gripes are and what they particularly appreciate – and then apply that knowledge to your own business.
- *Find out what people really think:* If consumers are posting reviews about your business, that sort of feedback is pure gold – reinforcing what you're doing well and pointing out areas where you can improve. It's market research – for free.

Social network sites

These are your archetypal social media sites – the Facebooks, MySpaces, Bebos and LinkedIns – the ones people automatically think about when you mention the words 'social networking'. They are – to paraphrase Facebook's opening gambit – 'social utilities that connect you with the people around you'. They basically let users build up a group of 'friends' with whom they can share things in all sorts of ways – from videos, to articles, to games, to groups and causes, to... well, if you haven't got one already, sign up for a profile of your own and you'll soon get the idea.

Huge numbers of people use social networking sites, and those numbers are growing all the time as more people join and invite all of their contacts to join them. At the time of writing MySpace, the global leader, reports around 200 million active users, while Facebook, the up-and-coming social network hot-shot, reports some 70 million users and climbing. Those are impressive numbers when you consider that MySpace was founded only in 2003, while Facebook started in 2004 but wasn't opened up to non-students until April 2006.

Jeremiah Owyan, a senior analyst at Forrester Research, confirmed on his blog in January 2008 that Facebook had the highest growth rate of the two, and Forrester predicts that it will catch its rival in terms of user numbers by late 2008 or early 2009.

Social network sites are popular because they offer users the ability to find and connect with people they already know in novel, convenient ways: rekindle old acquaintances and reinforce new ones. They make the process of communicating with a large network of people easy and painless. You post information to your profile and it's instantly available to those of your friends who are interested. You can broadcast information to all of your friends simultaneously or choose who you want to share specific content with.

Talking to a room full of software developers in San Francisco in 2007, Mark Zuckerberg, Facebook's youthful founder, summarized the company's mission thus: 'At Facebook we're pushing to make the world a more open place, and we do this by building things that help people use their real connections to share information more effectively.' This pretty much encapsulates the social networking phenomenon that's gripping the online world today.

What's in it for marketers

- *Advertising:* Social networks offer flexible advertising options for businesses looking to target their ads based on the profile information of users and/or particular actions. While the targeting angle is a compelling one, and social network audiences are large and growing, the jury is still out on the potential of the social network as an effective advertising medium. The audience is undoubtedly there, but many experts question whether advertising on social networking sites converts effectively. It's something to consider, certainly, if it's a good 'fit' for your business and you have a clearly defined audience that's interested in your product or brand, but be cautious and track your results carefully.
- *Improve your online exposure/reputation:* Social network sites usually allow organizations to set up their own profile or page. Members of the network can then link to these pages as 'friends' or 'fans'. Your page is essentially your business hub within the network and can be a great way to monitor what consumers think about you, to find out more about them and to offer them valuable content in return. Having a presence on these networks, keeping your content up to date, relevant and valuable to your audience, and responding positively to the feedback you receive are another great way to boost your online reputation.
- *Nurture social evangelists:* Your social network can be a great place to attract brand advocates and to recruit and nurture brand evangelists. People on social networks love to share. Find the people who are passionate about your industry, your brand and your products, reward them with valuable information and content, and then watch as they put all of their passion, zeal and social media acumen to work promoting your brand to the rest of their social network.

Blogs

In the space of a very few years the widespread popularity and adoption of the blog (an acronym of weB LOG) as a medium of self-expression and communication have caused one of the most fundamental shifts in the history of modern media. Suddenly, anyone can be a publisher. Barriers to entry have come crashing down, and easy-to-use blogging platforms have liberated millions of individuals, giving them access to a global audience. Setting up a blog can take as little as five minutes of your time on a free hosted service like Blogger (www.blogger.com) or WordPress (www.wordpress.com), and setting up a blog on your own domain is only marginally more complicated. People all over the world are using blogs to report local news, vent their frustrations, offer their opinions, share their visions and experiences, unleash their creativity and generally wax lyrical about their passions. And the world is listening and answering.

The blogosphere (the collective name applied to the global blogging community) is *the* home of internet buzz. If something is worth talking about online (and often even if it's not) it will be written about, commented upon and propagated through the blogosphere. There are, of course, millions of blogs out there that simply don't make the grade – but they don't get an audience. The best blogs float to the top (largely through online word-of-mouth, effective search engine ranking and the effect of social media submission and social bookmarking sites).

It's not just private individuals who are blogging, of course – the blog is becoming an important component in the business arsenal too, adding a personal component to the bland corporate façade, helping companies to reach out and make human connections in an increasingly human online world.

Bloggers read each other's posts, they comment on them, they link to each other prolifically, and the best of them have a massive following of avid and loyal readers. These readers go on to elaborate on what they've read in their own blogs, and spread the word through their own online social networks.

If you choose to do only one thing in the social media space, then get to know the popular blogs in your industry. Who are the people behind them? What are they writing about? What turns them on (and off)? Which topics generate the most comments? Prominent bloggers tend to be the biggest online influencers of them all – you need to be aware of them, build a relationship with them, and leverage that position where possible to help spread the word.

Never underestimate blogs. Their simplicity belies an unprecedented power to mould and influence online opinion. For a digital marketer, blogs and bloggers can be your salvation – or your damnation. Treat them with the respect they deserve.

What's in it for marketers

- *Potentially massive exposure:* Traditional press releases to your local media outlets are all very well, but get your story picked up and propagated by prominent bloggers and you'll get more online exposure, traffic and inbound links (think SEO) than any traditional press release could ever hope to achieve (for more tips on getting online press releases picked up by bloggers, see Chapter 8).
- *Consumer engagement:* Use your own corporate blog to add your voice to the blogosphere. Show your customers a personal side to your business, give them valuable information they can use, provide answers and improve their overall experience of dealing with your company. Try not to use your blog as a vehicle for blatant product and brand promotion but rather as a vehicle to offer your readers a personal insight into your company and brand. Sure, product announcements and press-release-like posts are fine, but look further afield too. You could offer your opinions and insight into industry news and events, comment on and link to other blogs that are discussing relevant issues, or get your resident expert to post 'how-tos' of getting the most out of your products. Engage with the online community, and they'll engage with you in turn. The more you give of yourself, the more you'll get back.

Podcasts

Podcasts are, in many ways, just the rich media extension of the blogging concept. A podcast is simply a series of digital media files (audio or video) distributed over the internet. These can be accessed directly via a website or, more usually, are downloaded to a computer or synchronized to a digital media device for playback at the user's leisure. They tend to be organized as chronological 'shows', with new episodes released at regular intervals, much like the radio and television show formats many of them emulate. Users can usually offer their feedback on particular episodes on the accompanying website or blog.

Although podcasting is still considered a nascent technology, there's already plenty of choice in the 'podosphere', and podcast portals like Podcast.com (www.podcast.com), Podcast Alley (www.podcastalley.com), Podomatic (www.podomatic.com) and even Apple's iTunes (www.apple. com/itunes) offer a convenient way to find, sample and subscribe to podcasts of interest.

What's in it for marketers

- *Listen and learn:* Leading podcasters in your industry will very probably be talking about things that are relevant to you as a business and to your customers. Podcasters also tend to be social media enthusiasts – influencers who have their finger on the digital pulse of their audience. You can harness their understanding of the online community in your particular space by analysing their podcasts, and the comments and feedback from their audience, to feed into your own digital marketing efforts.
- *Do it yourself:* Podcasting requires a little more technical know-how than blogging, but not as much as you might think to get started. At its most basic, all you really need is a digital audio recorder, some editing software and a website that you can post your files to. Depending on your business, your audience and your goals (back to strategy again!), podcasting may well offer you a valuable additional channel to reach your market. It could also help position you as a progressive digital player in your industry.

Micro-blogging

Micro-blogging is a relatively new craze that's sweeping through online early adopters, and looks set to explode as more people embrace social media and learn of its existence. It is essentially a short-message broadcast service that let's people keep their 'friends' up to date via short text posts (usually less than 160 characters). Twitter (www.twitter.com) is the biggest player in this space, with similar services being offered by the Google-acquired Jaiku (www.jaiku.com) and Pownce (www.pownce.com), a service that marries the micro-blogging short-messaging concept with file sharing and event invitations. Leading social network sites, like MySpace, Facebook and LinkedIn, also offer a kind of micro-blogging functionality within their 'walled garden' networks through their 'status updates' features.

At first glance micro-blogging may seem a bit pointless. After all, what can you really say in the Twitter-imposed limit of 140 characters? Well, think about SMS text messages on your phone – 160 characters maximum, and billions of people use them to communicate effectively every day.

The real value of micro-blogging isn't necessarily in the individual posts; it's in the collective aggregation of those mini-posts into more than the sum of their parts. When you receive frequent, short updates from the people you're connected to, you begin to get a *feel* for them, to develop a better understanding of what they're all about, and to feel a stronger connection with them.

What's in it for marketers

- *Your finger on the digital marketing pulse:* Micro-blogging platforms give you, as a marketer, access to high-profile thought leaders in the industry. They're using micro-blogging services to post snippets about what they're doing and how they're doing it, links to new online resources and thought on developments at the bleeding edge of the industry. By 'following' these thought leaders you can harness that valuable intelligence and use it to inform your own marketing decisions.
- *Understand the influencers:* Follow the influencers in your industry, and influence them in return. Identifying influencers is easy – they'll be the most active participants talking about topics relevant to your business with the most followers. You'll be amazed how much insight following the micro-blogging streams of a group of industry influencers can provide. By demonstrating your openness in adopting the latest in social media technology, you'll be seen as progressive and, as long as your contributions are constructive, will likely rise in their estimation.
- *Communicate with your customers:* Why would you want to micro-blog to your customers? Well, some very high-profile companies do (including Dell, the *New York Times*, ITN News, BBC, Southwest Airlines and British Airways to name but a few), not to mention prominent politicians (Barack Obama and Hillary Clinton, for example, were both prominent on Twitter during the 2008 Democratic presidential candidate campaign) and other high-profile public figures. In a world where e-mail has become increasingly noisy, offering a micro-blog feed provides beleaguered consumers with a convenient alternative way to subscribe to your updates without adding yet another newsletter to their cluttered inbox.
- *Raise your online profile:* Micro-blogging offers you yet another opportunity to get in front of your online audience and establish your expertise. Be forthcoming, answer questions, provide interesting snippets of news and advice, and direct people to useful blog posts, articles and other resources – yours and other people's. Help people, learn about them, listen to them, and give your online reputation another boost.
- *Generate traffic:* While not the primary goal, links on your micro-blogging profiles, and in your posts, can have the residual benefit of directing traffic to your website.

Wikis

Wikis are online collections of web pages that are literally open for anyone to create, edit, discuss, comment on and generally contribute to. They are perhaps the ultimate vehicle for mass collaboration, the most famous example, of course, being Wikipedia (www.wikipedia.org), the free online encyclopedia.

As at April 2008, Wikipedia reported that it had a staggering 2,349,270 English-language articles in its database. To put that number into context, the *Encyclopaedia Britannica* (www.britannica.com), a leading commercial encyclopedia, contains just over 65,000 articles. Despite criticisms from some quarters over the accuracy of some of its articles and the perceived authority of the information it contains, according to independent web tracking company Alexa (www.alexa.com) in the first quarter of 2007 Wikipedia received roughly 450 times the online traffic of its commercial rival Britannica Online (www.britannica.com).

The name 'wiki' originates from the Hawaiian word for 'quick', although it's sometimes also used as what's been dubbed a 'backronym' (a sort of reverse-engineered acronym) of 'what I know is'. And essentially, that's what wikis do – they let large communities of people collaborate to share their knowledge, experience and expertise online. Wikis are created by, and policed by, the community. Because of their open nature, inaccurate or misleading information can find its way on to a wiki, but if the wiki is active and vibrant inaccuracies are usually picked up quickly and eradicated by other community members. So wiki articles are constantly evolving and tend to become increasingly accurate and authoritative over time as the community grows, and they tend to be updated with new information as it becomes available.

What's in it for marketers

The concept of using wikis as a marketing tool is a very new phenomenon, and their value may not be as readily apparent as with some other forms of social media. However, they are a powerful collaborative tool and, with collaboration between companies and their customers in the ascendancy, look out for increasing use of wikis by innovative organizations in the very near future.

- *Build a strong collaborative community of advocates around your brand:* Wikis can be a great way to encourage constructive interaction and collaboration between people inside your organization and people outside it (your customers). Consumers begin to feel ownership and connection with a brand that encourages, facilitates and values their contribution. That ownership evolves into loyalty and then advocacy: powerful stuff from a marketing perspective, especially when you consider that these contributors will often be online *influencers* who will go on to sing your praises on other social media sites.

- *Harness the wisdom of the crowd:* How much talent, knowledge and experience do you have inside your organization? Probably quite a lot – but it pales into insignificance when compared to the massive pool of talent, experience and expertise you can access online. Retired experts, up-and-coming whizz-kids, talented amateurs, undiscovered geniuses – they're all out there. Wikis give you a simple, powerful and compelling way to draw on and capture some of that collective intelligence. Why not harness a wiki, for example, to help refine the design of your products, come up with your next great marketing campaign, define a more efficient business process, produce and/or augment product documentation, develop a comprehensive knowledge base – or anything else that might benefit from a collaborative approach?

The rules of engagement

Social media, then, offers a wealth of opportunity for consumer engagement and building brand awareness, but in such an open and dynamic space it's critical to consider what you're doing carefully. Social media is consumer driven, and the very characteristics that makes it such an enticing proposition for marketers – the interconnected nature of online consumers, and the staggering speed at which information traverses the network – can just as easily backfire.

The 'rules' of social media are really about applying a bit of common sense to what are essentially human relationships. The key thing to remember is that this is *social* media – people are going online to interact and exchange information and content with similar, like-minded people. They're unlikely to be interested in your latest sales pitch, and they're certainly not interested in promotional hype. They want interesting, fun, informative, quirky, addictive – whatever turns them on. When it comes to social media, you're not just sending out a message; you're inviting a response, and what you get might not be quite what you're expecting. You need a plan to engage in social media marketing, but you also need to be flexible and respond to the community.

- *Draw on what you already know:* You already have a wealth of knowledge about your customers – who they are, what they like to do and where they hang out online. OK, so one of the main reasons you're getting involved in social media is to get to know them a little better – but the point is that you're not going into this blind. Use that knowledge: apply what you already know about your customers, your business and your brand to your social media strategy. As you learn more, refine what you're doing accordingly.

- *Don't jump in unprepared:* Have a clear plan before you start – know who you're trying to engage with and what you want to achieve. Define ways to gauge and measure your success, with frequent milestones to help keep you on track. But remember to be flexible, and modify your plan as necessary in response to community feedback.

- *Look, listen and learn:* Before you engage in social media marketing, spend some time 'lurking' (hanging around without contributing). Familiarize yourself with the different types of social media sites that you plan to target. Go and use the sites; read the blogs; immerse yourself in the media. Look, listen and learn. Just as in real life, every online community is different. Familiarize yourself with the various nuances before you dive in.

- *Be open, honest and authentic:* Nowhere is the term 'full disclosure' more appropriate than in social media. Don't go online pretending to be an independent punter extolling the virtues of your brand. You will get found out, and when you do your company will go 'viral' for all the wrong reasons. There are some high-profile examples of companies getting this spectacularly wrong, with disastrous results. Never pretend to be someone or something you're not.

- *Be relevant, interesting and entertaining:* Everything you do should add value to the community, as well as moving you towards your business goals. Be helpful; be constructive; be interesting and entertaining. Join the conversation, and offer valuable, authoritative and considered advice. Make a real effort to engage with the community on their terms, and you'll usually find them more than happy to engage with you in return.

- *Don't push out a spammy message:* Don't join social media sites just to submit a mass of links and push information about your own products or flood the community with posts on why your company is the best thing since sliced bread. It smacks of spam and adds nothing to the conversation. At best, the community will ignore you. At worst, well, we're back to the negative viral effect again.

- *Respect 'rules':* If the site you're frequenting has policies, guidelines and rules, read them and abide by them.

- *Respect people:* Always be respectful to your fellow community members. That doesn't mean you always have to agree with them; healthy debate is good in any community. When you do disagree, though, always be polite and respectful of other people. They have as much right to their opinion as you do to yours. Don't get personal.

- *Respond to feedback:* If users give you feedback, that's invaluable. Let them know that you appreciate it and that you're interested in what they have to say. Be responsive, and show them how you've used that feedback constructively.

Adding social media to your own site

Remember, social media isn't the exclusive province of specialist social and community websites. You can integrate social media components into your own website and begin to harness the collective talent and intelligence of a vibrant community of users. Perhaps the most obvious example is Amazon's reviews and ratings system – emulated around the web – which allows consumers to review the books and other products the site sells.

Another area where social media really comes into its own is in allowing your consumers to collaborate with you. Forums like Dell's IdeaStorm (www.ideastorm.com), for example, allow customers to suggest and vote on features they'd like to see implemented in the computer manufacturer's product line-up. It's like a next-generation business suggestion box and focus group rolled into one. The ideas that get the most votes from the IdeaStorm community rise to the top of the heap, much like items on social media submission sites like Digg. The top ideas are then evaluated and selected to go into production.

Through IdeaStorm, Dell's customers are having a direct, positive and tangible influence on the design and development of Dell products. The consumer feels more involvement and connection with the brand, while the company enjoys an improved reputation in the community and ultimately delivers a better end product to its customers. It's a classic win–win scenario.

Then, of course, there are customer support forums – where the community can answer each other's queries about your products and services. People get answers to their questions quickly, and over time you build an invaluable, searchable knowledge base of solutions to common problems. Because consumers are responding to each other's queries you improve the overall customer support experience, while reducing the burden on your own support resources – again a win–win. There are literally hundreds of ways to use social media to harness the collective intelligence, experience and latent talent of your customers and the broader online community. Imagination, openness and a willingness to engage with and learn from others are all that it takes.

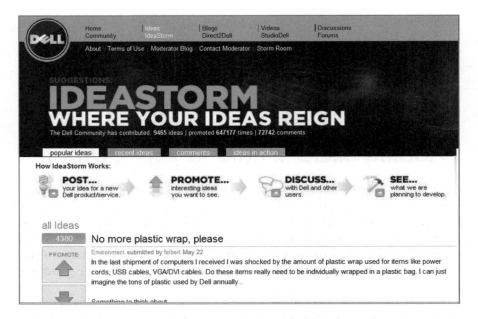

Figure 7.4 Dell IdeaStorm is a great example of a company harnessing the collective intelligence and creativity of consumers to inform real business decisions that ultimately foster consumer buy-in and deliver what customers want

Whatever social media strategy you choose to implement, remember that, even when you host social media components on your own sites, the same rules of engagement apply: be open, be honest, be considerate – and most of all *listen* to your customers, hear what they have to say and *respond* in a proactive and positive way.

Welcome to the conversation; welcome to the future of marketing!

Case study: Powerade Never Give Up 2007: Will Cullen Triathlon Challenge

Campaign background

Powerade is a sports drink that is part of the Coca-Cola family of products in Ireland. The Irish market for sports drinks is very strong; consumption levels are at 2.9 litres per capita per annum as against a European average of 1.8 litres.

In 2006 Lucozade Sport dominated the category at 54.4 per cent share, with Powerade (19.4 per cent) about to lose the number two position to the 2004-

launched, faster-growing Club Energise Sport (19.0 per cent). Powerade had two key issues: 1) share was in decline (19.4 per cent in 2006 as against 19.8 per cent in 2005); 2) it was losing its loyal consumers. In 2006 one in five weekly drinkers of Powerade were drinking Lucozade Sport daily – Powerade was a second-choice sports drink.

Key drivers were: 1) Powerade lacked differentiation. Its advertising caused consumer confusion as, like its competitors, it used sports stars in leading roles. This led to only 34 per cent correct brand attribution for Powerade advertising. 2) There was a lower media spend (share of voice 2006: Lucozade Sport 67 per cent, Club Energise 21 per cent, Powerade 12 per cent).

This low recall, coupled with low awareness of the brand's functional credibility, had led to the slow growth, a loss of space in-store and ultimately a loss of confidence. Powerade needed a direction change fast. It needed to think differently and act smarter if it was to consolidate the number two slot and begin to challenge Lucozade Sport.

Towards a big idea

1. Break category rules and reposition Powerade as a challenger.
2. Champion an idea that tapped into the mindsets of sports enthusiasts.
3. Avoid the category cliché of using big sports celebrities.

Campaign brief

Reposition Powerade in the competitive sports drink category.

- Differentiate Powerade from other competitor brands.
- Increase Powerade's market share.
- Drive Powerade brand sales.
- Engage and connect with the audience, and increase brand equity.

Target market

The overall target market for this campaign was 12- to 30-year-old males. The bull's-eye target market was 18- to 25-year-old males who were active sport participants.

Brand platform

With no global campaign available, the Irish team conducted workshops to uncover untapped insight to differentiate Powerade and leverage the Powerade pre-hydration claim. Powerade's DNA was agreed and then a new consumer insight was uncovered: 'When consumers want to perform, all that holds them back is self-belief.' From this came the core idea: 'Powerade prepares you mentally (self-belief) and physically (pre-hydration) to Never Give Up.' 'Never Give Up' became the creative expression.

The campaign concept was to communicate 'Never Give Up' by following a 22-year-old challenger, Will Cullen, as he trained for his first triathlon with Powerade's support. Will was followed over the eight months of his challenge from training to completion. The digital campaign produced the following marketing elements:

- website www.nevergiveup.ie;
- online and viral advertising;
- PR activity.

Digital strategy

A fully integrated Web 2.0 strategy was developed, which was a real innovation for an FMCG brand campaign. Web 2.0 is the use of internet technology and web design in order to enhance creativity, information sharing and most importantly collaboration among users. This strategy delivered a rich consumer experience with strong design, which was carried through each of the following elements:

- A multimedia campaign website – which included video, PDF guides, blog and viral video. This captured Will's training and progress throughout the campaign.
- Personalized video viral – a first in the market. Powerade used, as brand ambassador, Irish international rugby player Paul O'Connell to develop a unique personalized video message where users could send personalized messages to friends delivered through video by Paul O'Connell.
- Social network profiles on Bebo and MySpace for the website.
- Blogs were created on the site and received weekly updates from Will Cullen, detailing his progress. The blog was an interactive element providing increased communication between Will Cullen and online users.
- Photo sharing – a full suite of campaign images was uploaded and tagged on Flickr.com, increasing online campaign visibility.
- Online advertising was used to generate awareness on a range of Irish and Northern Irish sites and to drive traffic to the site and create wider online visibility.
- Search marketing was activated on the Google pay-per-click network.
- Online PR – campaign seeding was targeted at sport blogs and forums. Campaign seeding is an element of viral marketing and consists of planting your communication within the right online community focused on your target market. The members will then pass on your message by word of mouth and through links, tags and bookmarks. This is at the heart of Web 2.0 and represents another first for this campaign.

Results

After 12 months of the campaign, Powerade reversed its positioning in the market and became the number two brand in this sector. It's now the fastest-growing sports drink on the Irish market, growing four times faster than the category (+11 per cent), and it consolidated its number two position a full year ahead of plan. Here are the key results:

1. Sales volume grew by 42.5 per cent in 2007 (6.7 per cent in 2006)!
2. Its share of the sports drinks market grew 4.6 percentage points from 19.3 per cent in 2006 to 23.9 per cent in 2007.

3. Over 50 per cent of the target tried Powerade, up 5 percentage points on 2006.
4. Finally, there was a massive 625 per cent return on investment.

A strong idea can travel. 'Never Give Up' is considered best in class across Coca-Cola in Europe, with other markets looking to replicate. A strong idea is campaignable. For 2008 the concept has been adapted for other sports, and a local football team's training progress will be followed as it strives for championship glory. With Powerade's support, it will Never Give Up!

Digital results

- Site visitors generated 339,000 page views from 43,000 visitors.
- The average time per site visitor was five minutes. The typical duration for visits to brand sites is two to three minutes.
- Sixty per cent of site visitors downloaded a training or nutrition PDF on the site.
- The total number of personalized video creations was over 21,000 from 44,182 viral page views, a conversion rate of 48 per cent.
- The Powerade TV ads were viewed 13,814 times on YouTube.
- The campaign profiles on Bebo and MySpace were viewed 7,302 times.

Awards

Powerade has won:

- Digital Media Awards: Best Digital Advertising Campaign Award;
- APMC Awards: Gold Award, Non-Alcoholic Beverages;
- APMC Awards: Gold APMC Award, Best Use of Digital Media;
- APMC Awards: Grand Prix Award.

Agency comment

'The Powerade campaign offered Cybercom an opportunity to place digital at the centre of this campaign. The integrated digital approach maximized the impact for the campaign online, with the Paul O'Connell video viral being a first, as it used a celebrity to communicate to the online audience on a one-to-one basis.'

Campaign credits

Powerade Brand Manager, Coca-Cola Ireland: Aengus King
Digital agency: Cybercom Marketing Consultants
Advertising agency: McCann Erickson, Ireland
Public relations agency: Hartnett PR

Campaign images

http://cybercom1.com/cybercom/cannes/powerade.html

8 Online PR and reputation management

People don't really care how much you know until they know how much you care.

(Mike McNight)

It is not the strongest of the species that survives, nor the most intelligent that survives. It is the one that is the most adaptable to change.

(Charles Darwin)

It isn't what they say about you, it's what they whisper.

(Errol Flynn)

Our chapter pledge to you

When you reach the end of this chapter you'll have answers to the following questions:

- What is online PR, and why is it pivotal to your online success?
- What channels can you use to get your message out there and raise your profile online?
- Why is looking after your online reputation so critical?

- How can you get the right people talking about your brand online?
- How can you find out where people are talking about you and your brand online?
- What should you do to manage negative online conversations and repair your online reputation?

Fostering a positive online image

Spin and hype, those old stalwarts of marketing and public relations professionals around the globe, are falling by the wayside; 'open, honest and engaging' is the new mantra of communications in the connected and interactive online world.

There are a number of reasons why online PR is and will remain a crucial component of your digital marketing success. For a start, there's the undeniable fact that traditional media channels are constricting – while digital channels are expanding at a phenomenal rate. Digital channels, as we discovered in the last chapter, are also two-way. In a world where you're judged not just by your own words and actions but by the reactions and influences of others, a world where information traverses the network in a heartbeat and online conversations blossom and flourish in a thousand different places simultaneously, a world where social influencers can make or break your online reputation with a single online post to a blog or forum, promoting, monitoring and *managing* your online image are more important than ever.

First impressions matter; lasting impressions matter more

Making a good first impression is just as important online as it is when dealing with your customers face to face. But online PR is about taking a broader view: first impressions matter, but lasting impressions are what you really want to cultivate online. You want your relationship with your customers to flourish, grow and endure: you want a positive image of your brand at the forefront of their minds whenever they consider your products or services. And more than that: you want them to tell their friends.

Online PR and reputation management is about sowing seeds in fertile ground, tending them carefully as they grow, creating the conditions for them to thrive, pulling the occasional weed and ultimately reaping a bountiful harvest.

Defining online PR

In 2007 the Chartered Institute of Public Relations in the UK defined online PR as: 'Communicating over the web and using new technology to effectively communicate with stakeholders.'

That's a broad statement that encompasses a huge array of different disciplines. From a digital marketing perspective some of the things it would typically include are:

- raising the profile of your business or brand using online channels;
- monitoring conversations and managing your online reputation;
- developing online word of mouth and creating 'buzz';
- identifying online advocates and detractors (fostering the former, minimizing the impact of the latter);
- identifying online trends and issues in your industry;
- managing information flow;
- seamless integrations with the other elements of your digital marketing campaign.

Essentially it distils down to two key things: *raising the online profile of your business, products and services* by contributing positively to the online community; and *managing your reputation* by monitoring, assessing, responding to and influencing online conversations about you.

Promoting your business through online channels

When it comes to getting your business and brand out in front of online consumers, there are a number of tools you can use. First and foremost, of course, you can and should use your own website as a vehicle to make your PR-related content available to both media professionals and consumers. It's perhaps the only place online where you have direct control over every aspect of your content: how it looks, how it's presented and how people interact with it. Your site is also the ideal place to host added-value content that supports your broader off-site PR campaign, enticing people to click back to your own online real estate, where you can *track and measure* their engagement.

But having compelling content on your own site is only a very small part of the online PR story. The whole point of online PR is to raise awareness of your business and brand among the broader online community and to generate interest that exploits the viral potential of online social media. When word-of-mouth marketing meets online social networking, the result is massive latent potential – a groundswell that savvy online marketers can tap into.

To do that effectively, of course, you need to know who your customers are, where they congregate online and what turns them on – all the strategic stuff we covered earlier in the book. Use your knowledge of your customers to find them online; then join them. Engage with them on as many different platforms as you can effectively manage. Your ultimate goal may be to guide visitors to your site but, rather than relying on them coming to you, go out to them. Seed your best creative content and put it to work for you in the places *where your customers are already engaged.*

By adding genuine value to the conversation on sites that your customers frequent regularly, you not only raise your online profile but you also establish a willingness to enter into a productive two-way relationship with them. That in turn builds trust and makes them far more likely to engage with you. As your network of contacts grows and your relationship with the community develops, you can begin to generate a bit of buzz around your brand, build advocacy and develop that groundswell of positive influence we mentioned earlier.

Getting the word out with online press releases

Just like their offline equivalent, online press releases are a way of getting prominent, *newsworthy* stories about your product, brand or company out in front of as many eyeballs as possible. In many ways they are similar to the standard press releases you'd submit to offline media contacts to announce significant developments and/or news in your business.

When writing your online press releases bear the following points in mind:

- *A story worth reading:* If you're going to pique the interest of online publishers and make them want to pick up and run with your story, you'll need to do more than simply announce a new product, website or special once-in-a-lifetime offer. Your press release needs to be compelling, interesting and relevant. Tell a story – this is no place for a sales pitch; that can come later when the reader clicks through to your website. Your press release is designed to inform publishers about your story and encourage them to write or comment about it online. Think beyond your immediate readership, and write your press release to appeal to *the publisher's readers.*

- *You need a strong 'hook':* Your headline and first paragraph should capture the readers' attention and draw them in. As with any other form of online content, you literally have seconds to catch them before they click on something else.
- *Story first, detail later:* Use an 'inverted pyramid', journalistic style of writing. Distil the main elements of your story into the first few sentences; then use the rest of your press release to elaborate on specific and relevant details. As a guide, your readers should be able to break off at any point and still get the gist of your story.
- *Keep it concise, objective and to the point:* Keep your press release short and to the point. Don't over-elaborate, and avoid excessive use of adjectives, descriptive prose and flowery language. Keep it balanced and objective, and steer clear of promotional spin. Be ruthless. If a sentence doesn't add to the substance of your story, strip it out.
- *Use active, compelling language:* Your press release should zip along at a healthy pace. Use short, snappy sentences to keep it moving. Make use of the active voice in your PR writing – instead of statements like 'The ground-breaking report was commissioned by Company X', try active-voice equivalents like 'Company X commissioned the ground-breaking report' (for more examples of active/passive voice take a look at Purdue University Online Writers Lab page: http://tinyurl.com/6lowp).
- *Accessible and jargon free:* Remember, you don't know where your press releases are going to be picked up. Your story should be instantly accessible to a broad and general audience. Write your press releases in plain language, steer clear of industry jargon wherever possible, and when it is necessary give a brief explanation.
- *Contact details:* Your press release should *always* provide details of how to contact a real person in the organization, who *is ready* to provide any additional information or direct input required. This information should include your web address, contact telephone number and an e-mail address.
- *Be keyword optimized:* Your press release is going to end up on the web, so you should treat it a piece of web content. Write your copy to maximize its search visibility (see Chapter 4). Target specific, search-relevant keyword phrases in your writing – but not at the expense of human readability. Think people first and then search engines. Wherever it ends up, your press release will serve as an additional opportunity to rank for your chosen keyword phrases in the SERPs.
- *Link back to your site:* Some online press release distribution services may restrict the use of links, limit their number, or allow them only in the company boilerplate text ('About us' stuff) at the end of the piece. Where possible, aim to have at least one and possibly two or

three active back links to your website (but no more: too many and your carefully crafted press release will start to look like link spam). Links will direct traffic to your site and can potentially help with your SEO link-building efforts. If you want to track the responses to a particular press release, make sure you 'tag' your links so you can identify click-throughs using your web analytics solution (see Chapter 5).

● *Stick to the guidelines:* Whatever distribution service you choose to use, make sure that your press release adheres to its published guidelines for formatting, links, length, content, etc. Doing so will ensure your press release passes the editorial requirements and will maximize your chances of being picked up by content publishers.

Getting it out there

Once you've written your press release you'll need to distribute it. You will naturally want to add it to the 'press' or 'PR' section of your own website, and may have your own list of local, national and international media contacts you regularly send news items out to. However, to maximize the potential penetration and exposure from your press release you're going to want to spread it a bit further afield. You can do that by submitting it to one or more online press release/news distribution services like PRWeb (www.prweb.com), Business Wire (www.businesswire.com), Marketwire (www.marketwire.com), PR.com (www.PR.com) or ClickPress (www. clickpress.com). You'll find plenty more by searching for 'press release distribution' in your favourite search engine.

Some of these services offer free basic distribution, with paid upgrades, while others require payment on either a subscription or per-item basis. Which option best suits your business will depend on your particular needs.

As well as making your press release available on their own sites, these services also tend to distribute releases via news feeds to online and offline journalists, media websites and news aggregation services like Yahoo! News and Google News, which could result in a phenomenal amount of exposure for a newsworthy story.

Blogger outreach

'Blogger outreach' is the rather grand moniker that PR professionals apply to the process of reaching out into the blogosphere and persuading popular bloggers to write about your brand. It can be an incredibly effective way of raising your online profile, generating online traffic and improving your reputation. We've already seen that high-profile bloggers can have a disproportionate amount of influence and reach within their online community. What better way, then, to reach your prospective audience than to make advocates of these influential and vociferous commentators?

So, once you've submitted your finely honed press release to your distribution service of choice, you might be tempted simply to fire that same release to the top 10 bloggers in your industry. After all, you've done all the hard work, and sending out a group e-mail would be quick, easy and convenient, right?

It would also be doomed to failure. Why? Because bloggers are typically dismissive of generic, often highly irrelevant press releases pitching for free online exposure. Unless you're lucky and your generic release just happens to dovetail nicely with the blogger's specific interests, it will be painfully obvious that the pitch has come from someone who doesn't read the blog and hasn't taken the time to do any homework.

A 2007 study by APCO Worldwide and the Council of Public Relations Firms found that 42 per cent of bloggers receive an e-mail pitch from a PR professional at least once a day, 27 per cent reported getting more than one a day and 63 per cent were contacted by a PR professional at least once a week. That's a lot of press releases – most of which end up in the junk mail folder!

So how can you entice bloggers to give you some valuable exposure on their oh-so-popular websites? Well, it's important to remember that blogs are a form of social media, and the usual rules of engagement apply (see Chapter 7). Also, generally speaking, bloggers tend to be writing voluntarily about subjects that they're very passionate about. That's one of the things that makes bloggers so valuable when it comes to promoting your brand – but to harness that passion you need to show them that you understand and respect it.

- *Get to know the blogs you want to target:* It's important to get a feel for things before you jump in with both feet. Spend a bit of time familiarizing yourself with the top blogs in your industry, subscribe to their RSS feeds and *actually read* the posts (or, if you're in a hurry, you could skip to the archives and read up on some recent posts there): look, listen and learn. Before long you'll start to get a *feel* for the writers' style, their personalities, their likes and dislikes, what turns them on and what turns them off.
- *Engage through comments or by a linking from your own blog:* Make sure your pitch isn't the first thing the blogger sees from you. If you spot a post that sparks your interest or that makes a relevant point about your industry, engage by submitting a thoughtful, considered comment or

two – or, if you have a company blog, why not write your own post that links to the post in question? Make it a blogger–blogger interaction rather than a blogger–company or blogger–PR executive one. Engage in the conversation in an open, responsible and constructive way, and you'll find bloggers much more receptive to your 'pitch' when it does arrive.

- *Build a relationship:* If you attend trade shows in your industry, make a point of finding out if prominent bloggers are attending and get an introduction. If you can't meet them in person, leverage the power of social media to get to know them online. Bloggers who feel they already have a relationship with you will be far more receptive when your proposal lands in their inbox.
- *Make it relevant:* You know what each blogger you're targeting writes about – make sure what you're pitching matches the subject matter of the blog in question (you'd be amazed how often people get this wrong). Pitch to their passions!
- *Tailor made:* At the end of the day, bloggers write about the stuff that they care about. It's what makes blogs so compelling – and why more people in the United States today read a blog than buy a daily newspaper. Your proposal has to connect and resonate with the individual blogger. Tailor your message, and you stand a much better chance of success.
- *Transparency is crucial:* Always be completely open and honest about who you are and why you're contacting them. It's unethical to do otherwise and, besides, things don't stay hidden for long online and the last thing you want is a potentially nasty backlash.

Ogilvy PR's Blogger Outreach Code of Ethics

In September 2007, after rumblings in the blogger community about the way they were being approached by PR and marketing companies, Ogilvy PR drafted a code of ethics for marketers and PR professionals reaching out to bloggers. They posted it on their 360° Digital Influence blog. They then opened it up to the online community for discussion and feedback. The results of this ongoing discussion, as of 6 June 2008, are outlined below:

Our approach

- We reach out to bloggers because we respect your influence and feel that we might have something that is 'remarkable' which could be of interest to you and/or your audience.

- We will only propose blogger outreach as a tactic if it complements our overall strategy. We will not recommend it as a panacea for every social media campaign.

Outreach

- Before we email you, we will check out your blog's About, Contact and Advertising page in an effort to see if you have blatantly said you would not like to be contacted by PR/Marketing companies. If so, we'll leave you alone.
- We will always be transparent and clearly disclose who we are and whom we work for in our outreach email.
- If you tell us there is a specific way you want to be reached, we'll adhere to those guidelines.
- We won't pretend to have read your blog if we haven't, and we'll make a best effort to spend time reading the blogs we plan on contacting.
- In our email we will convey why we think you, in particular, might be interested in our client's product, issue, event or message.
- As available, we will provide you with links to third party information/blog coverage of the campaign we are pitching to you. (via Web Strategy with Jeremiah and MC Milker)
- Our initial outreach email will always include a link to Ogilvy PR's Blog Outreach Code of Ethics.

Building a relationship

- Whenever possible, we will articulate how blogger outreach, and your blog in particular, fits in with our overall campaign strategy. (via Neville Hobson)
- We will seek to present you with a range of opportunities to work together around a campaign, so that you can create the best experience possible for your audience. We acknowledge that, when it comes to knowing your audience, you are the expert.
- We'll let you know who we are by providing you with a link to some background or bio information on the individual contacting you. (via 93 Colors)
- We won't leave you hanging. If your contact at Ogilvy PR is going out of town or will be unreachable, we will provide you with an alternate point of contact.

- We encourage you to disclose our relationship with you to your readers, and will never ask you to do otherwise.
- You are entitled to blog on information or products we give you in any way you see fit. (Yes, you can even say you hate it.)
- We understand that when you agree to blog about a campaign it's not going to happen overnight. We'll work with you to develop a reasonable time line for posting that fits with your schedule – and we won't pester you to put up your post. (via LA Daddy)
- If you don't want to hear from us again, we will place you on our Do Not Contact list – which we will share with the rest of Ogilvy PR.
- If you are initially interested in the campaign, but don't respond to one of our e-mails, we will follow up with you no more than once. If you don't respond to us at all, we'll leave you alone.

Compensation and product access

- If we reach out to you with news about a product, campaign or issue, we will not provide monetary compensation, because we believe it is unethical to 'buy' favourable reviews and not want to appear as if we are.
- If you have advertising opportunities on your blog, we will counsel our clients to consider purchasing advertising as a way to reach your readers. We will make it clear, however, that paying for advertising does not mean that you will post about the campaign or that, if you do, you will do so in a way that is favourable to them.
- If we ask you to review a product and, therefore, provide you with the product to enable you to 'experience' it, we will ask that you be transparent and reveal that you have been given the product temporarily, or permanently.
- If we engage you as an advisor on a specific project, we will consider providing you with compensation (agreed upon at the start of the project). This compensation will solely be for your time as an advisor and will not include an expectation that you will write about the project – favourably or unfavourably.

This Blogger Outreach Code of Ethics was created by the 360° Digital Influence Group at Ogilvy Public Relations Worldwide. You'll find it posted on their own blog at http://blog.ogilvypr.com/?p=243.

Article syndication

When it comes to boosting your reputation and demonstrating your expertise, writing helpful, authoritative articles has always been a very powerful marketing tool. In the past it meant pitching ideas to editors to get your articles into mass-market print publications or high-profile trade journals. Yet again, though, the internet has taken a traditional marketing avenue and turned it on its head. Now anyone can write articles and syndicate them online – for free.

We've all heard the adage that on the internet content is king. We even used it ourselves earlier in the book. But creating compelling, high-value content can be a resource-hungry, time-intensive process. For thousands of websites, webzines (web magazines) and e-zines (e-mail magazines) out there, getting fresh, cost-effective, high-quality content to fill the next issue is a constant challenge. That's where article syndication comes in.

How article syndication works

Online article syndication basically involves experts (you or somebody in your business in this case) writing authoritative, compelling, high-value articles in their area of expertise and then making that content available free of charge for use by online publishers on their websites, newsletters and e-zines. As a condition of using your content the publisher agrees to present the article in its entirety, carrying your byline and, crucially, retaining your unique 'author resource box' at the foot of your article – including biographical information, contact details and a live link back to your website.

Article syndication is available to anyone and offers a great way to increase your online exposure, build a reputation for expertise in your field and get some valuable back links that can deliver both direct traffic and search optimization benefits. The best articles can be picked up again and again by different publishers, offering cumulative long-term benefit to the author.

Writing effective articles

Writing effective articles can be tricky – but, remember, the whole point here is that you're writing in your area of expertise: you already know a lot about your subject matter. As in any other discipline, practice makes perfect – so give it a try, measure your results and refine things as you go. Try writing articles in different ways; then monitor the responses to see which approach gains more traction.

Here are our top tips to help you write more effective articles for syndication:

- *Write what you know:* A bit clichéd, but unless you're an experienced writer it really is better to stick to topics you know a lot about – especially if one of your goals is to build up your online profile as an expert in your field. You'll be more confident writing about subjects you're comfortable with, and that confidence will shine through in your writing, lending your copy more authority.

- *Write for your audience:* This can be tricky when you're writing for syndication, because you never really know who your final audience might be – but you can make an educated guess. Think to yourself 'What would a typical reader of this type of content be looking for?' Then write your article for that reader, not for yourself.

- *Write keyword-optimized articles:* Use keyword research (see Chapter 4) to find out what people are searching for; then write articles optimized for those target keyword phrases to maximize your article's potential search engine exposure. Just make sure that your optimization doesn't compromise the article's effectiveness for human readers.

- *Focus on your niche:* More focused, specialist articles may have narrower appeal in terms of overall readership, but they are much more likely to get picked up by publishers in the area you want to gain exposure in. That means your articles will ultimately reach readers who are interested in your area of business.

- *Make your articles valuable:* Share your expertise; offer advice; deliver genuine value to your readers. Remember, you're positioning yourself as an authority in your area of expertise.

- *Consider their longevity:* Whenever possible, you want to maximize the shelf life of articles that you write. A useful how-to or top-tips article could be just as useful (therefore just as likely to be syndicated) in two years' time as it is the day you write it. Try to keep your articles date-neutral to maximize the potential return on the time you invest in writing them.

- *Avoid the hype:* Your articles aren't the place for promotional language – stick to the facts and your unique expert opinion.

- *Write with a consistent style and voice:* While it's fine to experiment with a different style and voice between articles, within a single article stay consistent. If you're writing in the first person ('I', 'we', etc), retain that voice throughout, and keep the same tone and writing style throughout.

- *Keep them short:* Articles for online syndication should typically fit comfortably on a single web page. Readers typically don't like reading very long articles online, and the longer the article the more difficult it becomes to hold the readers' interest. Aim for a word count somewhere between 300 and 1,000 words per article, with 400–600 words as the ideal.

Where to submit your articles

Your content is an incredibly valuable commodity. There are literally thousands of online publishers whose businesses rely on sourcing high-quality, authoritative articles for their readers – articles just like yours. But how do you get your article out in front of as many prospective publishers as possible? As always seems to happen on the internet, where there's a need websites spring up to service it, in this case article directory sites.

Article directories are basically websites that bring article authors and online publishers together. They usually consist of a searchable article repository, where authors can sign up to submit articles on a wide variety of topics. Submitted articles are normally reviewed by a human editor before being published to the site, where they then become available for syndication by online publishers and through the site's own newsletters, e-zines and RSS feeds. Web publishers can subscribe to receive alerts when new articles are submitted in their topics of interest.

There are literally hundreds of article directories out there. Top sites like Ezine articles (www.ezinearticles.com) or GoArticles.com (www.goarticles.com) are a good place to start your foray into online article syndication. These sites cover a vast range of subjects and attract a lot of interest from online publishers, but bear in mind that you'll also be competing with more authors (at the time of writing Ezine articles

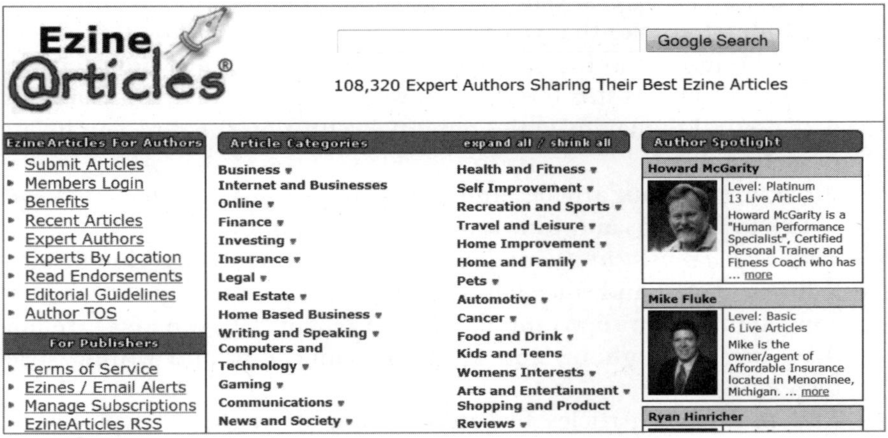

Figure 8.1 Writing articles and submitting them to online article directories like Ezine articles (www.ezinearticles.com) can be a very effective way of boosting your authority in your expertise, increasing your online exposure and driving qualified traffic to your website

reported 96,626 of them) and articles on the most popular sites. It's also worth looking at specialist sites that focus on articles in your particular vertical or subject niche and submitting articles to them too. They may not get the same traffic as the mainstream directories, but the traffic they do get will be much more targeted.

While in theory you could submit a small number of articles to a large number of article directories in the hope of increasing your exposure, in practice it's better to focus on writing a higher volume of high-quality articles and submitting them to a small number of quality article directories.

Company blog

A company or corporate blog is both quick and easy to set up. It offers you a platform that you can use to communicate and interact with consumers on a much more personal level than you can on a corporate website. Company blogs are typically written by an individual or a team of people, and offer a convenient way to publish news, announcements and helpful articles relating to your products and services, comment on industry developments and offer your customers a bit of insight into the culture of your organization and the personalities behind it.

You can also invite comments from readers on your blog – another medium where you can engage in conversation with consumers, ask their opinion and gauge their reaction to what's happening both in your company and in the marketplace.

While company blogs can be employed for a variety of different reasons, and the way you approach yours will very much depend on what it is you're trying to achieve, there are a few general guidelines that are worth bearing in mind when you embark on a company blog:

- *Blogs are social media:* This might be your site, but the social media rules of engagement from the previous chapter definitely apply.
- *Blogs are not promotional platforms:* Don't try to use your blog as a broadcast medium to push promotional messages to your audience – or before long you won't have an audience at all.
- *Engage:* Make your blog posts topical, interesting, entertaining and genuinely valuable to your readers.
- *Be yourself:* Leave the stuffy, corporate communication on your main site – keep your blog light, fresh, conversational and personal.
- *Update regularly:* Unlike your corporate site, your blog needs to stay fresh and current or it loses its value and appeal – having no blog is better than having a dead blog.

- *Encourage comments:* Write posts that encourage feedback from your readers. Ask for their opinion at every opportunity – your blog is an invaluable platform for information exchange: use it.
- *Don't censor comments:* Naturally you'll want to stop unsolicited link spam and obscenities from being published in your blog comments, but don't censor negative comments. They can often be among the most valuable feedback you can get, highlighting problems that you need to address and giving you the opportunity to show your customers that you listen and respond quickly and positively to the issues they raise.
- *Empower the blogger:* It's important that whoever is writing your company blog has the authority to respond to customers directly and to make decisions and commitments for the organization in response to comments received on the blog. The person running the blog shouldn't need to ask permission from a manager or supervisor before posting a response – if that person does, then perhaps the manager or supervisor should be the one writing the blog.
- *Optimize your blog:* Your blog is a website like any other – optimize it for search engines as you would your main site (see Chapter 4). Owing to their regular supply of topical content and their interactive nature, blogs tend to attract links more readily than corporate websites, and often do rather well when it comes to search rankings – improving your overall visibility.

Social media engagement

If you're looking to promote your business online today, you can't really avoid getting involved with social media. Nor would you want to. Social media offer the opportunity to get to know your customers in ways that simply weren't possible before. Engaging with consumers through social media gives you the chance to build real relationships with them.

We covered the relative merits of different types of social media in the last chapter and won't re-explore them here. Suffice it to say that, wherever your customers are congregating on social media websites, you have a priceless opportunity to get involved in the conversation, add value, build trust, improve your reputation and foster advocacy for your brand.

Monitoring the conversation – reputation management

As we discovered in the last chapter, people talk online all of the time – and, as social media continues to mushroom, people are talking more and more, about anything and everything, including your industry, your brand, your product. Some of these conversations may be incredibly positive, others benign and uninteresting, and a few may be damaging, but regardless of what's being discussed you absolutely need to know when people are talking about your organization online.

Whether it's to foster and encourage positive conversation and buzz, to engage productively with the online community or to respond to negative sentiment before it gets out of hand, the first step is to discover what's being said and where.

What to track

The specific terms you'll want to track will vary depending on your business, but you'll probably want to track a list something like the following:

- your company name, brand names, any trademarks you own and product names, including variations and mis-spellings (which applies to all of the other points here as well);
- the names of your CEO, executives and other key employees;
- your competitors, their brands, trademarks and products, and the names of their key employees;
- all of the above, prefixed or suffixed with common negative modifiers (eg 'Your Company Name sucks');
- terms specifically related to your industry.

How to track them

The first and most obvious option is to get involved in the online conversation wherever your customers are active. If you're an active member of an online community you'll generally be aware of who the main influencers are and what they're saying. With the best will in the world, though, you're unlikely to be able to maintain an active presence across all of the online communities where people could be discussing your brand.

There are quite a number of online services that specialize in monitoring online conversation and buzz – and as this topic gains in prominence there are more joining them all the time. Services like Nielsen Buzz Metrics (www.nielsenbuzzmetrics.com), BuzzLogic (www.buzzlogic.com), TNS Media Intelligence's Cymfony (www.cymfony.com) and Trackur (www.trackur.com) offer different reputation monitoring options ranging from very expensive enterprise-level solutions to more affordable basic services.

If you need a less comprehensive but more cost-effective monitoring solution, you can set up your own system using freely available online tools and services:

- *Set up alerts:* The first thing to do is go to Google Alerts (www.google.com/alerts) and Yahoo! Alerts (alerts.yahoo.com) and set up alerts for the terms you want to monitor. These services will send you an e-mail alert with links to news articles, blog posts and web pages they index that mention your terms.
- *Set up RSS feeds:* Go to the social media sites and content aggregations sites (Bloglines, Technorati, Google News, Google Blog Search, BlogPulse, Icerocket, Tweetscan, FriendFeed, etc) that you want to monitor. Many will let you search for keywords and subscribe to customized RSS feeds based on your search terms. You can then aggregate and organize all of these feeds in your RSS reader of choice (Google Reader, Feedreader, Newsgator, FeedDemon, etc – for an introduction to the concept of RSS feeds check out this video on YouTube by Common Craft: http://tinyurl.com/5w36v3).
- *Custom search engines:* A useful way of searching across multiple sites that you want to monitor, but which don't offer the RSS search functionality outlined above, is to create a custom search engine using a service like Google Co-op (www.google.com/coop) or Rollyo (www.rollyo.com). You could cover all of the sites you want to monitor with an individual custom search engine or create a different one for each type of site you want to monitor, eg one for consumer review sites, another for complaint sites relating to your industry and another for your industry-specific news sites.

Once you have your monitoring system up and running, establish a procedure for checking it regularly. Time is often of the essence, especially if there's something negative afoot, and it's important to catch things early. The key thing with reputation management is to engage as soon as possible and try to influence the conversation in a positive way, or at least to give your side of the story to the community. Ideally you want to prevent negative commentary from spreading through social networks

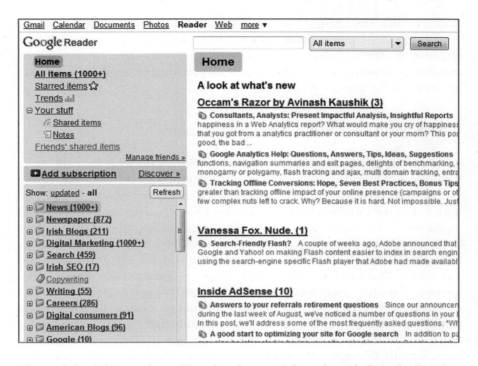

Figure 8.2 RSS readers, like the free web-based tool Google Reader (www.google.com/reader), allow you to subscribe to website 'feeds'. The reader aggregates and sorts all of your feeds and presents them in one convenient location for you to read at your leisure. Feed readers can also be invaluable monitoring tools to help you manage your online reputation

and, crucially, from reaching the SERPs, where they could be presented to literally millions of people.

Damage limitation: turning the tide when things go wrong

Bad things happen sometimes. That's life!

When they happen and people start talking about them online, word can spread quickly, and unless you do something to limit the damage it can escalate to become a groundswell of *bad* publicity. The power of social media, the ubiquity of the internet and everything that works so effectively to help you build a good online reputation can tarnish that reputation even more quickly. Whether it's a genuine grievance, a simple misunderstanding or a malicious rumour, you need to act, and act quickly, to mitigate the potential damage.

Prevention is always better than cure

Do everything you can to avoid negative online publicity occurring in the first place. Minimizing bad online press is much easier than mitigating the damage in its aftermath. That sounds like obvious advice, but with so much at stake it bears a mention. Review your processes and procedures; make sure customers have a clear and straightforward way to air their grievances with the company rather than taking them into the public domain. Deal with customer correspondence quickly, professionally and effectively. Make it your goal to turn negative customer sentiment into a positive customer outcome before it becomes a bigger problem.

Another effective way to minimize negative online publicity is to actively participate in the online communities that matter most to your business. Don't just monitor them remotely; get in there at the coalface and actually become part of the community. If people know and trust you within that community they'll be much slower to lend credence to spurious negative remarks.

Do something

Once you identify a negative post that carries any significance or weight you will need to do something about it. Don't bury your head in the sand in the hope it will all sort itself out. Quite often it's not the negative sentiments themselves that do the most damage to a company's online reputation; it's the lack of response, or an inappropriate response, that fans the flames of malcontent.

- *Analyse what's been said:* Get a handle on what you're dealing with: before you dive into the conversation, do a bit of digging. Does the grievance have merit, is it just a misunderstanding, or is it malicious gossip? Know where you stand and have a plan of action before you engage.
- *Engage positively in the conversation:* Don't try to hide the truth. It won't just come back to haunt you; it could come back and bury you! Be open, honest and forthcoming. If you have made a mistake, admit it,

and ask what you can do to help resolve the matter amicably. Look for a win–win.

- *Politely point out any misunderstandings:* If the problem was caused by a misunderstanding, clarify the matter publicly. Put all the facts on the table and let other community members make up their own minds. Be professional and courteous, and point out what you'll be doing to prevent such a misunderstanding arising in the future.

- *Stay calm, professional and respectful:* Aggrieved people can be touchy, and our immediate human instinct is to protect what's ours – in this case our reputation. Don't overreact. Keep calm – far better to fight fire with water, not more fire. You might even try thanking the poster for the valuable feedback – analysis of negative comments can often prove more valuable than positive ones, pointing to things that your business could be doing more effectively. Never, ever lose your cool and resort to vitriol – it helps nobody.

- *Post additional and supporting information on your website:* Whatever response you make, action you take and resolutions you agree, post updates and additional supporting information on your website, and link to it from the original conversation and other places you frequent online. Your site is the first place people will look for clarification – make it easy for them to find.

- *Be responsive and informative:* Respond to what people are saying to you online. Don't become entrenched – this is not a battle. Be open and flexible. Look, listen, learn and respond in a positive way.

- *If it's malicious, counter it:* If the negative statements are malicious (competitors posting inaccurate and damning consumer reviews of your products, for example, or an unjustified smear campaign by a disgruntled former employee), you should contact the website owners and ask them to remove the offending material. You should also ask to publish clarifying remarks on the site in question, and publish a prominent and comprehensive counter-statement on your own site. As an absolutely last resort you may have to resort to legal action, although it's not generally necessary, and you should avoid getting the lawyers involved if at all possible.

When negative pages hit the SERPs

Hopefully, by having an effective monitoring system in place, being active on popular sites and following the mitigation strategies outlined here and elsewhere, you'll be able to counter negative publicity before it makes its way into the SERPs and gets in front of millions of eyeballs. If negative stuff does hit the search engines, with any luck your own content around the web will be well enough optimized to outrank it for the keywords that matter to you. If not, you have two choices – live with it, or work to optimize your own content so that it outranks the offending material and pushes it down the SERPs.

Dell learns to listen: the computer maker takes to the blogosphere to repair its tarnished image

Jeff Jarvis

In the age of customers empowered by blogs and social media, Dell has leapt from worst to first.

Start with the worst. In June, 2005, I unwittingly unleashed a blog storm around the computer company. Terminally frustrated with a lemony laptop and torturous service, I vented steam on my blog under the headline: 'Dell sucks.' That's not quite as juvenile as it sounds, for a Google (GOOG) search on any brand followed by 'sucks' reveals the true Consumer Reports for that company's customers. Thousands of frustrated consumers eventually commented on and linked to my blog, saying, 'I agree.' They were a leading indicator of Dell's problems, which the company – and analysts and reporters covering it – should have heeded. My story ended, I thought, that August when, after returning the Dell and buying a Mac, I blogged an open letter to Michael Dell suggesting his company read blogs, write blogs, ask customers for guidance, and 'join the conversation your customers are having without you.'

The following April, Dell (DELL) did join that conversation. It dispatched technicians to reach out to complaining bloggers and solve their problems, earning pleasantly surprised buzz in return. That July, Dell started its Direct2Dell blog, where it quickly had to deal with a burning-battery issue and where chief blogger Lionel Menchaca gave the company a frank and credible human voice. Last February, Michael Dell launched IdeaStorm.com, asking customers to tell the company what to do. Dell is following their advice, selling Linux computers and reducing the promotional 'bloatware' that clogs machines. Today, Dell even enables customers to rate its products on its site.

Has Dell really gotten the blog religion? I recently visited the company's Round Rock (TX) headquarters to find out. Founder Dell, who took back the CEO reins in January, acknowledges its problems – 'We screwed up, right?' But then he starts to sound like a blogger himself: 'These conversations are going to occur whether you like it or not, OK? Well, do you want to be part of that or not? My argument is you absolutely do. You can learn from that. You can improve your reaction time. And you can be a better company by listening and being involved in that conversation.'

New metrics for success

Dell's worst problem had been that customers were having too many of the wrong conversations with too many service technicians in too many countries. 'It was a real mess,' confesses Dick Hunter, former head of manufacturing and now head of customer service. Dell's DNA of cost-cutting 'got in the way,' Hunter says. 'In order to become very efficient, I think we became ineffective.'

Hunter has increased service spending 35 per cent, cut outsourcing partners from 14 to 6 (and is headed to 3), and retrained staff to take on more problems and responsibility (higher-end techs can scrap their phone scripts; techs in other countries learn empathy). Crucially, Hunter also stopped counting the 'handle time' per call that rushed representatives and motivated them to transfer cust-omers so they would be someone else's problem. At Dell's worst, more than 7,000 of the 400,000 customers calling each week suffered transfers more than seven times. Today, the transfer rate has fallen from 45 per cent to 18 per cent. Now Hunter tracks the minutes per resolution of a problem, which runs in the 40s. His favourite acronym mantra (among many) is RI1: resolve in one call. (Apple (AAPL) claims it resolves 90 per cent of problems in one call.) He is also experimenting with outreach e-mails and chatty phone calls to 5,000 selected New Yorkers before problems strike, trying to replace the brother-in-law as their trusted adviser.

Has it made a difference?

The crucial word you hear at Dell is 'relationship.' Dell blogger Menchaca has led the charge in convincing bloggers that 'real people are here to listen,' and so he diligently responds and links to critics, and holds up his end of the conversation. 'You can't fake it,' he says. Dell's team is stanching the flow of bad buzz. By Dell's measure, negative blog posts about it have dropped from 49 per cent to 22 per cent. And the Dell Hell posts on my blog, which used to come up high on a Google search for the company, are now relegated to second-page search-engine Siberia. 'That change in perception just doesn't happen with a press release,' Menchaca says.

But reality still has to catch up to perception. To this day, I get blog comments and e-mails from disgruntled Dell customers. The University of Michigan's PC satisfaction scores show Dell dropping from 78 per cent in 2006 to 74 per cent this year. Internal Dell measurements showed satisfaction was actually much worse than that. A year ago, it was 58 per cent among core users, even lower in the high end. That, Hunter says, made the boss 'go ballistic.' Today, Hunter's measurements show satisfaction among high-end customers at more than 80 per cent and among core consumers at 74 per cent – numbers that he says must further improve. 'I think what the Web has brought is the voice of that 25 per cent,' Hunter says.

Customer collaboration

But the opportunities created by the conversation go far beyond dousing fires. The cant among executives trying to play the Web 2.0 game is that the customer is in charge. Well, if you really mean that, if you cede control to your customers, they can add tremendous value. Dell's customers not only make product suggestions and warn of problems, they help fellow customers fix them. Today, customers share their knowledge in so many ways that Dell's team says the challenge is to manage that knowledge and spread it.

To enable collaboration, the company is starting wikis that users can edit together. To encourage interaction, Dell plans to experiment with loyalty programs, rewarding good customers with gifts, opportunities to meet Michael, service upgrades, and possibly discounts. I ask whether they'd compensate helpful users, creating a marketplace of advice.

But Manish Mehta, head of e-commerce, is uncomfortable with payment, fearing it might compromise the credibility of these customers in their communities. And credible advocates are at the heart of the strategy Dell's new chief marketing officer, Mark Jarvis, is devising. 'By listening to our customers,' he says, 'that is actually the most perfect form of marketing you could have.'

I contend that this marks a fundamental shift in the relationship of customers with companies. Dell and its customers are collaborating on new forms of content and marketing, but note that they are doing this without the help of media and marketing companies.

Michael Dell predicts that customer relationships will 'continue to be more intimate.' He even speaks of 'co-creation of products and services,' a radical notion from a giant manufacturer. 'I'm sure there's a lot of things that I can't even imagine, but our customers can imagine,' Dell says, still sounding very bloggish. 'A company this size is not going to be about a couple of people coming up with ideas. It's going to be about millions of people and harnessing the power of those ideas.' Once you can hear them.

Online PR and reputation management, through monitoring, analysing and influencing online conversations, has become a crucial part of any digital marketer's arsenal. It serves to raise your profile, and to bolster and protect the hard-earned online reputation that is so essential to your online success.

Case study: Repak

Brief

Repak is Ireland's industry-funded organization (not for profit) whose aim it is to facilitate and grow packaging recycling. In addition to meeting Ireland's recycling target, Repak also has a key role in educating businesses and households with national campaigns and sponsorship.

There are two distinct audiences that Repak needs to communicate with: 1) consumers: Repak needs to increase awareness and the level of recycling; and 2) organizations that Repak targets as members, which in turn pay the recycling fees to fund recycling and help Repak run as a scheme.

The statement of objectives is:

- to increase the recycling message among a younger, more dynamic audience;
- to create an active level of engagement, dialogue and connection with 18- to 25-year-olds and to create a platform for future programmes;
- to personify the Repak brand and make it more attractable and approachable to a younger market;
- to promote and drive traffic through the Repak website;
- to mirror the traditional campaigns through a media-rich experience.

Programme planning and strategy

With the 18- to 25-year-olds or 'digital natives' it was decided that use of new digital media would be the best way of not only reaching but more importantly engaging with a community that could create a platform for future campaigns. In-depth research and focus groups were carried out, which supported the fact that new media were a new and innovative way to appeal to the youth market in support of Repak's information campaigns.

To enable two-way symmetrical communications, Slattery Communications decided to launch a new media campaign to supplement their national campaigns, using: 1) a Repak Bebo page – specifically used to target the 18- to 25-year-olds; and 2) a Repak blog site – targeted at more corporate entities and Repak members.

The Bebo page was interactive, fun and attracted the correct demographic that Repak sought to engage. Some of the highlights included the following:

- A 'Repak' skin with logo was developed especially for the site, and links were available not only to the Repak website and any releases issued but also to the blog site, YouTube page and later the online carbon calculator that was launched later in the year.
- The Bebo page was located at repakrecycling.bebo.com and was accessible to the public. It was highly interactive in that it had polls, blogs, a whiteboard drawing competition, photos, a quiz, a video and a blog section.
- There was an information section that explained what Repak is and what it does.
- There was a blog section, which gave lots of information, was regularly updated and was light-hearted and as fun as possible.
- A large network of over 1,000 friends was formed, which ensured that a large number of people were regularly alerted when the site was updated.
- The comment and whiteboard section allowed two-way interaction with people leaving comments and whiteboard drawings.

The blog site was run as a sub-page and link off the Repak website and was available at http://www.repakrecycling.blogspot.com/. All the content was entered by Repak, and all releases and events relevant to Repak were posted and commented on. This site allowed more and more search engines to pick up the blog sign and this then was linked back to the Repak home page, enabling Repak's corporate message to be communicated in a new and exciting way.

Results

With over 5,000 visitors in the first weeks after the launch and with over 1,000 unique friends to date, the Bebo site was a great success. As well as accessing the page, visitors invested time and effort in leaving comments, drawing pictures, answering quizzes and taking polls – all with a recycling theme. With Repak struggling to engage with youth post-primary and post-secondary education, the large uptake of third-level students accessing Bebo allowed Repak to further interact with a demographic that they considered they had neglected.

The statistics below were accessed in March 2008 (site launched October 2007):

- over 17,000 site views;
- over 1,000 friends;
- over 100 YouTube video views;
- international users from the United States, the UK, Germany and France.

Another objective of this campaign was to increase views to Repak's official website (www.repak.ie). When analysing the views over the course of the campaign (31 October 2007 to 13 March 2008) with the same period in the previous year, an increase of over 12,000 page impressions was observed. With no online advertising employed by Repak, much of this increase can be attributed to Slattery's new media campaign.

Campaign credits

Client: Repak Marketing Manager, Darrell Crowe
PR agency: Slattery Communications, Dublin
Slattery Communications Account Director: Eoin Kennedy

Images

http:// www.repakrecyling.bebo.com

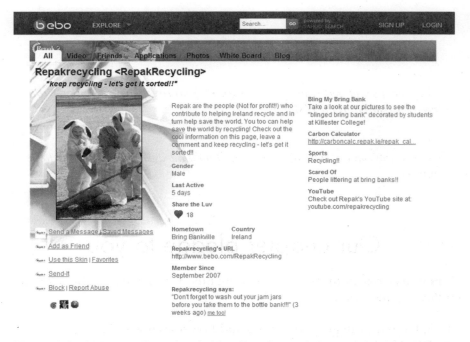

Figure 8.3 Irish recycling organization Repak used the popular social media platform Bebo to engage with its 18–25 year old target audience as part of this campaign

9 Affiliate marketing and strategic partnerships

Give me a set of golf clubs, fresh air and a beautiful partner and you can keep the clubs and the fresh air!

(Jack Benny)

In this new wave of technology, you can't do it all yourself, you have to form alliances.

(Carlos Slim Helú)

Our chapter pledge to you

When you reach the end of this chapter you'll have answers to the following questions:

- What is a strategic partnership and how does it work?
- Would a strategic partnership suit my business?
- How do I go about setting up a strategic partnership?
- What is affiliate marketing and how does it work?
- What can affiliate marketing do for my business?

Recognizing opportunities for strategic partnership

In the context of digital marketing, 'strategic partnerships' are most often defined by a deal between two (or more) parties where the desired outcome is a win–win for all concerned. Ideally a strategic partnership should be about synergy: all parties should come out of the relationship with more than any of them could have achieved alone.

One way to visualize a strategic partnership is in a bricks-and-mortar 'retail' context: suppliers rent space in high-traffic department stores in order to sell their products or services to customers who visit that store. The store brings in the traffic, suppliers sell their wares, the customer gets more choice – everybody wins.

Almost exactly the same process occurs online. A website that attracts large volumes of traffic will seek out long-term partnerships with suppliers to rent space in sections of their website; at the same time, online retailers or 'e-tailers' are looking for additional online 'venues' to peddle their wares. When they come together in the right circumstances you have all the ingredients for a mutually beneficial strategic partnership. Of course, the 64-million-dollar question in all of this is how to agree the balance of risk.

Online strategic partnerships usually go something like this

A large portal with a million visitors per day sells inventory (space) on its site to a travel company to advertise its products and special offers. In that scenario the burden of risk is entirely with the travel company – it is paying to advertise on the portal's website in the hope of attracting new customers. But, wait a minute, isn't that just a form of online advertising?

Yes, except that, in order to mitigate some of the risk, the travel company may negotiate with the portal to lower the cost of rental in exchange for certain incentives. The incentive could be exclusive products or offers for the portal's users (increasing the perceived value of the portal site, attracting and retaining more visitors).

With a tangible mutual benefit on the table, there's a good chance the portal site will be tempted to reduce the required advertising investment in return for:

- guarantees for their users in relation to a special offer – possibly around exclusivity;
- a revenue share of business accruing from the campaign, which can be tracked using page tags and analytics software;
- a long-term deal that can guarantee portal owners a healthy ROI.

Because portal owners now have a vested interest they also agree to do some editorial and PR around the advertising to build up the partnership.

Hold on, though – doesn't that smack a little of sponsorship? The burden of risk is still almost completely with the e-tailer. While there may certainly be some value in the 'exclusivity' element of the deal, it still doesn't feel balanced, because on the basis of no 'business being transacted' the only real loser is the merchant – in our case the travel company. And if it's a long-term deal that doesn't bode well for it.

A strategic partnership should be clearly balanced on both sides, with risk being shared throughout. Just because a portal has millions of users and a premium for advertising space on its site, that doesn't mean it is going to be worse off by adopting a revenue-share approach rather than one that consists of guaranteed cash. That view may not be the one regularly peddled by portal owners around the world, but nonetheless it is true!

Surely the aim of portal owners should be to maintain and grow traffic to their site, ensuring the content is up to date and up to scratch and that they offer users something of real value – in that respect they're like good old-fashioned media. How, then, does it suit users if the site offers a series of exclusive offers backed by marketers and ultimately paid for by the highest bidder? In a word, it doesn't, but it's a practice that has been rife among websites that, understandably, have been focused on using every trick in the book to maximize advertising revenue on the site, often enticing marketers with that tired old formula of advertising masquerading as editorial (or special offers) in an effort to bolster advertising opportunity.

Here's an example.

Damian Ryan shares first-hand experience of strategic partnerships:

In 2007 I spent several months working in the European and North American markets trying to secure 'strategic partnerships' for a client in the online video gaming sector. Most high-traffic sites would throw in an opening gambit along the lines of: 'Well, you'll need to give us two million bucks.' Despite my best efforts to minimize cash outlay, it didn't take me long to realize that these sites didn't particularly care *what* appeared on their sites: their job was to fill the space available and generate revenue, and they were doing that job extremely well.

Undeterred I realized that I had to take a different tack, and approached the sites with a 'content' rather than a 'commercial' angle. Essentially I was seeking their agreement and endorsement that 'Yes, this video games idea will definitely be of interest to our visitors.' Although this was a far more laborious approach, it worked much better for us, and as a result we found some really worthwhile strategic partnerships with minimal cash outlay and a genuine feeling that we were working together on the same team.

My advice to marketers seeking strategic partnerships with high-traffic sites is as follows:

- Do not enter into long-term arrangements without *fully testing the site* first. This is the real beauty of digital marketing – the ability to *test before you invest*.
- If you do decide to go for a long-term deal, make sure this is going to be of ongoing interest to the end users. Vary the content; change your offers regularly; use seasonality or other features to mix things up. You don't want to end up with the same message, day in, day out – except, of course, when it works!
- Talk to the site's other strategic partners – find out how long deals have been in place and how they value the association. Ask them how they go about tracking performance, etc. If possible, find out which strategic partnerships they *no longer* run on the site, and what happened. Marketers can be quite guarded with this kind of information, so you may not get it – but if you can overcome their reticence the information can be invaluable.
- Agree how performance will be measured from day one, and ensure your advertising and promotional messages are fully 'tagged' to track all necessary data – remember, it's not about clicks; it's about actual conversions.
- Be prepared to disclose profit margins; seek to build a close, transparent relationship with the site, a relationship where both parties fully understand the commercial realities and the mutual benefit involved. A little bit of patience and commitment up front will certainly help to establish realistic expectations.

What is affiliate marketing?

Wikipedia defines affiliate marketing thus:

> Affiliate Marketing is a web-based marketing practice in which a business rewards one or more affiliates for each visitor or customer brought about by the affiliate's marketing efforts.
>
> Affiliate marketing is also the name of the industry where a number of different types of companies and individuals are performing this form of internet marketing, including affiliate networks, affiliate management companies and in-house affiliate managers, specialized 3rd party vendors, and various types of affiliates/publishers who promote the products and services of their partners.
>
> Affiliate marketing overlaps with other internet marketing methods to some degree, because affiliates often use regular advertising methods. Those methods include organic search engine optimization, paid search engine marketing, email marketing and in some sense display advertising. On the other hand, affiliates sometimes use less orthodox techniques like publishing reviews of products or services offered by a partner.

In simplistic terms, therefore, affiliate marketing is the practice of driving traffic from one site to another in return for reward.

Where did all this start? Surprise, surprise, it's our friends from the oldest business in the world again! This time, though, we don't need to travel as far as ancient Pompeii to find them: a quick hat-tip here to Cybererotica.com, which is widely heralded as the site that introduced affiliate marketing to the world wide web.

At a more 'family-friendly' level, CDNow was the first site to really make *cents* (sorry, couldn't resist) out of this type of programme. It launched its affiliate marketing initiatives in 1994, and was soon followed by perhaps the most famous online affiliate marketer of them all, Amazon, and many others. As is so often the case with any new form of media, porn flexes its marketing muscles first and is rapidly followed by early adopters and then 'online transactional brands' before the rest of the world trundle aboard. Right now, affiliate marketing is very much the staple diet of adult, gaming and retail sites across the web, but it is rapidly extending its reach into other vertical markets like mobile phones and finance, which are, incidentally, the highest-spending categories in global online marketing.

The affiliate marketing ecosystem

Affiliate marketing is still treated by many as a bit of a dark art within the overall marketing mix. Many brands are wary of the potential for

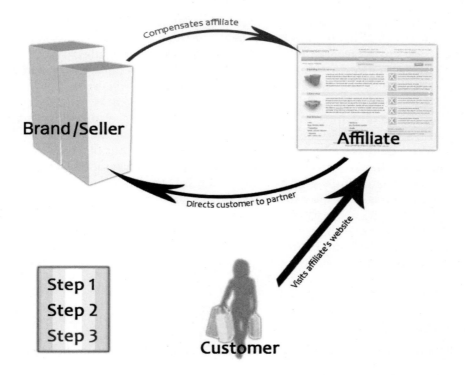

Figure 9.1 A diagram depicting how basic affiliate marketing works. For simplicity this diagram shows a 'do it yourself' affiliate arrangement, where the web merchant is running its own affiliate programme. Things can get a little more complicated when an affiliate network acts as an intermediary between merchant and consumer, but the basic premise is the same

misrepresentation and seek reassurances on a range of issues, including security, fraud and *brand bidding*.

'Brand bidding' is the term used to describe the practice of affiliates buying keywords on PPC programmes relating directly to brands or trademarks, with the sole objective of driving traffic towards the brand site and generating income for the affiliate. Many marketers want to maintain control over their own brand names, believing that this is, in essence, *their* traffic to begin with and that affiliates or other partners should stay away from these particular keywords and focus on more 'long-tail' keyword phrases to drive traffic. In other words, some marketers don't want to find themselves competing with affiliate partners in the SERPs.

Others are more enthusiastic about affiliate marketing and regard it as an integral part of their overall online marketing operations. On the plus side, affiliate marketing offers you a ready-made sales force operating on a reward or commission-only basis – in an age when marketers continuously seek ways to offset risk this surely has to be worth investigating, right?

On the negative side there are plenty of challenges surrounding measurement, and a lack of clear communication channels between affiliates and brands. For example, say a customer clicks on a special offer on an affiliate site, only to discover on arriving at the brand site that the offer has already expired – that's bad news for the affiliate and for the brand, because both lose revenue potential, but more seriously they also alienate a customer, perhaps for good (and, remember, online consumers are highly accomplished when it comes to letting their peers know about bad online experiences).

Today things are starting to hot up on the affiliate front. Early in 2008 Time Warner's AOL acquired affiliate network buy.at, and in the travel sector Expedia-owned TripAdvisor acquired Holidays Watchdog, deals that demonstrate how seriously investors are treating the whole affiliate business model.

But who are these people?

Meet your affiliates

The most *basic affiliates* are individuals (or companies run by individuals) or larger organizations who leverage their web properties to suck traffic from around the web and then push that traffic out to brand sites in return for commission. A click on an affiliate site can pay handsomely for high-value transactions. One web hosting company, for example, pays its affiliates up to $600 for new business. More traditional affiliates, such as poker rooms and casinos, pay up to $400 for a new account and a decent share of all revenue earned too. So there's plenty of incentive.

Affiliates may be considered by some as the bottom feeders in the affiliate ecosystem, but they are a vital component in achieving any sort of scale through investment in the affiliate marketing channel. You should look after your affiliates as well as you'd look after your own sales force. Equally, the age-old adage 'Be wary of strangers bearing gifts' applies, and you should make sure you have controls and measures in place to monitor your affiliates: there is no point in signing up 100 affiliates who are unchecked, unmotivated and unproductive.

Moving up a notch, you have what are known as *super-affiliates*. These would typically include price comparison sites like moneysupermarket. com and pricerunner.com as well as loyalty sites like the Irish-owned pigsback.com (the term 'on the pig's back' is derived from an old Gaelic expression that essentially means someone is 'on to something good'). Super-affiliates do pretty much the same thing as affiliates, but on a much larger scale. Companies like E-conversions, for example, operate as super-affiliates for major brands such as Dell, British Gas and SKY in the UK market. They are very much part of the marketing furniture for the brands they represent, and are ubiquitous players in the vertical markets that have been quick to embrace the opportunity presented by affiliate marketing: finance, electronics, travel and retail joining the already-established bastions of casinos, gaming and porn. The scope of affiliate marketing continues to grow, with other sectors, such as fashion, getting involved.

Sitting above super-affiliates in the hierarchy are the *affiliate networks* – these are significant enterprises like Commission Junction and TradeDoubler, and many others that specialize purely in affiliate marketing and essentially act as brokers between brands and affiliates.

One example we encountered at the 2008 Internet World show in London was the US-owned Affiliate Response Network; their proposition is very straightforward. Once you are set up as a client and they conduct some initial testing on search terms (to find out what keywords pull relevant, targeted traffic) they connect your brand to a high-performing online network of affiliates focused on getting results. They will work closely with you to assess the optimal channels to pull targeted traffic: this could be e-mail, search, display, emerging media and so on. Typical models of business they support include cost per lead, cost per sale, etc. The network also provides clients with real-time tracking and reporting systems, an essential ingredient in understanding the power of affiliate marketing and also in allowing marketers to get a more accurate picture of which digital marketing elements really work for them.

So who lives in this ecosystem? Consumers, clients, affiliates, super-affiliates, affiliate networks and not forgetting, of course, Google and the search engines (which sounds suspiciously like a dodgy 1970s rock band). Depending on your view of the world, Google with its distributed AdSense pay-per-click model is the biggest affiliate marketing player of them all. Then again, in the words of the great Jerry Reitman, former head of direct marketing worldwide for Leo Burnett's, 'at the end of the day... it's all advertising'.

The click that really counts

The reason affiliate marketing has been so successful is that advertisers pay only for the last click or the most recent click that creates an action – but as the business grows many are starting to question this way of measurement. Think about it like this: you want a new suit, so you nip down to the shops, try a selection on, then return home, head online and buy one exactly like the one you liked in the shop. The question: should the shop receive any kind of reward?

In the affiliate world this is an issue that doesn't look likely to be solved any time soon, but it is on the radar, and as online affiliate marketing continues to evolve there will be ever-increasing pressure to find a solution, necessity as ever being the mother of invention.

Taking our shop scenario and applying it to online affiliate networking we see an equally skewed scenario unfolding. Your affiliates can attract consumers to their site through investing in stunning e-mail marketing campaigns and their highly honed search marketing techniques (the best affiliates are extremely good at this, with many outperforming brand websites for competitive keyword phrases in the SERPs). They can educate those consumers, woo them and engage them through a host of special offers, help them to compare prices, engage with them and build a relationship. And then our fickle friend the digital consumer goes straight back into a search engine, types in the brand name and buys the product direct from the company website. For all their hard work and investment the affiliates get zip, nada, zilch! Is that right?

There's also the issue that, from a marketing investment standpoint, it is crucial that you, the marketer, know exactly where the actual 'sale' was made. When and where did the consumer's level of interest in your product suddenly pass the tipping point and become a desire to purchase?

Fundamentally, the more we know about the steps consumers go through in purchasing our products, and the further back we can track that interaction between consumers and brands online, the more we'll see investment shifting from offline to online marketing. Transparency in marketing is key as we move from the era of interruption into the age of digital engagement.

What advertisers should do

- Job number one is to crank up the computer and have a good look around that interweb thingamajig. Examine both affiliate sites and other brands in your particular space. You'll quickly get a feel for whether your product or service is suited to the affiliate marketing model. There's a good list of vertical markets available on www. affiliatetips.com.
- Decide if you want to manage the affiliate process in-house or out-source it to a third party like an affiliate network. Initially you could

decide to test a series of propositions in-house to avoid paying fees to finance an affiliate network's learning curve, but if yours is a common, widely used product there's a good chance the network already know what they're doing.

- Start off small and build it. Test everything: creative messages, day parts, channels, regions, etc. You may also need to establish your policy in relation to brand bidding.
- If you allow affiliates to bid on your brand name and trademarks to generate traffic it is important that you have some controls in place. You may decide to limit this to your top (best-performing) affiliates only, for example. As with many other things in marketing, the Pareto principle applies: 80 per cent of your revenues from affiliate channels are likely to accrue from your top 20 per cent of affiliates.
- Measure as much as you can. While we may have to live with the 'last click' metric for a while yet, trying to understand the true potential of affiliate marketing is now part of the job for marketers.
- Love your sales team. There aren't many situations in the real world where you'll find a team of experts waiting to hand you business for what amounts to very little investment on your part. Seize the opportunity, and treat your affiliates as part of your extended marketing team, because essentially that's what they are.

As it becomes tougher to compete for consumer mind-share in the digital marketplace, brands are going to need all the friends they can get. In the future, affiliate marketing could well mesh with mainstream marketing to form a hybrid marketing landscape, where the marketer is leader of a wide and varied series of sales channels, each doing its own thing, each one accountable and each rewarded based on performance.

In the UK alone affiliate marketing was worth £3 billion in 2007, up 45 per cent year on year (e-consultancy). It's growing quickly, and it's here to stay.

TravelAffiliate – overview of a successful affiliate programme

TravelAffiliate is an Irish-based affiliate programme that helps travel companies to sell their products online through a network of affiliate website publishers using a cost-per-acquisition medium. That means that advertisers who join the TravelAffiliate network pay only when *an actual booking* is made. TravelAffiliate works closely with large travel brands including Gohop, the Irish Hotels Federation, the

Star Alliance, ebookers, Tour America, Sunway, the Louis Fitzgerald group and Holidaysonline.

The basics

TravelAffiliate essentially does the following:

- provides Irish travel suppliers with an online marketing tool that is cost-effective, measurable and results focused;
- gives website owners an opportunity to generate additional revenue and to get useful, relevant and up-to-date content for their sites;
- provides all clients (advertisers and affiliates) with transparent and accurate real-time reporting;
- maintains a reliable and productive network of publishers;
- helps publishers to identify the best 'mix' of ad partners for their particular site;
- promotes new advertisers to its network of publishers.

Keeping track of online transactions

The TravelAffiliate programme uses cookies and tags (see Chapter 5) to track advertiser sales and leads. The TravelAffiliate cookies are used solely for the purpose of tracking performance and paying publishers the relevant commissions when a consumer completes an agreed transaction (ie fills in a lead generation form or makes a booking). Because more than 99 per cent of all internet users have cookies enabled in their browsers, cookies provide a very effective way of tracking conversions from the initial click-through to the actual transaction.

How it works

Travel suppliers upload their advertising content to the TravelAffiliate system. It could be text links, banner or display links, or even a complete booking engine. Website publishers can select the partners they want to feature on their websites, and are rewarded financially whenever a sale is generated through a referral originating from their site, as long as the transaction happens within 30 days of the original click-through.

What TravelAffiliate is essentially doing is brokering the relationships between advertisers and publishers, and facilitating independent management of those relationships. Advance tracking and reporting technology helps to minimize potential disputes and allows both advertisers and affiliates (publishers) to track performance in real time. TravelAffiliate tracks and reports on a wide variety of metrics, including impressions, clicks, sales and sales values. Suppliers upload their campaign content only once, and TravelAffiliate manages the process of establishing relationships with publishers and assigning unique tracking IDs and all of the administration.

Affiliates have access to metrics on merchant performance, including earnings per click (EPC), conversion and average approval time. For each ad creative/campaign there are detailed statistics on impressions, clicks, click-through rates (CTR), earnings per click (EPC) and conversion rates.

TravelAffiliate demonstrates how an effective affiliate marketing programme can offer a clear win–win–win for suppliers/marketers, online publishers and affiliate networks.

Case study: O2 Live 8 mobile ticketing

Brief

O2 has a long-standing involvement in the music space, and through its already-established relationship with the music industry O2 was able to launch the ultimate ticketing competition for Bob Geldof's Live 8 event. The proposal aimed to support the 'Make Poverty History' campaign, raising awareness of Third World poverty, prior to the G8 summit in Scotland.

O2's communication objectives were:

- to demonstrate how mobile technology can be used to support the music industry for other mobile activities, in addition to ring tone and content downloads;
- to show that the mobile can be used as a force for social good;
- to engage the UK population in entering the competition via text to win their tickets and attend the Live 8 event;
- to distribute 130,000 tickets in a two-week time frame, in advance of the concert in Hyde Park on 2 July 2005;
- to ensure that the ticketing added to the sense of occasion championed by the Band Aid Trust and the Live 8 Make Poverty History campaign.

Campaign strategy

In order to meet the communication objectives, O2 developed a campaign strategy that promised to create mass awareness of the text mechanic through all media channels. This was to include details of how to enter, steps to follow and how to collect the Live 8 tickets. The strategy was developed to ensure that coverage continued in the run-up to the event and to help create a sense of occasion around the text ticketing.

Campaign details

At 8 am on 6 June, a press conference was hosted with Bob Geldof, and a release was issued across all media, including national press, radio and TV stations, announcing the O2 text ticketing mechanic. (The text mechanic was developed via a 'free, network independent competition' that required people to answer a multiple choice question about Live 8.)

Statements on how the network was coping and the initial text numbers were released the following day. A follow-up release detailing the total number of text entries was released to generate further widespread coverage. Ticket collection events were organized at flagship O2 retail stores throughout the UK, with broadcast crews and photographers in attendance interviewing the first customers to collect their tickets.

Story angles on the whole campaign were developed for new media and mobile correspondents.

Results

- Nearly 2.1 million people sent in messages applying for tickets (around 70,000 of these were sent via post). This was the first mass text ticketing event ever to be held in the UK and set a new Guinness world record.
- At messaging peak, O2 received 611 messages per second.
- The ticket lottery raised over £3 million for Live 8 and delivered a fair and fast way to distribute the much-treasured tickets in a two-week window.
- A total of 53 pieces of print media coverage appeared, totalling an ad value of £353,771 and a PR value of £1,061,313.
- Over 100 pieces of broadcast coverage were achieved, communicating the text mechanic and ticket collection figures.
- The Live 8 ticketing story was extensively covered online by over 50 news, music and entertainment sites.
- O2's branding and messaging were heavily present in all coverage.
- The ticketing worked – thousands of people were in Hyde Park on 2 July championing 'Make Poverty History' ahead of the G8 summit.
- Text ticketing has become a key focus for O2 as part of its music strategy and has since been successfully rolled out at the O2 Wireless Festival.
- Ultimate ROI will be measured in numbers of people who have a chance to change their lives as a result of the G8 policies generated through public support for Make Poverty History and Live 8. O2 was part of a team of people and companies that helped to facilitate that voice.

Client comment

Sally Cowdry, Marketing Director, O2 UK:

> Live 8 was a landmark moment for mobile ticketing in the UK. Whilst O2 and other operators had forecast huge potential in this technology, the response for the Live 8 event exceeded our greatest expectations.

Glenn Manoff, Director of Communications, O2 UK:

> 2.1 million people made their voices heard by texting O2. The Live 8 mobile ticketing platform was not only successful in a logistical sense, but also helped the Live 8 foundation champion the cause to Make Poverty History, which we are extremely proud to be a part of.

Campaign credits

Marketing Director, O2 UK: Sally Cowdry
Director of Communications, O2 UK: Glenn Manoff
Advertising agency: Cohn & Wolfe, London

10 Digital media creative

For every idea out there, there's a way to get to it. Ask advertising's creative thinkers about their personal road maps to The Answer, and you confront a mix of fear and bravado, chilly logic and warm emotion. The process is one part reason, one part heart, and one (big) part pure, simple intuition.

(Terence Poltrack)

Creativity is a type of learning process where the teacher and pupil are located in the same individual.

(Arthur Koestler)

Life is 'trying things to see if they work'.

(Ray Bradbury)

Our chapter pledge to you

When you reach the end of this chapter you'll have answers to the following questions:

- How do businesses tackle the challenge of developing their digital creative?
- What are the key phases involved in the digital creative process?
- How do you evaluate the success of your creative campaign?
- What are the top tips for online creative success?

Creative application of digital media

The question of what actually constitutes a winning creative idea has been perplexing marketers the world over since the dawn of advertising. Way back in 1919 a young copywriter called Raymond Rubicam developed the 'copy in the drawer' approach to the conundrum. Rubicam simply jotted down his favourite campaign idea and put it in his desk drawer. After a few days of considering other options, Rubicam went back to his scribblings in the drawer and, if they still seemed to resonate with him, he ran with the idea. His unsophisticated approach was developed in a pre-digital world, a world where consumers weren't bombarded with thousands of marketing messages every day. Still, even in today's incredibly complex, hyper-connected world, the concept of keeping things simple retains much merit.

Estimates suggest that each of us receives a staggering 5,000 to 13,000 marketing messages, on average, *every single day*. This marketing communication 'noise' fills our lives and makes it increasingly difficult for individual marketing campaigns to be heard above the din. To stand out from the crowd demands something extraordinary, and that's why hitting the 'right' creative note with a digital campaign is so important.

Using an agency

Because of the substantial challenges involved in developing a cohesive and coherent digital campaign, many companies choose to bring in the experts to help: engaging the services of advertising or public relations professionals to guide the creative elements of their marketing campaigns.

Professional agencies and consultants don't come cheap, but if you have the budget to accommodate them they can help to get you off to a flying start with your digital marketing. Agencies employ 'creative' talent with the skills to take the germ of a marketing idea and transform it into an engaging, compelling and holistic multi-channel marketing campaign. The new challenges thrown up by digital technology over recent years have led to the rise of specialist digital marketing agencies to apply that creative process in the virtual realm. These agencies focus their efforts on harnessing the power of interactive technologies to reach out and engage with online consumers.

So, assuming you have the budget for it, you could draft in a digital marketing agency (or a traditional agency with a dedicated digital team) to meet your needs. Ideally you'll want to identify a number of potential agencies based on their expertise in digital media, the reputation of their previous work, and their perceived reputation in online communities.

The beauty of digital media creative is that it's so visible and accessible online. A quick search should reveal examples of digital campaigns created by your shortlisted agencies – along with plenty of online discussion about what they got right or otherwise (if you struggle to find digital campaigns by your shortlisted agencies perhaps it's a sign that you need to rethink your shortlist). Make sure that all agencies on your shortlist have relevant expertise in the digital arena and that they are up to speed with the current and emerging opportunities that digital media creative offers (after reading this book, you'll have a fairly good foundation for making that assessment).

When you've identified your shortlist of prospective agencies, you'll typically provide them with a comprehensive brief that covers background about your business, brand(s), target market, campaign goals and budget. Based on that brief your selected agencies will pitch for your business, presenting their ideas on how to execute your campaign.

You can choose to bring in a specialist agency on a project-by-project basis, engaging them to undertake a specific marketing activity, such as developing an e-mail marketing campaign, or to manage online advertising for the launch of a new product. Alternatively, you can choose to hire a full-service agency to look after your entire digital marketing portfolio for a specified time period.

Doing it yourself

The other option, of course, is to handle your digital marketing needs in-house. The decision of whether to choose an agency or carry out your own digital marketing normally depends on a combination of factors:

- *Your marketing budget:* Depending on how much is in the pot for digital marketing, hiring an agency may or may not be financially viable.
- *Your in-house digital marketing skills:* You'll need to have, hire or be prepared to spend both time and money developing your own in-house digital marketing skills if you want to manage your digital campaigns yourself.
- *Time:* If time to market is important, you may want to lean towards external expertise: people who can hit the ground running and get your digital campaign off to a flying start. You can always build your in-house expertise alongside the professionals – learn from working with them, and bring things in-house once your own team is ready.

Generally the larger your marketing budget, the more potential benefit you're likely to accrue through bringing in an agency. That said, the very essence of digital technology is the way it can empower people to achieve remarkable things. With the right tools there's absolutely no reason why you can't manage your digital marketing in-house.

If you decide to hire an agency, that's great – they'll look after you from here. For the rest of this chapter we're going to assume that you're taking on the development of your own digital campaign. But where do you start?

Coming up with a great idea

Eminent US scientist Linus Pauling once observed that 'the best way to have a good idea is to have lots of ideas'. He had a point. If you want to come up with great digital marketing ideas you need to be thinking them up constantly, considering new approaches and different ways to reach out to and engage with your audience. You should mull them over and write them down. Share them; get input from others. Many will wither and die under scrutiny, but some will survive and grow, perhaps even flourish.

When you're nurturing your ideas, it might be useful to consider the following process of exploration, insight, execution and evaluation.

Exploration

This phase involves the gathering of relevant information: facts, experiences, history, knowledge and feelings. The important thing here is to use all of the resources at your disposal to gather accurate and relevant facts. You need to *really* know your market, its demographics, lifestyle and needs.

According to Esther Lee, CEO of Euro RSCG North America and President of Global Brands, it's vital that we as marketers stop thinking of consumers as passive information receivers, but rather as co-authors of a brand's personality. Consumers develop strong feelings of attachment to a brand and can identify very strongly with a particular product. The internet has enabled groups of passionate consumers to communicate, share their experiences and build virtual communities around their affinity for well-known brands. An example of this phenomenon is the growth of Apple Mac User Groups online (www.apple.com/usergroups).

It is essential to know your market intimately – in terms of not just hard figures and demographic data but the softer human aspects: their beliefs and feelings about your brand, and their relationship with it. You want to preserve and enhance that relationship, not inadvertently destroy it.

To communicate effectively with your market through digital media you have to know your market's online behaviour. What are the most popular sites visited by your target market? How do they interact online? Do they prefer to get their information by e-mail, through social networks or by internet search? Do they shop online? You also need to be clear about exactly what you're trying to achieve in your campaign. You need to set specific goals. Are you looking to increase market share? By how much? Or perhaps you're aiming to recruit a certain number of new users to your online community or to increase product awareness. The list is practically endless, but the point is that you need to define explicit objectives against which the success of your campaign can be measured effectively.

Insight

Brainstorming with a group of people is always a great way to bounce around ideas and let those with promise float to the top. If you're familiar with the TV series *Mad Men*, which is based on a 1960s advertising agency, you'll remember the stereotypical scenes of men lounging in smoke-filled rooms, brandishing scraps of paper with scribbled ideas and lots of alcohol!

In the 1980s, advertising creative teams eschewed the sedentary approach of their forebears. Creative thinking became synonymous with activity: pacing a room, throwing scrunched-up paper into miniature basketball hoops and generally getting more physical. TV shows like *Thirtysomething* depicted many such scenes as characters grappled with the challenge of generating campaign ideas.

Some advertising creatives prefer to clear their minds completely and let their subconscious work on the problem. They actively don't focus on the creative challenge, believing that the 'big idea' will come when they're not looking for it!

Other techniques for idea generation include things like changing the context in which you set the product or service, asking 'What if?'-style questions, looking for connections between seemingly disparate ideas, identifying opposites, altering set patterns, making unusual comparisons and looking for humour. The identification of opposites may have unearthed some of the zany characters introduced in the CFMP Advisory Board's 'GetTheGlass' campaign (www.gettheglass.com; see the case study in Chapter 4). In the campaign, each member of the Adachi family suffers from an ailment caused by milk deprivation.

Unexpected juxtaposition – putting the brand into unconventional situations and seeing what evolves – is another useful approach to idea generation. Diesel favour this approach in their marketing, and the 'Heidies' campaign concept of models stealing the latest 'Heidies collection' and holding a Diesel sales assistant hostage live online could have evolved from just such a technique.

How will you know when you have come up with a winning idea? The legendary David Ogilvy developed a useful five-point checklist for traditional media that applies equally well in the digital age:

- Did it make me gasp when I first saw it?
- Do I wish I had thought of it myself?
- Is it unique?
- Does it fit the strategy to perfection?
- Does it have longevity?

Answer 'yes' five times and there's a good chance you've hit on a winner. An alternative approach is revamping Raymond Rubicam's 'copy-in-a-drawer' concept. Let the campaign idea rest in a virtual drawer – or folder – on your computer. After a few days of exploring alternatives, go back to it and, if you still feel it has merit, perhaps it is the 'big idea' you've been searching for.

The benefits of unearthing the right idea can be immense. A great idea will give your campaign broader reach, improved longevity, increased resonance with your audience, and in special cases a universal appeal that results in it transcending the boundaries of your original market. That's exactly what happened with Dove's Self-Esteem Fund, a campaign originally developed by Unilever Canada for the Canadian marketplace but adopted globally to phenomenal acclaim (see the case study in Chapter 2).

Execution

Once you have your idea, the next step is choosing what form of digital communication best suits your campaign. Is it online advertising, e-mail marketing, content sponsorship, viral marketing, mobile marketing, social networking, e-couponing, e-competitions, a combination of the above or something else entirely?

Online advertising typically consists of banner (display) ads and the contextual ad units typified by search engine pay-per-click advertising. Banner ads are generally created as flat image file (a GIF, JPEG or PNG), embedded HTML snippets, a JavaScript applet (a sort of mini-application) or a multimedia object (using technologies like Java, Flash or AJAX to combine text, animation, sound, interactivity, etc). The 'banner' moniker is a throwback to the early days of online advertising, when the typical ad was a horizontal banner-like strip across the top of a page full of text. These days banner ads come in a wide variety of standard shapes

Figure 10.1 The Dove Self-Esteem Fund campaign was originally devised for a local campaign by Unilever Canada, but its global potential was soon realized

and sizes (see the standards and guidelines on www.iab.net), as well as a few less standard ones. Whenever a banner ad is displayed on a web page an 'impression' is generated.

There are a number of creative choices when it comes to online display ad formats:

- *Floating ads:* banners that float above the content of a page.
- *Rich media ads:* These ads feature an opportunity for the viewer to interact with the communication. They generally incorporate dynamic features such as sound, video or Flash animation.
- *Wallpaper ads:* ads that change the background of the page being viewed.
- *Trick banners:* banners designed to look like operating system or browser dialogue boxes rather than ads, complete with buttons. They may even contain an error message to capture attention and entice viewers to click. (*NB:* We're not advocating duplicitous ad

formats here but are including them in this listing for the sake of completeness. If you value your online reputation, be very wary of anything that attempts to hoodwink the user.)

- *Polite ads:* a large ad that downloads in sections rather than all at once, thereby minimizing the disruption of the viewing experience for the user.
- *Pop-up ads:* a new window displaying the advert that opens up in front of the current page.
- *Pop-under:* similar to the pop-up but the advert opens behind the active window and won't be seen until the user closes the window.
- *Leaderboard ads:* These are the horizontal banners located at the top of a page. Given their prominence and large area, these tend to be the first ads to hit the readers' eyeballs. Leaderboards offer plenty of space for eye-catching graphics and with their prominent placement are the most popular (and therefore expensive) display ad positions.
- *Big Box ads:* These are located on content pages where readers spend large amounts of time reading full-length articles. This is also among the largest display ad formats available, and offers the broadest scope for getting creative with your marketing message. It's also more difficult for people to ignore, as it's sitting smack in the middle of content they're reading. Examples of Big Box-style ads can typically be found on home pages, editorial content pages, photo galleries or any other content-rich pages.

Normally with display ads you purchase space on a particular page based either on a set number of impressions or on a performance-based pricing model (see 'The rise of performance-based advertising' in Chapter 5), and your ad will be served up in rotation each time a user requests that page. Contextual ads, in contrast, are served up according to keywords purchased by the advertiser, and will be displayed alongside contextually relevant content on a particular site *or network of sites*. Until relatively recently contextual ads were typically text ads (the classic example being search engine pay-per-click ads), but image and even rich media contextual advertising is becoming more common, as is a wider variety of ad formats as advertising and affiliate networks broaden their scope.

Other execution options include:

- *E-mail marketing:* creating an e-mail campaign to target new consumers, increase consumer loyalty or increase consumption of your product. E-mail marketing is a low-cost and potentially high-yield option. See Chapter 6 for more on e-mail marketing.
- *Content sponsorship:* You could choose to sponsor a section of a popular website whose content is likely to appeal to your target audience.

Sponsorship can be costly, so for it to be worthwhile you need to be sure that the site in question attracts significant traffic and that it has particular appeal to your target market. The value in sponsorship stems from the close connection between a site's content and your customers.

- *Viral marketing:* Viral marketing is all about harnessing online word of mouth to pass on your digital marketing message. Seeding specifically tailored viral content on social media sites, when you get it right, can result in a dramatic ripple effect, as your content is picked up and passed from friend to socially connected friend across the web. The DeAPlaneta case study (in Chapter 6) features a great example of the power of this form of communication. The personalization features in the e-mail sent as part of this campaign encouraged recipients to adapt the e-mail before forwarding it to their friends, family or online connections.

- *Mobile marketing:* The most popular form of mobile marketing in Europe and Asia *at the moment* is SMS messaging. It is important to note that, as with e-mail marketing, it is vital that recipients 'opt in' to get SMS messages and are given an easy way to opt out again at any time. Given the potentially invasive nature of SMS communication, it is key that the consumer is in control. The use of mobile marketing in the Live 8 campaign was a key factor in its success (see the case study in Chapter 9). Mobile marketing is on the verge of becoming much more than simple text messages (see Chapter 11 for a discussion on how the mobile sector looks likely to evolve over the coming years).

- *Social networking:* Social networking sites are essentially online communities of people with shared interests and activities (see Chapter 7). The most popular sites are MySpace and Facebook in the United States, Bebo, MySpace and Facebook in Europe, and Friendster, Orkut and CyWorld in Asia. Social media include blogs, groups and forums, wikis like Wikipedia, user-generated content sites like YouTube and Flickr, and product-rating and review sites like Epinion, LouderVoice and Amazon. These all facilitate online social interaction between peers. The Repak case study (Chapter 8) features an interesting use of Bebo to target the Irish youth market.

- *E-couponing:* the online distribution of printable money-off coupons that are redeemable at points of sale. E-sampling operates on the same principle; however, in this instance the product is redeemed without payment.

- *E-competitions:* digital competitions targeted at your market with a view to obtaining e-mail addresses, marketing information or product trial.

Table 10.1   Choosing a digital marketing execution

Aim of Campaign	Suggested Execution Methods
Grow brand awareness	Online advertising, content sponsorship and viral marketing.
Enhance brand image or consumer sentiment	Develop website, online advertising, e-mail marketing, mobile marketing or online competitions.
Product trial	Mobile marketing, e-mail marketing, online competitions, e-couponing and e-sampling.
Create brand loyalty	E-mail marketing, website creation, online newsletters, social networking and virtual communities.
Generate sales and/or leads	Search marketing, website creation, e-mail marketing and online advertising

Your digital marketing strategy and your goals for a particular campaign will guide your selection of execution method. The guidelines in Table 10.1, adapted from suggestions by P De Pelsmacker, M Geuens and J Van den Bergh in *Marketing Communications: A European Perspective* (Pearson, Harlow, 2006), will help to point you in the right direction.

Evaluation

One of the strengths of digital marketing is the fact it's so measurable. However, as we saw in Chapter 5, it is vital to choose the right metrics for your campaign and to ensure that the measurement of those metrics is accurate and meaningful. Some of the evaluation tools for assessing your campaign success are:

- *Online advertising metrics:* Pay-per-click (PPC) advertising service providers provide tracking information in your control panel on the number of viewers who actively engaged with your advert. It is important to note that this metric ignores the value of exposure: many people who view the advert may not act on the information until long after viewing your ad. If you confine your measurement to clicks you essentially miss an important component in your online campaign. (*NB:* You can also typically integrate click-through stats from your PPC campaigns into your web analytics package.)

- *Ad impressions:* Impressions measure the number of times your specific ad is requested by a user's browser. It is generally considered to be a reasonable measurement of the viewer's opportunity to see your advertising message.
- *Performance-based advertising:* Some advertising models allow you to choose the user behaviour you want to track in your digital campaign and to purchase your campaign advertising based on that behaviour. Performance measurement can be the number of e-mail addresses captured as part of the campaign, the online sales generated, the number of visitors to your website, subscriptions to your online newsletter, etc. This model is also referred to as pay per action or pay per acquisition (PPA).
- *Website analytics:* Page views, conversion rates, absolute unique visitors, new and returning visitors, bounce rate and abandonment can all be measured using appropriate web analytic software (see Chapter 5) and, if set up correctly, will allow you to establish what proportion of your visitors are arriving from each advertising campaign and how well they are converting, allowing you to tweak your campaigns accordingly.
- *E-mail marketing measurement:* E-mail delivery, bounce rates and opening rates are routinely measured. Further metrics will depend on the goal of the e-mail campaign. For example, do you want to collect e-mail addresses, sell something (direct marketing), conduct market research, etc? Whatever you're looking to achieve, you can set up your e-mail campaign to work with your web analytics solution to track overall performance.
- *Social networking metrics:* Social media expert Beth Kanter advocates tracking the following metrics for your social media campaigns: page views, visits, visitors, visitor info, time on site, bounce rate, referrers, entry and exit pages, click-through analysis and search engine entry. Since the use of social media involves an ongoing campaign that builds over time to achieve its objectives, it is necessary to identify trends emerging in your measurement rather than focusing on a snapshot of results at any given time.
- *E-couponing and e-sampling:* These strategies can be measured by tracking the numbers of users who interacted with the e-coupon or e-sampling communication compared to those who then go on to redeem the coupons. Users can be profiled and their behaviour analysed for future targeting.
- *Mobile marketing:* Most mobile handsets at the moment still don't support JavaScript, which is the usual mechanism used to tag ads so that they feed into your web analytics. The balance, however, is shifting as more powerful devices like Apple's iPhone and other

smartphones, integrating multimedia, web, data and connectivity features into a single unit, become more mainstream. Companies like Bango (http://bango.com), Quattro Wireless (www.quattrowireless. com) and others have developed services that specialize in mobile advertising and tracking. Mobile advertising, and the metrics to measure it, is an emerging field that's developing rapidly. Look out for some major advances in the ability to track, measure and manage your mobile campaigns over the next few years. (See Chapter 11 for a discussion on the future of mobile marketing.)

● *Viral marketing:* Viral is typically considered to be the creation of buzz, or getting consumers to spontaneously share your content with their network of online connections. Viral content spreads organically, distributed by consumers through their network of online connections. The specific metrics for measuring a viral campaign will vary depending on the campaign's execution – be it e-mail, online video, rich media interactive content or whatever else. Always ensure you consider how you're going to measure your viral campaign, and build tracking and measurement into the creative design from day one.

By tracking the campaign metrics of specific creative content you can quickly identify what does and doesn't resonate with your audience and adapt your campaigns accordingly. In the Dove Self-Esteem Fund campaign, Big Box ads were outperforming Leaderboard formats, so the campaign managers decided to weight the campaign in favour of Big Box ads, increasing response rates.

Digital creative: what works and what doesn't

We've moved from the age of interruption to the age of engagement, from a passive consumer to an active consumer who basically doesn't just sit back and wait for things to be delivered, but who goes and seeks things out. A whole new mind-set is needed in the way you create and develop work and how you plan your media.

So says Sir John Hegarty, founder of award-winning agency Bartle, Bogle, Hegarty. He reminds us that the internet is not a single medium but a mash-up of multiple media that's owned and controlled by its users. Digital technology encourages conversation, engagement and *listening*.

This view is shared by Goodby, Silverstein & Partners' Creative Director, Will McGinness:

> In creating work in a digital context, I think it's really important to treat the consumer with respect. With over 100 million websites online, people tend to think that you need to shout to get noticed. If the internet has illustrated anything, it's that you need to be relevant and smart to earn the respect of your customers. OK, so you don't always need to be smart. I guess the important thing is to create content that people like and want to engage with. It's that simple.

The specifics of your digital campaign, and the creative content you design to support it, will vary significantly depending on what you're promoting, the outcome you're looking for, the channels of engagement you choose to employ and the particular target audience you're hoping to connect with. That said, there are some overriding principles that it makes sense to embrace whatever the form of digital creative you're using:

- *Relevance:* Your digital marketing creative *must* be in tune with your market to have any chance of resonating with them and delivering results. Irrelevant material equals ignored message.
- *Interaction:* Online consumers increasingly expect an interactive experience when they choose to engage with online advertising. Design your creative with that in mind, acknowledge that the users are in control, and allow them to interact with the ad itself, with each other or with you, the advertiser.
- *Relationships:* Your digital campaigns are about much more than one-off promotion – they should focus on fostering productive long-term relationships with your target audience. Design your online creative to inspire conversation among your target community; then engage and participate in that conversation. Look, listen, learn and respond.

Marketing on the internet, as we've already discovered, is becoming less about broadcasting a message and more about engaging in ongoing dialogue with consumers. The internet has had a greater effect on consumer engagement than any other marketing medium (IAB Brand Engagement Study 2006, see www.iabuk.net) and, in the hyper-connected social web, engagement has become a critical success factor for digital marketers.

How do you make sure your advertising creative is engaging? Well, engaging campaigns typically share the following characteristics:

- *Respect your audience:* Fail in this one simple consideration and at best you risk alienating potential customers; at worst you could unleash an online backlash that will leave your reputation in tatters.
- *Offer a compelling value proposition:* Give your consumers something in return for their investment of time. It could be information, a useful application or simply entertainment – just make sure their engagement with your ad is rewarded with something relevant and genuinely valuable.
- *Employ an irreverent, informal or conversational tone:* Don't be officious or formal – but always bear the first point above in mind, and never be disrespectful of your audience.
- *Avoid hype:* Overt advertising or marketing speak will simply be ignored – use clear, simple language to spell out your value proposition.
- *Address an audience of one:* Speak to the individual rather than the entire demographic.
- *Play to digital's strengths:* Integrate intelligent metrics and analysis into your campaign; use the data to refine your offering so that it delivers what consumers actually want.

Nine top tips for successful online creative

Finding a compelling idea, choosing the right online execution channels, developing the creative content to support your campaigns and tracking and analysing the results can be challenging – but it's a challenge that, if you can rise to it, will bring substantial reward for your business. Below we outline nine top tips for creating compelling online creative to support your digital marketing campaigns.

1. Know what you're trying to achieve and how you plan to achieve it

Set specific, measurable goals for your campaign at the outset and decide on the psychological vehicles you'll use to engage your consumers. Your goal might be to increase sales of a particular product line by 20 per cent over a given time period. Psychological mechanisms you might select in order to achieve that goal include:

- *Reminder:* Use reminders to keep your brand front and centre in the consumer's subconscious. What you're aiming for here is to put your particular brand at the forefront of your customers' minds when they next come to make a purchase. This mechanism tends to work best with well-established brands in low-involvement categories like consumer packaged goods, where people make regular low-value purchases.

- *Reinforcement:* This is designed to strengthen the consumer's overall perception of an existing brand. It can be effective in both high- and low-involvement purchases, as long as the consumer is already aware of the brand.
- *Repositioning:* This is about changing the consumer's perception of your brand. To achieve this, online advertising needs to focus on strong brand imagery and powerful, iconic messaging to shift consumer perception in the desired direction (but remember to avoid the marketese).
- *Introduction:* This is used when you want to let people know about a new product or brand. Highlight brand presence and keep the message simple. If you need to communicate a more complicated message to introduce your new brand, product or service, consider high-visibility ad formats like rich media ads, floating ads or pop-ups (use pop-ups judiciously – they can be obtrusive, interrupt the user experience and get routinely blocked by pop-up-blockers).
- *Direct response:* This is used when you want to capture leads or generate sales. A prominent call to action and an emphasis on the benefits of the product are the key ingredients of direct-response advertising – online and offline.

2. Deliver tangible value

Simple really: make sure you give something back in exchange for your viewers' attention – whether it's information, entertainment or application. Deliver something of genuine value to people who give you their most valuable asset of all: their time.

3. Use simple iconic messages

In the digital medium, users are empowered to take control of their online journey. Internet users are, by and large, experienced web navigators in pursuit of information, products, communication and, increasingly, entertainment. They move quickly and aren't inclined to take time out in order to decipher your 'clever' play on words.

If your message is ambiguous, regardless of how 'clever' you think it is, you will probably lose your audience. Your message has to be simple, compelling and *instantly understandable* if you want any hope of engaging savvy web consumers.

The same rule applies to images. Keep your visuals simple in your banner and display ads. If you opt for animation, use it to grab attention rather than trying to tell a story. User attention is fragmented online, and many will be unwilling to invest undivided attention on your impressive animated narrative.

That's not to say you can't use narrative effectively – it can be an incredibly powerful weapon in your creative arsenal – but telling a story is better suited to rich media ad formats that let users dictate the pace of the story ('Click to read more', etc). Their attention can wander, without them missing the next part of the story. When they're ready to proceed they can return to your thrilling narrative and pick up where they left off. Perfect!

4. Tailor your creative to your choice of execution

Whatever execution you choose – banner and display ads, e-mail campaigns, viral, mobile – all have their own specific best-practice guidelines (we covered some of them in Chapter 6). By all means push the boundaries, be as imaginative as you like, but let your creative impulses be guided and tempered by the constraints of your chosen campaign execution media. Work with your technology of choice, rather than against it, cater for the needs of your target audience, and always put the user experience first.

Banner ads and ad boxes are the most widely used advertising formats. Rich media ads are best suited to animation, and facilitate the use of narrative or storytelling. Websites or micro-sites demand an emphasis on user experience above everything else if you want to retain your audience (if your site isn't intuitive and doesn't deliver results quickly, they'll simply leave).

5. Maintain brand consistency

It's essential to maintain a strand of continuity through visual elements of your online campaign. Brand consistency ensures the key visual message is linked directly to the brand. You can test this using what's called the 'glance test'. Ensure your logo stands out prominently in the banner and/or in all frames of an ad when you take a quick look at the screen. Remember, most viewers will give your ad only a cursory glance at best, so you have to capture their attention in a split second and make sure your brand identity registers.

6. Match your landing page to your creative

Landing pages are an important extension of advertising creative; in some ways, perhaps, they can even be considered a *part of the ad creative*. Landing pages are specifically tailored pages on your website on which people arrive when they click your ad. They are the conversion mechanism that gives your ad value and ultimately delivers that all-important ROI.

You should aim for a seamless user experience, matching the look and feel of your advertising creative to that of your landing pages to maintain brand continuity (see above), build confidence and trust in your brand and ultimately entice consumers to buy, sign up, fill in a form or whatever your conversion goal for a particular campaign happens to be.

7. Optimize your creative – test before you invest

The beauty of the digital medium is that it's very easy to test different elements of your online creative and to hone it until it resonates with your market and delivers the results you're looking for. By monitoring real data on the response of actual users you can tweak and optimize your online creative as necessary throughout your campaign to maximize its performance.

8. Learn from your experience

As you become more experienced at digital marketing you will gain greater understanding and insight into the medium and will learn how to play to its many strengths. Become a student of other people's digital campaigns; analyse them ruthlessly to identify what's effective and what's not. Always be on the lookout for opportunities to add to your bank of digital creative knowledge.

9. Focus on relationship development

Each digital campaign should form part of an overall online marketing strategy that is in tune with your market's needs. Rather than embarking on a series of disparate and disjointed campaigns that lack real cohesion, you should ensure your campaigns work in harmony to develop and enhance your relationship with consumers while moving your business inexorably towards its defined goals.

Remember that every campaign you run is an opportunity not just to reach out and connect with consumers but also to learn from them. Listen, and allow their feedback to inform the creative direction of your next campaign. The conversation keeps evolving; make sure your digital marketing creative continues to evolve along with it.

Case study: the Big Shadow

Brief

The 'Blue Dragon' was the killer title of an Xbox 360 game. This title had the responsibility to increase the sales of Xbox 360 in the Japanese market. The target market for the campaign was to reach not only 'game freaks' but also 'casual game players'.

Concept

The game 'Blue Dragon' involves the hero's shadow: the shadow turns into a giant dragon, which goes through fights and plays an important role. The agency therefore chose 'shadows' as the core concept of the campaign. GT believed that the use of shadows would capture consumers' interest in both the campaign and the 'Blue Dragon' game.

The location of this campaign was also a key issue. The best location was found to be at Shibuya in Tokyo, as teenagers consider it a cool place to visit and large numbers of people come to this location for shopping. Over a million passers-by can be reached from this location.

Campaign

GT focused on the primordial human experience of shadow play. Magnified shadows of ordinary people were projected, and a system was created whereby people could play with their own shadows. A person's shadow was projected as a giant shadow image, which suddenly changed into the shape of a dragon, creating a new and engaging interactive experience.

A shadow could also be manipulated via the web while viewing a webcam image. The campaign wanted to provide a fresh experience that linked the city and the internet as well as people and shadows. The 'shadows' were not real shadows but rather projections of images captured by a video camera and manipulated with a specially developed program and then cast on to the wall by four powerful projectors. This combination of technology enabled the 'shadows' to morph into shapes such as the dragon shadow images. The program transformed people's projected shadows into dragons or one of 10 other characters that featured in the actual game.

Shadows of people moving in front of the lighted wall were captured and processed in real time, projecting the dragon shadow on a building wall (27 metres wide, 45 metres high) from a projector. A webcam at the location was able to capture a person's 'shadow' via the internet and included the off-site 'shadow' in the on-site wall projection in real time. The relayed images were archived and could be viewed as a sequence of still images arranged in a spiral along a time axis.

The goal was not to show off advanced technology but rather to see how close it could get to the primordial experience of shadows, which everyone carries in their memory.

A news release issued an invitation to both online and offline media to the campaign launch.

Results

Sales of 'Blue Dragon' exceeded the campaign target. Over 3 million people viewed the campaign. The innovative nature of the campaign won it coverage across all media. It was featured in over 30 blogs. GT had planned to upload the campaign on YouTube, but when the agency sought to upload its video it found that the video had already been placed on YouTube by a viewer.

The innovative nature of the campaign won it many awards, including a Clio Award, a Grand Prix at Cyber One Show Interactive, a Gold at Tokyo International Ad Awards, a Gold Creata Award, and a Bronze Cyber Lion at Cannes.

Client comment on the campaign

Joji Sakaguchi, Director, Xbox Marketing Department, Home and Entertainment Division, Microsoft:

> 'A shadow will be cast by the bright rays of light from our hearts' – this is the core concept for Xbox game 'Blue Dragon'. To express such a concept was the main object for this project.

Shu, the main character of this game, uses his 'shadow' as a weapon to fight enemies that confront him on his journey to save the world. The biggest challenge for this project lay in the part of designing a method to show the users the core concept of this game that couldn't be expressed via TV commercials or Flash ad banners. Also, the concept had to be expressed with a sense of the grand scale of this next-generation role-playing game spectacular created by the great master creators.

The significance of the 'Big Shadow' was that it enabled users to feel the sense of actually controlling their shadows just like they would in the game. The users experienced a 'real' and 'outdoor' experience through an innovative measure. The concept of the game was also expressed in three dimensions via the internet – a virtual world.

An interactive shadow was cast upon the huge walls of a parking lot in Shibuya, a city crowded with teenagers, who are the main target of this game.

This method not only expressed the new experience, but also succeeded in producing buzz. Passengers would take a picture of the event with their cell phones, and send them to their friends. Such communication style using cell phones is popular in Japan, and worked well with this project. Also, users who couldn't come to the real venue were given an 'online entry chance'; this campaign generated another series of buzz, hence succeeding in expanding the community.

Campaign credits

Client: Microsoft
Product: Xbox 360 'Blue Dragon'

Advertising agency: GT Inc, Tokyo
Creative Director: Koshi Uchiyama
Art Director: Naoki Ita

Campaign visuals

www.gtinc.jp/tiaa/bigshadow_image_300dpi/

Figure 10.2   The 'Big Shadow' campaign took the concept of shadow-play to a new level, allowing people to interact with giant shadows projected onto the side of a Tokyo building. The public could interact with the 'shadows' both on-location and remotely over the internet

11 A lot to look forward to

For marketing to service the new needs of business, and for it to profit from rather than suffer from the changing world of media, it will have to adapt in a radical way.

(Chris Ward, Microsoft MSN, The future of digital marketing)

I look to the future because that's where I'm going to spend the rest of my life.

(George Burns, 1896–1996)

The best way to predict the future is to invent it.

(Alan Kay)

Our chapter pledge to you

When you reach the end of this chapter you'll have answers to the following questions:

- What are the key trends that are shaping the digital marketing landscape of the future?
- How is the relationship between consumers and marketers evolving?
- What are the main challenges digital marketers will face over the next three years?
- What can you do to future-proof your business?

The future's bright: head towards the light

If the last five years have taught us anything in the digital marketing space, they've taught us to expect rapid and unprecedented change. In a few short years online marketing has gone from talent show wannabe to headlining Broadway act, emerging from the wings of cyberspace into the centre-stage spotlight.

Spending on online advertising continues to grow rapidly, poaching budget from more 'traditional' channels as businesses realize that the future is online – and so are their customers. In 2007, US internet advertising revenues totalled \$21.2 billion, 26 per cent higher than in 2006, which was itself a record year (Interactive Advertising Bureau (IAB)/PricewaterhouseCoopers (PwC), *2007 Internet Advertising Revenue Report*) and, while industry analyst company eMarketer predicts that growth will slow slightly in 2009, it predicts growth will bounce back in 2010 and continue to grow strongly through 2012.

And this is only the beginning. Mainstream business is just starting to understand and tap into the rich vein of potential that digital marketing represents. Right at the start of the book we mentioned that this is an incredibly exciting time to be involved in the digital marketing space. We're at a tipping point. Digital channels are on the cusp of entering the mainstream: the crazy, lawless, 'wild frontier' days of the pioneers are behind us. As digital marketing starts to mature, we're entering a new and exciting era of opportunity, accountability and sustainable growth. It's shaping up to become the biggest revolution in marketing history. And we can all be a part of it.

Word of mouth: savvy consumers control the future

Technology continues to evolve at a startling pace – getting faster, more capable, easier to use and more affordable – and that trend doesn't look set to slow any time soon. But the technology itself is a very small part of the digital marketing story: what's really exciting for the digital marketer is the way *technology is enabling people*. It's the way people are adopting and using technology that is a catalyst for rapid and enduring change. Consumers are using technology to redefine their consumption of media, their relationships with brands and marketers, and their relationships with each other. It's changing the nature of the game – and marketers either have to adapt or be left behind.

'The reality is communication technology has always made consumers savvier, more educated and amplified their diversity', explains digital marketing visionary Jonathan Mendez in his Optimize & Prophetize blog (www.optimizeandprophesize.com):

> We will all agree that power has shifted in the marketplace to consumers as they take on an ever-active voice in the marketing and the ultimate success of products. Reviews, recommendations and social networks necessitate factual and helpful messages and marketing that quantifies benefits to consumers. This is the only way consumers will accept your voice. Some might say straight talk lends itself to more direct response focused marketing – and it does – but it can also become best friend of a brand builder.

There's little doubt that, as the population of digital-savvy consumers continues to grow around the world, so too will the imperative for marketers to engage with them online: listening and learning from them, and including their input in the evolution and development of brands. Some forward-thinking companies, like Dell and Procter & Gamble, are already embracing this consumer-driven trend, and it's something that will continue to grow.

For marketers, our biggest challenge moving forward is how we manage that transition from broadcasting a message to entering an ongoing dialogue: how do we make sense of this plethora of new communications tools and use them to connect with customers who are ever more fragmented and dispersed? How can we engage in a way that adds mutual and enduring value? The answers demand a paradigm shift in the marketing mindset – a change that's proving painful for a lot of old-school marketers and agencies but which opens up a whole new world of opportunity to those nimble enough to adapt.

We need to harness the power of digital media to talk *with* our customers, not *at* them, and to recognize that in the online space *the consumer really is controlling the conversation.* That's not to say that message-based advertising will die out – it almost certainly won't – but to be effective the message will need to become more targeted, focused and relevant. Advertising will have to *add tangible value* through delivering useful information, entertainment or a practical tool or application in exchange for the user's attention.

We're in a period of transition: broadcast-style interruptive advertising will continue to coexist with more engaging formats for some time yet. Ultimately though, engagement-based marketing delivers more all-round value. As more marketers start to understand and accept that fact, we'll see engagement becoming the dominant model in online marketing.

Search: a constantly evolving marketing powerhouse

Because search is so central to the online experience it can be difficult to believe that, as an industry, it is still very much in its infancy. People who predict that search marketing has peaked (and there are some out there) are fundamentally underestimating both the power of search engines to innovate and adapt and the overwhelming desire of a continually expanding user base to find relevant, valuable information on an increasingly cluttered web.

At the time of writing Google, by far the dominant player in search, is still less than a decade old. The technology underpinning search, while it has developed extraordinarily quickly, is still very young. It has a lot of growing up to do over the coming years.

Blended search is already with us, and will be refined and developed over the coming years; search engines will continue to hone their ability to understand context in search queries – to divine exactly what users are looking for and to deliver ever more relevant results. Personalized search based on both profile information and preferences we explicitly provide (or give permission for them to collect) will be combined with information inferred from aggregated search histories to deliver more relevant search results to individuals.

The method search engines use to rank the pages will certainly change over time. At the moment inbound links are one of the dominant factors in determining the quality, authority and relevance of a site for search rankings. Over time, as search engines get better at evaluating the actual content of a site, perhaps incorporating some form of distributed human input model to determine quality, or tapping into social media to get a more human-centric perspective, the emphasis could well shift away from link-based ranking. How the ranking algorithms will evolve is anybody's guess, but they will evolve, and search marketing will continue to evolve alongside them.

At the forefront of these developments, for the foreseeable future at least, will be Google, and despite the best efforts of leading competitors it's difficult to see how anyone in the current search marketplace can seriously challenge the wily incumbent for the top spot over the next few years. That's not to say they won't try, or that others won't emerge with a whiz-bang new search technology that will ultimately blow Google out of the water. This is an incredibly disruptive arena, as Google themselves have proved, and there are any number of search start-ups out there, working frantically on what they believe to be Google-killing search technologies. Watch this space!

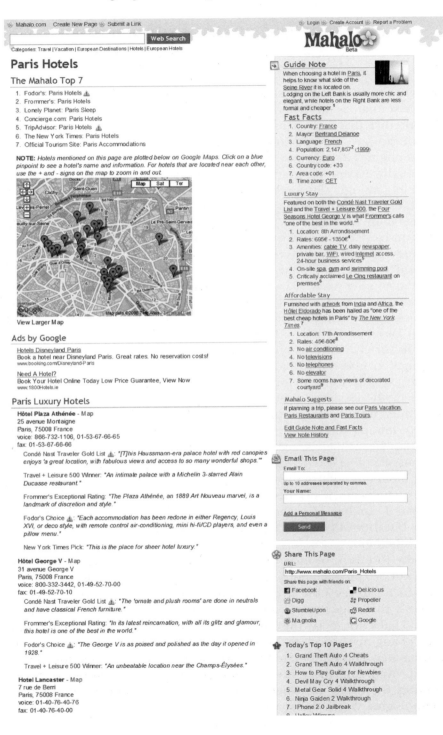

Paris Hotels

The Mahalo Top 7

1. Fodor's: Paris Hotels
2. Frommer's: Paris Hotels
3. Lonely Planet: Paris Sleep
4. Concierge.com: Paris Hotels
5. TripAdvisor: Paris Hotels
6. The New York Times: Paris Hotels
7. Official Tourism Site: Paris Accommodations

NOTE: *Hotels mentioned on this page are plotted below on Google Maps. Click on a blue pinpoint to see a hotel's name and information. For hotels that are located near each other, use the + and - signs on the map to zoom in and out.*

View Larger Map

Ads by Google

Hotels Disneyland Paris
Book a hotel near Disneyland Paris. Great rates. No reservation costs!
www.booking.com/Disneyland-Paris

Need A Hotel?
Book Your Hotel Online Today Low Price Guarantee, View Now
www.1800Hotels.ie

Paris Luxury Hotels

Hôtel Plaza Athénée - Map
25 avenue Montaigne
Paris, 75008 France
voice: 866-732-1106, 01-53-67-66-65
fax: 01-53-67-66-66

　　Condé Nast Traveler Gold List : *"[T]his Haussmann-era palace hotel with red canopies enjoys 'a great location, with fabulous views and access to so many wonderful shops.'"*

　　Travel + Leisure 500 Winner: *"An intimate palace with a Michelin 3-starred Alain Ducasse restaurant."*

　　Frommer's Exceptional Rating: *"The Plaza Athénée, an 1889 Art Nouveau marvel, is a landmark of discretion and style."*

　　Fodor's Choice : *"Each accommodation has been redone in either Regency, Louis XVI, or deco style, with remote control air-conditioning, mini hi-fi/CD players, and even a pillow menu."*

　　New York Times Pick: *"This is the place for sheer hotel luxury."*

Hôtel George V - Map
31 avenue George V
Paris, 75008 France
voice: 800-332-3442, 01-49-52-70-00
fax: 01-49-52-70-10

　　Condé Nast Traveler Gold List : *"The 'ornate and plush rooms' are done in neutrals and have classical French furniture."*

　　Frommer's Exceptional Rating: *"In its latest reincarnation, with all its glitz and glamour, this hotel is one of the best in the world."*

　　Fodor's Choice : *"The George V is as poised and polished as the day it opened in 1928."*

　　Travel + Leisure 500 Winner: *"An unbeatable location near the Champs-Élysées."*

Hotel Lancaster - Map
7 rue de Berri
Paris, 75008 France
voice: 01-40-76-40-76
fax: 01-40-76-40-00

Fast Facts

1. Country: France
2. Mayor: Bertrand Delanoe
3. Language: French
4. Population: 2,147,857[2] (1999)
5. Currency: Euro
6. Country code: +33
7. Area code: +01
8. Time zone: CET

Luxury Stay

Featured on both the Condé Nast Traveler Gold List and the Travel + Leisure 500, the Four Seasons Hotel George V is what Frommer's calls "one of the best in the world."[3]

1. Location: 8th Arrondissement
2. Rates: 605€ - 1350€[4]
3. Amenities: cable TV, daily newspaper, private bar, WiFi, wired Internet access, 24-hour business services[5]
4. On-site spa, gym and swimming pool
5. Critically acclaimed Le Cinq restaurant on premises[6]

Affordable Stay

Furnished with artwork from India and Africa, the Hôtel Eldorado has been hailed as "one of the best cheap hotels in Paris" by *The New York Times.*[7]

1. Location: 17th Arrondissement
2. Rates: 45€-80€[8]
3. No air conditioning
4. No televisions
5. No telephones
6. No elevator
7. Some rooms have views of decorated courtyard[9]

Mahalo Suggests

If planning a trip, please see our Paris Vacation, Paris Restaurants and Paris Tours.

Edit Guide Note and Fast Facts
View Note History

Today's Top 10 Pages

1. Grand Theft Auto 4 Cheats
2. Grand Theft Auto 4 Walkthrough
3. How to Play Guitar for Newbies
4. Devil May Cry 4 Walkthrough
5. Metal Gear Solid 4 Walkthrough
6. Ninja Gaiden 2 Walkthrough
7. iPhone 2.0 Jailbreak

Figure 11.1 Human power: searching for Paris hotels on Mahalo (a human-powered search engine) lists top Paris hotels, whereas Google's SERPs for the same keyphrase are dominated by hotel group booking sites and affiliates like TripAdvisor and ParisHotels.com (Google's one saving grace here is universal search, which means a map and links to actual hotels appear in the SERPs). The human input to the Mahalo page makes it much more focused and relevant, with useful information and recommendations down the right, and *actual hotel websites* graded from luxury through moderate to affordable in the SERPs

Humanizing and personalizing search

Introducing a human recommendation element into search makes all sorts of sense. Human-powered search engines like Mahalo (www.mahalo.com) present search results that have been screened and recommended by a real, live editorial team rather than a computer program. Obviously this approach can and does deliver more relevant and useful search results for the most popular search terms, but even when a social media or wiki-esque model is adopted, as it is at Mahalo, it's difficult to see how purely human-powered search will ever scale up to become a real contender as a comprehensive and universal search engine.

Chris Sherman, Executive Editor with Search Engine Land, points out that human-powered search is nothing new and has been happening for more than a decade. While he recognizes that human editors are better than any algorithm at judging relevancy, he's also sceptical about the scalability of human-powered search when it comes to offering a comprehensive solution. 'Human beings are great at making judgements and recommendations, but they don't scale', he told us when we caught up with him at the Search Marketing World conference in Dublin (April 2008, www.searchmarketingworld2008.com). 'They can't possibly keep up with the way the web is growing.'

Chris and other leading experts in search believe the future will see hybrid search engines emerge that combine the best elements of algorithmic search with human recommendation, personalization, behavioural profiling and geo-location to deliver uniquely tailored search results. That evolution is already happening, with personalization, behavioural profiling and geo-location all playing a role in defining relevancy on major search platforms: what I see in my Google SERPs today could be different to what you see for the same search phrase, weighted according to where I'm searching from, my personal preferences and the behavioural profile Google has built up based on what I've searched for before, the results I've clicked on, etc.

Over time the personal differentiation of search results – ranking according to relevancy to an individual rather than to the masses – will become more pronounced. For marketers, of course, personalized search results are a great thing. They mean that our search marketing efforts should yield more qualified search traffic that's far more likely to convert when it arrives at our website.

Social search – taking things a step further

In an interview with VentureBeat in early 2008, Google's Vice President of Search Products and User Experience, Marissa Mayer, defined social search as:

> any search aided by a social interaction or a social connection... Social search happens every day. When you ask a friend 'what movies are good to go see?' or 'where should we go to dinner?', you are doing a verbal social search. You're trying to leverage that social connection to try and get a piece of information that would be better than what you'd come up with on your own.

While social media sites allow us to connect with our 'friends' and find out what they recommend, to see what they consider 'hot or not', delivering social search in a web search engine context introduces a variety of complications – not least of which is privacy. Think about it – do you really want what you enter into a search engine to influence the search results of all your online social connections? Do you want your search results influenced based on what they've been searching for? Some may; many more will not.

So just how our online social connections and interactions might influence our personal search results in the future is unclear, but there's no doubt that leading search engines are looking into the possibility and that social elements *will* factor in determining the ranking and relevancy of search results in some way moving forward.

'If we look at a search engine ten years from now, we know it will be better than Google is today', said Mayer.

> Google itself gets better every single day because we're constantly making changes to the relevance... I think one way it will be better is in understanding more about you and understanding more about your social context: who your friends are, what you like to do, where you are. It's hard to imagine that the search engine ten years from now isn't advised by those things.

What all this means for marketers

In marketing terms search is by far the biggest platform in the digital marketing space. All of the developments in search – universal search, human-powered search, social search, etc – are ultimately being driven by a single universal goal: the prime objective we mentioned back at the start of Chapter 4. Search engines need to deliver the most relevant, authoritative results to their users if they want to maintain and expand their user base. By giving users what they want, search engines attract more users, which in turn attracts more advertisers – and that means more money for search engines.

More relevant, focused search results, as we've mentioned, are great news for marketers – because, as long as you're targeting the right keyword phrases in your SEO and paid search campaigns, it means the traffic coming your way will be more qualified and more likely to convert. Search marketing looks set for continued and sustainable growth moving forward, in terms of both organic SEO and paid search campaigns.

While paid search has to date attracted the lion's share of the search marketing dollar, we'll probably see more of that spend drifting towards SEO over the coming years as businesses feel the pinch of rising costs per click in their paid search campaigns and realize the ongoing value of organic rankings to deliver traffic for their targeted keyword terms.

Overall more business are going to realize the benefits of establishing coordinated search marketing campaigns, running paid search and SEO in tandem, choosing their keywords wisely to garner the most valuable traffic from both.

Mobile: marketing on the move

Mobile marketing – or, more accurately, marketing to consumers through mobile devices – has been heralded as the next big thing in the digital space for some years now. So far it's failed to deliver, but few doubt its potential – or the fact that mobile internet usage is set to explode. It's just a question of when.

Speaking at a conference in 2006, Sir David Brown, Chairman of Motorola, recounted a tale from the mid-1980s, when mobile industry analysts forecast a global mobile phone market of just 900,000 units by 2000. Their prediction fell a little short. As we rolled into the new millennium the global mobile industry was selling *900,000 handsets every 19 hours* ('Mobiles still ringing in New Year', www.bbc.co.uk, 23 December 2006).

By the end of 2007 there were a staggering 3.3 billion active mobile phone subscriptions in the world – that's about one phone for every two people – a figure that makes the mobile phone the most widely adopted piece of consumer technology on the planet. To put it into context there are an estimated 1.3 billion fixed-line phones in the world and also, coincidentally, around 1.3 billion internet users; there are about 850 million cars in use, 1.5 billion TV sets and 1.4 billion people use at least

Mobile user numbers in context

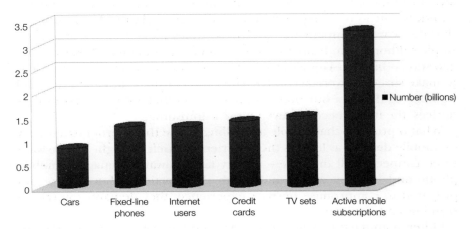

Figure 11.2 The latent potential of mobile: putting 3.3 billion handsets into perspective

one credit card globally. The potential reach of mobile internet access dwarfs fixed-line.

In 2007 over 798 million people around the world accessed the internet using a mobile phone rather than a personal computer. Until relatively recently, though, accessing the internet in any meaningful way through your mobile phone was unwieldy and impractical. Limited bandwidth, poor functionality and horrific user interfaces meant that phones, by and large, were used for making phone calls, sending and receiving text messages and, perhaps, sending the occasional urgent e-mail.

The mobile internet finally becomes useful

Mobile data bandwidth has now increased to the sort of levels that make accessing the internet on the move practical. It's also becoming more affordable, and devices are emerging that take advantage of this increased bandwidth and innovative user interface design to deliver a rich and engaging mobile internet experience.

The trigger for this refinement of the mobile device was the introduction in 2007 of Apple's iPhone and iPod Touch, both of which featured the same outstanding multi-touch user interface and a fully functional web browser capable of displaying full-fledged web pages rather than the dumbed-down mobile web typical on other devices.

The impact: more people are using them to access the web than any other mobile device. How many more? On 13 February 2008 Vic Gundotra, head of Google's mobile operations, told the *Financial Times* that the search company was getting 50 times more search traffic from Apple's iPhone than from any other mobile handset on the market. The gap was so big that Google got its engineers to recheck the server logs to make sure they were accurate. When you consider the relatively small number of iPhones out there compared to other web-enabled mobile devices, the figure becomes even more astonishing.

What it proves is that people are willing to use the internet extensively on mobile devices, as long as the experience is rich enough. People want to be connected all the time – just try taking away a teenager's mobile phone and internet access and watch the reaction – but they're not prepared to compromise on user experience: they demand something seamless and intuitive.

Other manufacturers are following Apple's lead, and a number of mobile devices with slick, easy-to-use interfaces, fully functional web browsers and feature-rich web-enabled applications are beginning to enter the marketplace. The potential is enormous, so much so that Google predicts mobile internet search volumes will surpass those of standard internet search 'within the next several years', to quote Vic Gundotra. That, of course, means more advertising revenue for Google and more opportunities for marketers.

Open development platforms encourage innovation

Playing its part in making that prophecy come true will be Google's own open source mobile operating system and software platform, Android, along with the US$10 million incentive it has set aside to reward developers of the best applications on Android. Apple too has re-evaluated its decision to close the iPhone platform and has opened it up to third-party developers; leading handset manufacturer Nokia has done the same with its own software platform.

All of the ingredients are in place for mobile internet usage to explode – it's a question of when, rather than if, it will happen. When it does, the implications for digital marketers will be profound, in terms of the scope and reach of our digital campaigns, and the ability to target and connect with consumers wherever they are and whatever they're doing.

At the moment we have the standard web and the mobile web – essentially a minuscule subset of the web that's been shoehorned to fit the constraints imposed by today's mainstream mobile devices. In the not-too-distant future, widespread adoption of much more capable devices will herald the demise of the 'mobile web'. What we'll be left with is just the web, complete with search, rich media, video, graphics, engagement and everything else we've come to know and love, all seamlessly accessible, wherever we happen to be and using whichever device we choose.

The day when more people in the world access the internet through their mobile phone than their computer isn't very far away.

Knowing where you are and who's nearby

Another aspect of mobile technology that's something of a hot topic, especially in relation to mobile, is geo-location – or the ability to work out exactly where the device is at any given time. Some high-end devices have a built-in global positioning system (GPS) but, even for those that don't, software can triangulate the phone's position based on its proximity to the nearest masts. Once again Google is spearheading the charge to help build location-aware applications by looking to make geo-location services freely available to developers through its Google Gears application programming interface (API) (TechCrunch, www.techcrunch.com, 31 May 2008).

Combine the ability to accurately place your phone on the map with the software's ability to use your phone's built-in Bluetooth capability to detect other devices (and hence people) near to you, and you have all the ingredients for enhanced real-life networking in the palm of your hand. The possibilities are mind-boggling.

Feel like eating Mexican food? Your mobile will serve you up all the spicy details of places nearby, complete with reviews, ratings and menus. It could even work out that it's lunchtime and suggest locations you might like to eat based on your past preferences.

At a party, but don't know anyone? No problem: a quick look at your mobile will tell you that three of the people in the room are friends of friends in your online social network and that two of them have similar interests to you. Recognizing them is easy – you've seen their profile picture – and, with a bit of background to help break the ice, you're soon chatting away about those common interests.

Or perhaps you're attending a business conference and are on the lookout for a new job? Your mobile lets you know there are four CEOs scheduled to be at the conference whose companies are looking to hire someone with your skill set. It can show you their online profile information and tell you that one of them is standing approximately 10 metres away. That evening, when you get back to your hotel, there's a record of everyone you've met that day waiting for you on your laptop, complete with links to their online profiles. You log on and check your social network and see that three of your friends are in town (based on geo-location data from their phones), so you contact them. Instead of dining alone in the hotel you spend a social evening at a local restaurant with friends – all thanks to your mobile.

While there are still some fairly large hurdles to overcome before this happens – issues relating to privacy, security and data protection to name a few – all of it is technically possible right now. It will take a little time for it to permeate into the mainstream, but it is just around the corner. From a marketing standpoint the possibilities are staggering; they will help businesses to engage with customers more effectively and deliver timely, valuable, focused, location-specific content to them as and when they need it.

Tracking and measuring human behaviour

Tracking, measurement and accountability in the digital marketing space have come a long way in a few short years. Now powerful web-based analytics tools are available for free, and even small businesses can track and measure their ROI with some degree of confidence over much of their online marketing investment. We can track everything from impression, through clicks, to conversion; we can even analyse exactly where the process is breaking down and take steps to remedy the problem. With a little bit of effort we can establish what's working and what's not; we can test, make changes and refine our campaigns in real time. All of this measurement makes marketers more accountable for the investment they make – and that's a great thing.

Web analytics and measurement will continue to grow, and if anything will become even more important to digital marketers over the coming years. The model of delivery may change, with more online agencies developing their analytics capabilities and offering the service as a value-added option for their clients – an option many may choose in preference to in-house teams and external consultants. Regardless of the model that emerges, measuring and tracking performance online are going to be critical to success, and will involve tracking new and fairly unconventional metrics.

With standard analytics we can measure what people are doing and when; where things tend to fall down is when it comes to pinpointing the one thing people really want to know: why. Why are people abandoning their shopping cart at stage X? Why aren't people who click on ad Y going on to sign up for our newsletter? Why aren't visitors clicking through to deeper content pages on our website? Why won't people engage with the latest social media campaign?

Web analytics is great for collecting, aggregating and reporting on the where and the when – the quantitative empirical data of online transactions. Clicks, impressions, visits: all straightforward, all measurable – observable actions where one equals one, two equals two, etc. However, quantitative data alone can never truly describe the subtleties of human behaviour.

And therein lies the problem, because the brave new world of conversational marketing that we've described, where consumer engagement reigns supreme, is *all* about identifying and responding to the subtleties of human behaviour and interaction. But how do you accurately measure qualitative concepts like engagement, influence, trust and authority in a repeatable and comparable way? How do you consistently and comparably measure the evolution of online conversation?

There are already plenty of speculative suggestions, theories and formulae out there, but little consensus to date. Over time, gradual consensus will emerge on how and where to measure these qualitative online metrics and how they can best be used in conjunction with existing web analytics to help us improve both our relationship with consumers and our ROI.

In-game advertising

Computer and video games have become a fertile ground for advertisers over recent years. Since Sony launched its first PlayStation back in 1995 the games console market has exploded. Video games are one of the fastest-growing areas of entertainment and are perfect for hitting the desirable 18- to 34-year-old male demographic. Predictions vary wildly, but estimates suggest that in-game advertising could be worth between US$800 million and just shy of US$2 billion by 2012.

With the advent of always-on broadband internet connections, modern games consoles can connect players with each other – and crucially allow advertisers to connect with the games. In-game advertising is a particularly attractive proposition because, unlike in most other media, gamers tend to welcome the presence of real-world brands within games. It brings an added sense of realism to their gaming experience. In fact a study by Nielsen Interactive Entertainment found that some 70 per cent of gamers responded positively to the presence of real brands and advertising in their games, as long as it was *contextually relevant* and served to enhance rather than disrupt their game play.

Static billboard-style advertising in games is rapidly being replaced by dynamic ads served up in real time over the internet by specialist in-game advertising networks. Ads can be geo-targeted and contextual, and can be modified at will by the networks, offering changing and ongoing advertising opportunities throughout the lifetime of the game. There are also product placement opportunities in games, in much the same way as there are in feature films – only in games the gamer actually gets to interact with the placed product, making for a more engaging experience. Because these ads are served over the internet, their performance can be tracked in much the same way as that of any other form of online advertising.

A little further down the track there are also likely to be opportunities to link in-game purchases to online stores. For example, buying a pair of jeans or sunglasses for your in-game character could generate a corresponding purchase for the same items with an online retailer. Brands will also be able to sponsor specific sections or 'challenges' within gaming environments and offer real-world rewards and incentives for gamers to complete the challenge, generating brand engagement and positive online and offline publicity.

As the in-game advertising market continues to mature and grow it will become an increasingly dynamic and imaginative arena for marketers – definitely one to watch.

Holistic marketing: blurring lines and integrating media

Digital marketing is a big part of the future, for sure, but it's important to remember that it's not the only game in town. In fact, even thinking of media in terms of digital and traditional is becoming an increasingly invalid position. The lines are blurring as traditional media are used to drive traffic online and increasingly start to embrace digital channels to deliver 'traditional' content on consumers' terms. TV, radio, newspapers, magazines: all of these traditional media are embracing digital channels through necessity; consumers demand it, so they deliver it, and they're getting better at it all the time. In their favour, of course, is their content. People know their content and trust their brands. The success of initiatives like the BBC's on-demand TV service, iPlayer, is ample testament to the fact that traditional media can learn to 'play' the digital game.

So we're not forecasting the death of traditional media advertising here, rather the continued evolution and diversification of media as a whole. For marketers, that diversification presents both significant challenges and boundless opportunity. Fragmentation of the market into ever-smaller niche groups across an array of different media means that each potential marketing channel reaches a smaller audience, but it also means your campaigns can be more targeted, relevant and engaging than ever before.

Technology is also helping marketers to address fragmentation by providing us with ever-more-sophisticated tools to track multiple, integrated campaigns that span numerous channels and audiences. As mentioned earlier in the book, digital marketing, uniquely, allows us both to broaden our scope and to narrow our focus at the same time.

Over the next five years or so we'll see a much more holistic view of the marketing landscape emerge, a view with less emphasis on 'traditional' versus 'digital', and more focus on integrating campaigns to span not just the different elements of digital marketing – search, display, e-mail, affiliate, social media, etc – but also a seamless integration with offline channels.

Thought leaders predict the future

We asked some leading figures in digital marketing for their insight into the future of digital marketing. Here are their thoughts.

Richard Eyre, Chairman of the Internet Advertising Bureau

Q. Where do you think digital marketing is heading over the next two to three years?
A. Continued blurring of the lines between 'traditional media' and digital media. Continued march to mobile.

Q. Which components of 'digital' (ie search, affiliate, display, etc) do you believe will be more widely used in say three years' time?
A. I think search will continue to bring in new advertisers who could not previously afford much more than a slot in *Yellow Pages*. The ability of online advertising to be highly targeted and deliver high and manageable ROI will make advertising a more regular component of more companies' marketing efforts, and the networks make buying cheap, so I think they will continue to take a significant share of the online dollar. Meanwhile, the larger advertisers will continue to discover the value of online advertising in the mix, and will favour display.

Q. Which components of digital (ie search, affiliate, display, etc) do you believe will be less *widely used in say three years' time?*
A. Interruptive formats. Though pop-ups account for quite a small share of spend now, they will disappear. Users will complain about rich media that are too clever and distracting, forcing advertisers to think hard about their use.

Q. What are the main challenges and opportunities you think these developments will hold for the digital marketer?
A. I think the main challenge is that the digital advertising offer has not stopped developing yet. Advertisers and agencies are painfully slow to adapt to the new, so I think they're in for more of the same, ie evaluation of new approaches, trying to separate the good from the just new.

I think we'll see derivatives in search and display that help advertisers get closer to consumers without annoying them as much as today's interruptive formats are wont to do.

Advertisers will have to get their heads around mobile advertising. This will have to be cleverer than spam texts.

Q. Are there any other trends in the digital space that you think marketers need to be aware of?
A. Knowing more about your consumer opens up a new opportunity in mainstream advertising, which has so far had to opt for one message for many. This development will make it possible and in time necessary to tailor advertising messages by audience member. Big one! On-demand TV will obviously reduce the effectiveness of the commercial break.

Q. If you could give one piece of advice to someone who's about to embark on a digital marketing adventure, what would it be?
A. Get great advisers and listen to them.

Q. Do you think the disruptive nature of digital technology will eventually sound the death knell of traditional advertising as we know it? When?
A. No. I think it's too easy to proclaim the death of the old on the birth of the new. I don't see newspaper or magazine reading or radio listening stopping, so there will remain an advertising opportunity here.

Q. Why do you think traditional full-service advertising agencies are struggling to make the transition to digital? What are the obstacles, and how are they overcoming them?

A. I think one reason is the age of the senior people – usually a man of a certain age who is hoping like hell that all this digital malarkey will hold off till he can retire. One senior media player recently described the internet to a meeting I was in as 'those things which we do not understand'.

Yet for all their lack of instincts, they know they have to participate. The approach then is to try to buy in specialists. But there are few of them, and the best are unlikely to go into an agency where digital media are second sister. So then they buy an agency. OK, but the digital mentality never quite makes it into the DNA of the agency – it's grafted on. Clients are not daft – mainly. This is obvious, so they split the budget for the agency and hire their own digital specialist.

The obstacles lie in the heads of the senior people and they are not easily overcome till that generation retires to Portugal.

Alain Heureux, President, IAB Europe and IAB Belgium

Q. Where do you think digital marketing is heading over the next two to three years?

A. Digital will take centre stage in any strategic media strategy, and will top €25 billion in terms of European advertising expenditure. It will be *the* medium through which consumers engage with brands, deliver brand impact and communicate their purchase intentions.

Q. Which components of 'digital' (ie search, affiliate, display, etc) do you believe will be more widely used in say three years time?

A. We'll see much more targeted marketing emerge: marketing that combines and consolidates search, display and content; delivered through social network platforms and information sites on PCs, portable and mobile devices.

Q. Which components of 'digital' (ie search, affiliate, display, etc) do you believe will be less widely used in say three years time?

A. I think, unfortunately, due to the global spam epidemic, that e-mail marketing has difficult times ahead.

Q. What are the main challenges and opportunities you think these developments will hold for the digital marketer?

A. Changing current marketing habits, and changing existing measurement currencies and metrics while simultaneously improving efficiency, and becoming more effective, accountable and results driven.

Q. Are there any other trends in the digital space that you think marketers need to be aware of?
A. Mobile marketing and mobile in-game marketing.

Q. If you could give one piece of advice to someone whose about to embark on their digital marketing adventure, what would it be?
A. Think outside the box. Remember that defining successful marketing strategies in the digital space is about much more than cutting and pasting content from traditional media and marketing collateral.

Q. Do you think the disruptive nature of digital technology will eventually sound the death knell of traditional advertising as we know it? When?
A. I think traditional media will become more and more digital or at least develop a digital element. The trend will make cross-media strategies that are tailored to both the needs of the market and the objectives of the advertiser much more common.

Q. Why do you think traditional full service advertising agencies are struggling to make the transition to digital? What are the obstacles, and how are they overcoming them?
A. Lack of know-how, and of best practice and expertise. Their business models are not yet adapted to digital marketing and media. As long as traditional marketing metrics and currencies prevail it will be very difficult for these agencies to fully integrate digital practices into their cross-media campaigns.

Martin Murray, CEO, Interactive Return

Q. What do you believe are the greatest challenges facing the digital marketing business over the next five years and why?
A. Total media penetration: Digital media will be so omnipresent and potentially obtrusive that the 'banner blindness' that was experienced in the early years of digital marketing will extend to all digital media channels and formats. The solution to this problem is consumer-initiated, customized, value-added messaging.

Social media: From the publisher's perspective, it must be monetized; from the advertiser's perspective it must be a workable, convertible and measurable medium; for the consumer, it has to deliver value beyond rating your teacher and twittering that you are now sitting at your desk.

The 30-second TV ad: Allow it to die a natural death and let's move on to media and executions that work for advertisers and consumers.

Q. What do you think will be the digital marketers' key channel in the future – mobile or online or both – and why?
A. Everything else has gone mobile so presumably digital marketing will too. We just haven't seen the correct interface, bandwidth and price plan yet. Online from a fixed position – office, home, home-office – will continue to grow in importance relative to offline channels.

Dynamic, unpredictable, exciting – and essential

Digital marketing is going places – of that there's no doubt. Where exactly it's going and how it's going to get there are all part of the adventure. In this chapter we've offered just a few suggestions of what might lie in store – but finding out for yourself is all part of the fun.

In this dynamic and unpredictable place, fortune favours not just the brave but also the nimble. Your organization has to be able to adapt quickly to change, recognize the opportunities it presents and capitalize on them quickly. If you build a digital marketing strategy and team that can give you that flexibility, you'll find plenty of opportunity opening up for you as digital marketing continues its stellar evolution.

So stick around for the ride – it's shaping up to be a very interesting one indeed.

Case study: Heidies

Brief

To launch Diesel's new Intimate collection Diesel wanted to continue its youth-oriented marketing with a dynamic online campaign.

Concept

A fake hostile takeover occurs of diesel.com. Two gorgeous crazy girls, the 'Heidies', steal the new and unreleased Diesel Intimate collection, kidnap a Diesel sales assistant and lock themselves (and him) in a hotel room. At all times the

Heidies are seen wearing Diesel underwear in pursuit of their 15 Mb of fame. They want the world to see what they are doing. The essence of the concept was 'Acting weird on the internet makes you famous.'

Campaign

Six cameras streamed everything live for five days on diesel.com. Viewers could change camera angles. All pictures were taken as they happened and then uploaded without any retouch. Almost all were taken by the Heidies and their hostage. Diesel.com became their blog, and their images were uploaded on many other popular sites as well. The images and video they uploaded attracted a worldwide online audience. The website was broadcast on a big screen in the Heidies' room. Viewers could send messages to be broadcast; they had their names written on the kidnapped sales guy's chest and by interacting were able to affect the Heidies' action.

Results

The response was beyond expectation. The Heidies received e-mails from all over the world as well as music videos, messages, creative drawings and all sorts of attachments. The campaign won many awards, including a Gold Cyber Lion at Cannes.

Campaign credits

Client: Diesel, Intimate collection
Agency: Farfar, Stockholm
http://www.farfarshowroom.com/diesel/casestudy/

Figure 11.3 Hostile takeover: the 'Heidies' essentially hijacked the Diesel.com website for five days for this campaign, streaming live from six cameras, and interacting in real time with site visitors over the internet

Glossary

Throughout the book we've avoided technical jargon wherever possible and have tried to present information in plain, clear English. Where specific digital marketing terminology was unavoidable we provided a brief definition in the text itself. To supplement the definitions in the text and to give you a handy reference for digital marketing terms, we've included the following glossary, reproduced here with permission from the UK's Internet Advertising Bureau (www.iabuk.net).

abandon   When a user does not complete a transaction.

ad impression   An advertisement impression transpires each time a consumer is exposed to an advertisement (either appended to an SMS or MMS message, on mobile web (WAP) page, within a video clip, or related media).

ad serving   Delivery of online adverts to an end user's computer by an ad management system. The system allows different online adverts to be served in order to target different audience groups and can serve adverts across multiple sites. Ad technology providers each have their own proprietary models for this.

ad unit   Any defined advertising vehicle that can appear in an ad space inside of an application. For example for the purposes of promoting a commercial brand, product or service.

advertiser   Also called merchant, retailer, e-retailer, or online retailer. Any website that sells a product or service, accepts payments, and fulfils orders. An advertiser places ads and links to their products and services on other websites (publishers) and pays those publishers a commission for leads or sales that result from their site.

affiliate marketing   An affiliate (a website owner or publisher) displays an advertisement (such as a banner or link) on its site for a merchant (the brand or advertiser). If a consumer visiting the affiliate's site clicks on this advertisement and goes on to perform a specified action (usually a purchase) on an advertiser's site then the affiliate receives a commission.

algorithm   The set of 'rules' a search engine may use to determine the relevance of a web page (and therefore ranking) in its organic search results. See also *organic search results* and *search engine optimization.*

application service provider (ASP)   An online network that is accessible through the internet instead of through the installation of software. It is quickly integrated with other websites and the services are easily implemented and scalable.

avatar   A picture or cartoon used to represent an individual in chat forums, games or on a website as a help function.

bandwidth   The transmission rate of a communication line – usually measured in kilobytes per second (kbps). This relates to the amount of data that can be carried per second by your internet connection. See also *broadband.*

banner   A long, horizontal, online advert usually found running across the top of a page in a fixed placement. See also *universal advertising package, embedded format.*

BARB   Broadcasters' Audience Research Board is responsible for the measurement of TV viewing.

behavioural targeting   A form of online marketing that uses advertising technology to target web users based on their previous behaviour. Advertising creative and content can be tailored to be of more relevance to a particular user by capturing their previous decision making behaviour (eg: filling out preferences or visiting certain areas of a site frequently) and looking for patterns.

blog   An online space regularly updated presenting the opinions or activities of one or a group of individuals and displaying in chronological order.

broadband   An internet connection that is always on and that delivers a higher bit rate (128 kbps or above) than a standard dial-up connection. It allows for a better online experience as pages load quickly and you can download items faster.

buffering   When a streaming media player saves portions of file until there is enough information for the file to begin playing.

button   A square online advert usually found embedded within a website page. See also *universal advertising package, embedded format.*

cache memory   Used to store web pages you have seen already. When you go back to those pages they'll load more quickly because they come from the cache and don't need to be downloaded over the internet again.

call to action (CTA)   A statement or instruction, typically promoted in print, web, TV, radio, on-portal, or other forms of media (often embedded in advertising), that explains to a mobile subscriber how to respond to an opt-in for a particular promotion or mobile initiative, which is typically followed by a notice (see *notice*).

click-through   When a user interacts with an advertisement and clicks through to the advertiser's website.

click-through rate (CTR)   Frequency of click-throughs as a percentage of impressions served. Used as a measure of advertising effectiveness.

click to call   A service that enables a mobile subscriber to initiate a voice call to a specified phone number by clicking on a link on a mobile internet site. Typically used to enhance and provide a direct response mechanism in an advertisement.

commission   An amount of income received by a publisher for some quantifiable action such as selling an advertiser's product and/or service on the publisher's website.

content sponsorship   Advertiser sponsorships of content areas (eg entire website, home page or a specific channel) to include the total value of the package including any embedded or interruptive formats. This category also includes revenue related to e-mail advertising or prioritized listing of results in search engines that are included as part of the sponsorship deal.

contextual advertising   Advertising that is targeted to the content on the web page being viewed by a user at that specific time.

conversion rate   Measure of success of an online ad when compared to the click-through rate. What defines a 'conversion' depends on the marketing objective, eg: it can be defined as a sale or request to receive more information, etc.

cookie   A small text file on the user's PC that identifies the user's browser and hence the user so they are 'recognized' when they re-visit a site, eg: it allows usernames to be stored and websites to personalize their offering.

cost per action (CPA)   A pricing model that only charges advertising on an action being conducted, eg a sale or a form being filled in.

cost per acquisition (CPA)   Cost to acquire a new customer.

cost per click (CPC)   The amount paid by an advertiser for a click on their sponsored search listing. See also *PPC*.

cost per mille (CPM)/cost per thousand (CPT)   Online advertising can be purchased on the basis of what it costs to show the ad to 1,000 viewers (CPM). It is used in marketing as a benchmark to calculate the relative cost of an advertising campaign or an ad message in a given medium. Rather than an absolute cost, CPM estimates the cost per 1,000 views of the ad. (Wikipedia definition)

CRM   Customer relationship management.

deep-linking advert   Linking beyond a home page to a page inside the site with content pertinent to the advert.

display advertising on e-mail   Advertising that appears around the unrelated editorial content of e-mail newsletters. This can take the form of embedded formats like banners, or as sponsorship, and includes both opt-in (sent to customers specifically requesting it) and opt-out (sent to customers with the option to be removed at their request) e-mails.

domain name   The unique name of an internet site, eg www.iabuk.net.

downloading   the technology that allows users to store video content on their computer for viewing at a later date. Downloading an entire piece of media makes it more susceptible to illegal duplication.

D2C   Direct to consumer.

DRM   Digital rights management is a set of technologies used by publishers and media owners to control access to their digital content. Access can be limited to the number of times a piece of content is accessed from a single machine or user account; the number of times access permissions can be passed on; or the lifespan of a piece of content.

dynamic ad delivery   Based upon predetermined criteria, dynamic ad delivery is the process by which a mobile advertisement is delivered, via a campaign management platform, to a publisher's mobile content.

e-commerce (electronic commerce)   Business that takes place over electronic platforms, such as the internet.

e-mail bounced   Those e-mails sent as part of a mailing distribution which did not have a valid recipient e-mail address and so generated a formal failure message. (ABC Electronic jargon buster definition)

electronic programme guide (EPG)   Is the electronic version of a television schedule showing programme times and content on the television screen or monitor. In the case of VOD, an EPG displays the content of all of the services available to a subscriber.

embedded format   Advertising formats that are displayed in set spaces on a publisher's page. See also *banner, skyscraper, button.*

emoticons   Emoticon symbols are used to indicate mood in an electronic mode of communication, eg e-mail or instant messenger. :-)

encoding   The conversion of an analogue signal to a digital format.

EPC (average earnings per one hundred clicks)   A relative rating that illustrates the ability to convert clicks into commissions. It is calculated by taking commissions earned (or commissions paid) divided by the total number of clicks times 100.

expandable banner/skyscraper   Fixed online advertising placements that expand over the page in the response to user action, eg mouseover. See also *rich media.*

firewall software   Provides security for a computer or local network by preventing unauthorized access. It sits as a barrier between the web and your computer in order to prevent hacking, viruses or unapproved data transfer.

flash   Web design software that creates animation and interactive elements which are quick to download.

flash impression   The total number of requests made for pages holding flash-based content by users of that site in the period being measured. (ABC Electronic jargon buster definition)

geotargeting   The process of only showing adverts to people on a website and in search engines based on their physical location. This could be done using advanced technology that knows where a computer is located or by using the content of the website to determine what a person is looking for, eg someone searching for a restaurant in Aylesbury, Buckinghamshire.

GPRS   General Packet Radio Service or '2.5G' is an underlying mechanism for the networks to deliver internet browsing, WAP, e-mail and other such content. The user is 'always connected' and relatively high data rates can be achieved with most modern phones compared to a dial-up modem. Most phones default to using GPRS (if capable), and Incentivated is able to develop services that utilize this delivery mechanism.

graphic banners   A graphic mobile ad represented by a banner featuring an image. Similar to a web banner but with lower size constraints. (See *banner.*)

GSM Global Standard for Mobiles. The set of standards covering one particular type of mobile phone system.

hit A single request from a web browser for a single item from a web server.

hot spotting The ability to add hyperlinks to objects in a video that enable viewers to tag a product or service. Hot spotting can be used as a direct response mechanic in internet video.

HTML Stands for HyperText Markup Language, which is the set of commands used by web browsers to interpret and display page content to users. (ABC Electronic jargon buster definition)

image ad An image on a mobile internet site with an active link that can be clicked on by the subscriber. Once clicked the user is redirected to a new page, another mobile internet site or other destination where an offer resides.

impressions The metric used to measure views of a web page and its elements – including the advertising embedded within it. Ad impressions are how most online advertising is sold and the cost is quoted in terms of the cost per thousand impressions (CPM).

instant messaging Sending messages and chatting with friends or colleagues in real time when you are both online via a special application.

Integrated Services Digital Network (ISDN) High-speed dial-up connections to the internet over normal phone lines.

Internet Protocol TV (IPTV) The use of a broadband connection to stream digital television over the internet to subscribed users.

internet service provider (ISP) A company which provides users with the means to connect to the internet. Eg: AOL, Tiscali, Yahoo!

interruptive formats Online advertising formats that appear on users' screens on top of web content (and sometimes before the web page appears) and range from static, one-page splash screens to full-motion animated advertisements. See also *overlay*, *pop-up*.

interstitial ads Which appear between two content pages. Also known as splash pages and transition ads. See also *rich media*.

IPA Institute of Practitioners in Advertising is the trade body representing advertising agencies in the UK.

IP address The numerical internet address assigned to each computer on a network so that it can be distinguished from other computers. Expressed as four groups of numbers separated by dots.

keyword marketing The purchase of keywords (or 'search terms') by advertisers in search listings. See also *PPC*.

LAN (local area network) A group of computers connected together, which are at one physical location.

landing page (jump page) The page or view to which a user is directed when they click on an active link embedded in a banner, web page, e-mail or other view. A click-through lands the user on a jump page. Sometimes the landing page is one stage upstream from what would ordinarily be considered the home page.

lead   When a visitor registers, signs up for, or downloads something on an advertiser's site. A lead might also comprise a visitor filling out a form on an advertiser's site.

link   A link is a form of advertising on a website, in an e-mail or online newsletter, which, when clicked on, refers the visitor to an advertiser's website or a specific area within their website.

location-based services (LBS)   A range of services that are provided to mobile subscribers based on the geographical location of their handsets within their cellular network. Handsets do not have to be equipped with a position-location technology such as GPS to enable the geographical trigger of service(s) being provided since the location of the cell-site can be used as a proxy. Assisted GPS combines cell-site information with satellite positioning for a more accurate read. LBS include driving directions, information about certain resources or destinations within the current vicinity, such as restaurants, ATMs, shopping, movie theatres, etc. LBS may also be used to track the movements and locations of people, as is being done via parent/child monitoring services and mobile devices that target the family market.

locator   An advertisement or service through which an advertiser's bricks-and-mortar location can be identified based on proximity of the consumer or their preferred location (can be LBS or user-defined postal code).

log files   A record of all the hits a web server has received over a given period of time.

meta-tags/-descriptions   HTML tags that identify the content of a web page for the search engines.

micro-site   A sub-site reached via clicking on an ad. The user stays on the publisher's website but has access to more information from the advertiser.

MMA   The Mobile Marketing Association (MMA) is the premier global non-profit association that strives to stimulate the growth of mobile marketing and its associated technologies. The MMA is an action-oriented association designed to clear obstacles to market development, to establish standards and best practices for sustainable growth, and to evangelize the mobile channel for use by brands and third-party content providers. The MMA has over 500 members representing 40-plus countries.

mobile data services   Includes SMS, MMS, WAP, LBS and video.

mobile internet advertising   A form of advertising via mobile phones or other wireless devices (excluding laptops). This type of mobile advertising includes mobile web banner ads, mobile internet sponsorship and interstitials (which appear while a requested mobile web page is loading) as well as mobile paid-for search listings. Mobile internet advertising does not include other forms of mobile marketing such as SMS, MMS and shortcode.

MP3   A computer file format that compresses audio files up to a factor of 12 from a .wav file.

MPEG   File format used to compress and transmit video clips online.

MSISDN   Mobile Subscriber Integrated Services Digital Network. The mobile phone number of the participating customer.

multiple purpose units (MPU)   A square online advert usually found embedded in a web page in a fixed placement. Called 'multiple purpose' as it is a flexible-shaped blank 'canvas' in which you can serve flat or more interactive content as desired. See also *rich media, universal advertising package.*

natural search results   The 'natural' search results that appear in a separate section (usually the main body of the page) to the paid listings. The results listed here have not been paid for and are ranked by the search engine (using spiders or algorithms according to relevancy to the term searched upon). See also *spider, algorithm, SEO.*

notice   An easy-to-understand written description of the information and data collection, storage, maintenance, access, security, disclosure and use policies and practices, as necessary and required of the entity collecting and using the information and data from the mobile subscriber.

NVOD   Near video on demand service is the delivery of film and television programming from a server via a cable network or the internet. Like VOD these services are nonlinear and navigated via an EPG. Programming must be downloaded and the majority of existing services require the same amount of time to download as the duration of the selected programme.

OB   Outside broadcast unit known as a 'production truck'. In the United States an OB unit is a truck containing a mobile TV production studio.

off-portal   Point of sale/access on the mobile network, but outside of the operator's 'walled garden'/portal/deck, where consumers can access/purchase information and mobile products/content/utilities.

online HD   Is the delivery of high-definition streamed video media. This typically conforms to 720p standards where 720 represents 720 lines of vertical resolution and p stands for progressive scan.

online video advertising   Video advertising accompanying video content distributed via the internet to be streamed or downloaded onto compatible devices such as computers and mobile phones. In its basic form, this can be TV ads run online, but adverts are increasingly adapted or created specifically to suit online.

on-portal   Point of sale/access within the operator's 'walled garden'/portal/deck, where consumers can access/purchase information and mobile products/content/utilities.

opt-in   An individual has given a company permission to use his/her data for marketing purposes.

opt-out   An individual has stated that they do not want a company to use his/her data for marketing purposes.

organic search results   The 'natural' search results that appear in a separate section (usually the main body of the page) to the paid listings. The results listed here have not been paid for and are ranked by the search engine (using spiders or algorithms) according to relevancy to the term searched upon. See also *spider, algorithm, SEO.*

overlay Online advertising content that appears over the top of the web page. See also *rich media*.

paid-for listings The search results list in which advertisers pay to be featured according to the PPC model. This list usually appears in a separate section to the organic search results – usually at the top of the page or down the right-hand side. See also *organic search results, pay per click (PPC)*.

paid inclusion In exchange for a payment, a search engine will guarantee to list/review pages from a website. It is not guaranteed that the pages will rank well for particular queries – this still depends on the search engine's underlying relevancy process.

paid search See *PPC*.

pay for performance program Also called affiliate marketing, performance-based, partner marketing, CPA, or associate programme. Any type of revenue-sharing programme where a publisher receives a commission for generating online activity (eg leads or sales) for an advertiser.

pay per click (PPC) Allows advertisers to bid for placement in the paid listings search results on terms that are relevant to their business. Advertisers pay the amount of their bid only when a consumer clicks on their listing. Also called sponsored search/paid search.

pay per lead The commission structure where the advertiser pays the publisher a flat fee for each qualified lead (customer) that is referred to the advertiser's website.

pay per sale The commission structure where the advertiser pays a percentage or flat fee to the publisher based on the revenue generated by the sale of a product or service to a visitor who came from a publisher site.

pay per view (PPV) Is an e-commerce model that allows media owners to grant consumers access to their programming in return for payment. Micro-payments may be used for shorter programming whilst feature films may attract larger sums.

personal video recorder (PVR) Is a hard-disc-based digital video recorder (most use MPEG technology) and enables viewers to pause and rewind live TV. PVRs also interact with EPGs to automatically record favourite programmes and have led to an increase in the number of consumers watching 'time sifted' TV and skipping advertising breaks.

pharming An illegal method of redirecting traffic from another company's website (such as a bank) to a fake one designed to look similar in order to steal user details when they try to log in. See also *phishing*.

phishing An illegal method whereby legitimate looking e-mails (appearing to come from a well-known bank, for example) are used in an attempt to get personal information that can be used to steal a user's identity.

placement The area where an advertisement is displayed/placed within a publisher's mobile content.

podcasting Podcasting involves making an audio file (usually in MP3 format) of content – usually in the form of a radio program – that is available to download to an MP3 player.

polite loading   Fixed online advertising placements that load and display additional flash content after the host page on which the advert appears has finished loading. See also *flash*.

pop-under   An ad that appears in a separate window beneath an open window. Pop-under ads are concealed until the top window is closed, moved, resized or minimized.

pop-up   An online advert that 'pops up' in a window over the top of a web page. See also *interruptive formats*.

portal   A browsable portal of links to content, pre-configured usually by the network operator, and set as the default home page to the phone's browser.

post-roll   The streaming of a mobile advertising clip after a mobile TV/video clip. The mobile advert is usually 10–15 seconds.

pre-roll   The name given to the adverts shown before, or whilst an online video is loading. There can be more than one and, although they all vary in length, they average 21 seconds in duration.

PSMS   Premium SMS. A text message that is charged at a premium over the standard rate.

publisher   Also referred to as an affiliate, associate, partner, reseller or content site. An independent party, or website, that promotes the products or services of an advertiser in exchange for a commission.

query string formation   In a search engine, a query string is the set of words entered into a search engine by an individual. For example, a search for 'search engine marketing information'. Query string formation is simply the process of thinking of the correct query string to get the results required.

reach   The number of unique web users potentially seeing a website one or more times in a given time period expressed as a percentage of the total active web population for that period.

real time   No delay in the processing of requests for information, other than the time necessary for the data to travel over the internet.

really simple syndication (RSS)   Software that allows you to flag website content (often from blogs or new sites) and aggregate new entries to this content into an easy-to-read format that is delivered directly to a user's PC. See also *blog*.

rich media   The collective name for online advertising formats that use advanced technology to harness broadband to build brands. It uses interactive and audio-visual elements to give richer content and a richer experience for the user when interacting with the advert. See also *interstitial ads, superstitials, overlay* and *Rich Media Guidelines*.

Rich Media Guidelines   Design guidelines produced by the IAB for effective use of rich media technologies in all forms of internet advertising. They aim to protect user experience by keeping them in control of the experience, eg: encouraging clearly labelled close, sound and video buttons.

sale   When a user makes a purchase from an online advertiser.

sales house   An organization which sells advertising on behalf of other media owners. These sales houses typically retain a percentage of the revenue they sell in exchange for their services. These organizations may combine a number of websites together and sell them as different packages to advertisers.

search engine marketing (SEM)   The process which aims to get websites listed prominently in search engine results through search engine optimization, sponsored search and paid inclusion. See also *PPC*, *SEO* and *paid inclusion*.

search engine optimization (SEO)   The process which aims to get websites listed prominently within search engines' organic (algorithmic, spidered) search results. Involves making a site 'search engine friendly'. See also *organic search results*.

serial digital interface (SDI)   Is a dedicated digital video interface used to carry broadcast quality video content.

server   A host computer which maintains websites, newsgroups and e-mail services.

session   The time spent between a user starting an application, computer, website, etc and logging off or quitting.

SIM   Subscriber identity module. A removable part of the mobile phone hardware that identifies the subscriber.

simulcast   Watching an existing TV service over the internet at the same time as normal transmission.

site analytics   The reporting and analysis of website activity – in particular user behaviour on the site. All websites have a weblog which can be used for this purpose, but other third-party software is available for a more sophisticated service.

skyscraper   A long, vertical, online advert usually found running down the side of a page in a fixed placement. See also *universal advertising package*.

SMPP   Short Message Peer-to-peer Protocol – used for exchanging SMS messages.

SMS   Short Message Service.

SMSC   Short Message Service Centre. A network switch for routeing SMS traffic.

sniffer software   Identifies the capabilities of the user's browser and therefore can determine compatibility with ad formats and serve them an advert they will be able to see/fully interact with (eg: GIF, flash, etc).

Solus e-mail advertising   Where the body of the e-mail is determined by the advertiser, including both text and graphical elements, and is sent on their behalf by an e-mail list manager/owner. Solus e-mail advertising is conducted on an opt-in basis where the recipient has given their consent to receive communications.

spam   Unsolicited junk mail.

spider   A programme which crawls the web and fetches web pages in order for them to be indexed against keywords. Used by search engines to formulate search result pages. See also *organic search results*.

sponsored search   See *pay per click (PPC)*.

sponsorship   Advertiser sponsorships of targeted content areas (eg entire website, site area or an event) often for promotional purposes.

SS7 Signalling System 7. A worldwide standard for telecommunications hardware to talk to each other.

stickiness Measure used to gauge the effectiveness of a site in retaining its users. Usually measured by the duration of the visit.

streaming media Compressed audio/video which plays and downloads at the same time. The user does not have to wait for the whole file to download before it starts playing.

superstitials A form of rich media advertising which allows a TV-like experience on the web. It is fully pre-cached before playing. See also *rich media, cache memory*.

tenancy The 'renting' out of a section of a website by another brand who pays commission to this media owner for any revenue generated from this space. Eg: dating services inside portals or bookstores inside online newspapers.

text ad A static appended text attached to an advertisement.

text link Creative use for mobile advertisements – represented by highlighted and clickable text(s) with a link embedded within the highlighted text. Usually limited to 16–24 characters.

traffic Number of visitors who come to a website.

UMTS Universal Mobile Telephony Service or '3G' offers comprehensive voice and multimedia services to mobile customers by providing very high data rates and new functionality such as data streaming. 3G phones are backward compatible and can access all the services that 2 and 2.5G phones can, except that in this case data can be transferred a lot quicker. This means that any service that Incentivated can currently provide will work on the newer phones whose experience can be enhanced specifically based on handset type.

uniform resource locator (URL) Technical term that is used to refer to the web address of a particular website. For example www.iabuk.net.

unique users Number of different individuals who visit a site within a specific time period.

universal advertising package A set of online advertising formats that are standardized placements as defined by the IAB. See also *banner, skyscraper, button, MPU* and *embedded format*.

universal player Is a platform-agnostic media player that will allow video and audio to be played on any hardware/software configuration from a single source file.

user-generated content (UGC) Online content created by website users rather than media owners or publishers – either through reviews, blogging, podcasting or posting comments, pictures or video clips. Sites that encourage user-generated content include MySpace, YouTube, Wikipedia and Flickr. See also *blog, podcasting*.

video on demand (VOD) Allows users to watch what they want, when they want. This can be either 'pay per view' or a free service usually funded by advertising.

viral marketing   The term 'viral advertising' refers to the idea that people will pass on and share striking and entertaining content; this is often sponsored by a brand which is looking to build awareness of a product or service. These viral commercials often take the form of funny video clips, or interactive flash games, images, and even text.

VMNO (Virtual Mobile Network Operator)   A company that uses the infrastructure of an existing (licence-owning) telecoms network operator. Tesco and Virgin are two of the largest VMNOs in the UK.

Voice Over Internet Protocol (VOIP)   Technology that allows the use of a broadband internet connection to make telephone calls.

WAP (Wireless Application Protocol)   Standard for providing mobile data services on hand-held devices. Brings internet content such as news, weather, travel, etc to mobile phones and can also be used to deliver formatted content such as wallpapers, ringtones, video, games, portals and other useful links.

Web 2.0   The term Web 2.0 – with its knowing nod to upgraded computer applications – describes the next generation of online use. Web 2.0 identifies the consumer as a major contributor in the evolution of the internet into a two-way medium. See also *user-generated content.*

web based   Requiring no software to access an online service or function, other than a web browser and access to the internet.

web portal   A website or service that offers a broad array of resources and services, such as e-mail, forums, search engines, and online shopping malls.

whitelist   An e-mail whitelist is a list of contacts that the user deems are acceptable to receive e-mail from and should not be sent to the trash folder. (Wikipedia definition)

Wi-Fi (Wireless Fidelity)   The ability to connect to the internet wirelessly. Internet 'hotspots' in coffee shops and airports, etc use this technology.

wiki   A wiki is a type of website that allows the visitors themselves to easily add, remove, and otherwise edit and change some available content, sometimes without the need for registration.

wilfing (What Was I Looking For?)   Seven in 10 of Britain's 34 million users forget what they are looking for online at work and at home. Wilfing is an expression referring to browsing the internet with no real purpose.

Wireless Markup Language (WML) aka WAP 1.0   Where the mobile internet started many years ago. Hardly supported any more.

XHTML (Extensible Hypertag Markup Language) aka WAP 2.0   The language used to create most mobile internet sites.

XML (Extensible Markup Language)   Language used by many internet applications for exchanging information.

Further reading

Here we have listed some of the books, sites, influencers and giants that make up the digital marketing landscape. Now we have finished our book, like good little 'digerati' we are turning our attention back to our own website, www.understand ingdigitalmarketing.com. So check in with us from time to time and, meanwhile, here is the list, which we hope you find useful.

Books

Berners-Lee, T (2000) *Weaving the Web: The original design and ultimate destiny of the world wide web*, HarperCollins, New York

Bird, D (2007) *Commonsense Direct and Digital Marketing*, 5th edn, Kogan Page, London

Castells, M (2000) *The Rise of the Network Society*, Blackwell, Oxford

Cocoran, I (2007) *The Art of Digital Branding*, Allworth Press, New York

Hafner, K and Lyo, M (1996) *Where Wizards Stay Up Late*, Touchstone, New York

McLuhan, M ([1964] 2001) *Understanding Media*, Routledge, London

Meerman Scott, D (2007) *The New Rules of Marketing and PR*, John Wiley & Sons, Hoboken, NJ

Palfrey, J and Gasser, U (2008) *Born Digital: Understanding the first generation of digital natives*, Basic Books, New York

Shiffman, D (2008) *The Age of Engage*, Hunt Street Press, Ladera Ranch, CA

Standage, T (1999) *The Victorian Internet*, Berkeley Publishing, New York

Tungate, M (2007) *Adland: A global history of advertising*, Kogan Page, London

Weber, L (2007) *Marketing to the Social Web: How digital customer communities build your business*, John Wiley & Sons, Hoboken, NJ

Wertime, K and Fenwick, I (2008) *Digimarketing: The essential guide to new media and digital marketing*, John Wiley, Singapore

Wind, J and Mahajan, V (2001) *Digital Marketing: Global strategies from the world's leading experts*, John Wiley & Sons, New York

Recommended websites for digital marketers

Here we list just some of the thousands of sites we have encountered during our intrepid writing spree! There are loads more references in each chapter of the book, and you can always use a search engine to find more yourselves!

History of the net:
http://www.isoc.org/internet/
history/
Thorough!

Web population:
http://www.internetworldstats.com/
Excellent reference point.

General digital marketing:
www.iab.net
www.iabuk.net
www.iabeurope.ws
The IAB has led from the beginning and continues to drive digital marketing forward.

http://adage.com/digital/
Punchy and required reading.

www.nma.co.uk
Brilliant best of British.

www.emarketer.com
One of the myriad of digital marketing sites, but always up to speed.

www.brandrepublic.com
Truly a great source of knowledge.

General web industry:
www.w3.org
It's all here, folks.

Building a site?
www.daniweb.com
Uncomplicated and quite cool.

Learning SEO:
www.seotoolset.com
Practical.

Search engine marketing:
www.searchenginewatch.com
Incisive.
www.searchengineland.com
Comprehensive.
Both sites also good for online PR info.

Web analytics:
www.google.com/analytics
Hard to beat.
www.alexa.com
Useful evaluation tool.

E-mail marketing:
www.emaillabs.com
Worth a look.

Social media marketing:
www.webcredible.co.uk
Order among chaos!

Online PR:
See 'Search engine marketing'.

Affiliate marketing:
www.affiliatetips.com
A great overview of the sector.

Digital creative:
http://www.canneslions.com/
winners/cyber/
www.webbyawards.com
Why not check out the awards?

Mobile marketing:
www.mmaglobal.org
Useful industry association website.

Viral marketing:
www.viralmanager.com
Good resource of case studies, etc.

In-game advertising:
See 'General digital marketing'.

Anything else?
www.wikipedia.org
The biggest and what would we do
without it?

Index